# SOVIET FOREIGN POLICY, 1917–1991
## A Retrospective

TEL AVIV UNIVERSITY   אוניברסיטת תל־אביב

The Cummings Center for Russian and East European Studies
The Cummings Center Series

Soviet Foreign Policy, 1917-1991
A Retrospective

Gabriel Gorodetsky, Editor

# THE CUMMINGS CENTER
## FOR RUSSIAN AND EAST EUROPEAN STUDIES
### TEL AVIV UNIVERSITY

The Cummings Center is Tel Aviv University's main framework for research, study, documentation and publication relating to the history and current affairs of Russia, the former Soviet republics and Eastern Europe. Its current projects include Fundamentalism and Secularism in the Muslim Republics of the Soviet Union; the Establishment of Political Parties and the Process of Democratization in Russia; Religion and Society in Russia; the Creation of New Historical Narratives in Contemporary Russia; and Soviet Military Theory and History.

In addition, the Center seeks to establish a bridge between the Russian and Western academic communities, promoting a dialogue with Russian academic circles through joint projects, seminars, roundtables and publications.

## THE CUMMINGS CENTER SERIES

The titles published in this series are the product of original research by the Center's faculty, research staff and associated fellows. The Cummings Center Series also serves as a forum for publishing declassified Russian archival material of interest to scholars in the fields of history and political science.

Managing Editor – Deena Leventer

# SOVIET FOREIGN POLICY
# 1917–1991
## A Retrospective

Edited by
## GABRIEL GORODETSKY

FRANK CASS

*First published 1994 in Great Britain by*
FRANK CASS AND CO. LTD.
Gainsborough House, 11 Gainsborough Road,
London E11 1RS, England

*and in the United States of America by*
FRANK CASS
c/o International Specialized Book Services Inc.
5602 N.E. Hassalo Street, Portland, OR 97213-3644

Copyright © 1994

British Library Cataloguing in Publication Data
Soviet Foreign Policy, 1917–91:
Retrospective
  I. Gorodetsky, Gabriel
  327.47

ISBN 0–7146–4506–0 (cloth)
ISBN 0–7146–4112–X (paper)

Library of Congress Cataloging-in-Publication Data
Soviet foreign policy, 1917–1991: a retrospective / edited by Gabriel
Gorodetsky
  p.cm.
  ISBN 0–7146–4506–0        0–7146–4112–X
1. Soviet Union — Foreign relations.  I. Gorodetsky, Gabriel, 1945–
DK266.45.S68 1993                                            93–30555
327.47'009'04-dc20                                               CIP

Typeset by University Publishing Projects, Tel Aviv, Israel

Printed and bound in Great Britain by
Bookcraft Ltd, Midsomer Norton, Avon

# Contents

# SOVIET FOREIGN POLICY, 1917–1991
## A Retrospective

# Introduction

Since Russia's emergence as a major power in the eighteenth century, the Western world has been reluctant to accept it as an integral part of Europe. This rebuff, embedded in a deep-rooted Russophobic tradition, was heightened by the Bolshevik Revolution. In 1839 the Marquis de Custine returned from Russia appalled, preaching to the Europeans that the Russians were no more than "Chinese masquerading as Europeans". Two centuries later Churchill referred to the Soviet Union as "an enigma wrapped in a mystery". Earlier on he had applied less flattering metaphors to the Russians, comparing them to "crocodiles" and a "plague of baboons". The continuity in the Western perception of Russia was conspicuous in Churchill's choice of the "Iron Curtain", a mere paraphrase of the "cordon sanitaire" with which Lord Curzon had hoped to isolate Western civilization from the Bolshevik "plague" during the Civil War.

Nor have the Russians been unanimous about their own destiny and identity. From the early 1830s the Russian intelligentsia pursued a fierce debate over the road which Russia should follow to surmount her political, social and economic backwardness. The debate has accompanied each twist in Russian history. Originally the Westernizers identified Russia as an integral part of European civilization, while the Slavophiles valued the unique features of a way of life which derives from Russia's position between West and East. The contemporary variation on the controversy is expressed by the liberal reformers, who look towards the West, and the nationalists who favour the establishment of a unique Eurasian entity. The reopening of the age-old dialogue on the nature of Russian nationalism and the place of Russia in world affairs reflects the search for a new identity.

On both the Western and Russian sides vindictiveness, resentment and suspicions have shaped perceptions which in turn have generated antagonistic policies. Russia has long been regarded as a cancerous element within the European community despite its military efforts in the First World War, its attempts to form a united resistance to Nazism, and its major role in the reshaping of postwar Europe. The Cold War ultimately cast a long shadow over Russia's contribution to the final victory over Nazism in Europe. This in turn encouraged isolationist and xenophobic tendencies in Moscow, fuelling Stalin's pathological suspicion of Western intentions.

The dismemberment of the Soviet Empire finds Russia once again at a crossroad. In its feeble state, troubled by internal havoc, instability and economic hardship, Russia is once again being forced to forfeit its connection to Europe. The move towards a united Europe continues with vigour and there is a clear sense of relief now that the menace from the East has been lifted. For a while it seemed that Russia's claim to membership in Europe might disturb the tranquillity of the European Home. The undeniable departure of Russia as a dynamic force from the European scene is welcomed, as long as Russian domestic chaos does not spill beyond its borders. In its present weakness Russia is once again being ostracized and left out in the cold.

For historians the dissolution of the Soviet Union permits an overall view of Soviet foreign policy. They are now in a position to explore archival sources which have been entirely inaccessible, and to examine topics which have been highly politicized in the past. For the Russian scholar, the historical journey cannot be divorced from the dynamics of the present reshaping of Russia. While it is commonly acknowledged that historical precedents cannot serve as a yardstick for forecasting the future, the search for a new identity relies heavily on the legacy of the past. Allusion to the past, whether the Communist or the Imperial one, is a means to reestablish Russia's international stature. In the best Russian tradition, further assisted by a diehard and less appealing communist practice, Russian historians still feel politically responsible and committed to their past history.

In the sphere of East-West relations the historical lessons are indispensable for the reevaluation of the perceptions and prejudices which have underlain the policies pursued. More than in any other field of history, both Russian and Western students of Soviet foreign affairs have been bound in differing degrees by political dispositions. The emergence of a new Russia provides a unique opportunity to shed biases and examine controversial historical precedents in a temperate fashion.

It was the need to put this historical experience into perspective which brought together leading Russian and Western historians in Moscow to sum up their research, identify contentious issues and ponder whether indeed past experience has any relevance for the emergence of a new Russia. While the present collection does not pretend to encompass the whole range of issues relating to the course of seventy years of Soviet foreign policy, it does address the crucial ones pertaining to the Soviet Union's relations with the West.

The mere opening of archival sources is not a sufficient guarantee of a proper re-examination of Soviet foreign policy. The encounter with the Russian scholars confirmed the need to set common paradigms in view of the basic discrepancy in methodology and conceptual outlook. Setting up a common platform for collaboration will facilitate future joint investigation with Russian scholars, whose proximity to and familiarity with the archival sources and acquaintance with the environment which they investigate are valuable assets.

Any revisionist approach requires the transcendence of biases and political beliefs. Bidding farewell to a familiar and congenial past with a smile, as Bezymensky astutely comments, can be an agonizing task. For instance, the attempts made by the Gorbachev administration to deny the existence of the Secret Protocols of the Ribbentrop-Molotov Pact in the Soviet archives manifest the need for a continuous dialogue which will maintain the momentum of reviewing Soviet history.

New facets of Soviet foreign policy should be explored, particularly the domestic aspects, as is pointed out by Alexander Dallin. Dallin sets the agenda for further study of the process of foreign policy decision making and the need to investigate institutional rivalry over matters of foreign policy. The neglect of these aspects has led to the total bankruptcy of Sovietology in its attempts to understand the workings of Soviet foreign policy.

Although Russian historians are no longer fettered by official diktats, their historical approach to the subject matter is understandably governed by their individual and collective attitudes to the colossal changes now sweeping Russia. They are once again joining hands with politicians in a search for clues and moral lessons in the past which can be applied to the future course of the country. A disturbing tendency is the attempt to erase the entire Soviet experience from the collective Russian memory and then pick up the threads back in 1914, dismantling the legacy, history and traditions of almost an entire century.

A number of historians feel compelled to come to terms with the Soviet legacy. The formulation of policy must be based, as Igor Lebedev observes, on a continuity which is grounded in constant geopolitical, national and psychological conditions. As is evident from most of the chapters in this volume, the Russian Federation will find it exceedingly difficult to dissociate itself from the communist legacy, just as the Bolshevik Revolution failed to sever its ties with the Tsarist heritage. Lebedev calls for a dispassionate reassessment of Soviet foreign policy, which will help to reconstruct Russia's identity on the basis of past legacy and establish its corresponding responsibilities. This is essential for the stability of the entire world. Others like Alexander Tchoubarian, apply a new blend of ethics and morality as the main criterion for passing historical judgment. The application of morality and ethics to the search for a new foreign policy seems to

Tchoubarian the best means of bridging the gap between science and politics.

A major historical debate, which had a direct political influence on the formulation of policy towards the Soviet Union, involved the evaluation of the nature and aims of Soviet foreign policy. Up to the very collapse of the Soviet empire, historians and politicians continued to haggle over the issue of whether the dual policy was based predominantly on ideology or *realpolitik*. The first decade of the Bolshevik Revolution is now recognized as a dramatic epoch in which ideology and statesmanship clashed in a still relatively pluralistic environment. The majority of the historians writing in this volume agree that from the beginning Soviet foreign policy was characterized by a gradual but consistent retreat away from unbending hostility to the capitalist regimes and towards peaceful coexistence based on mutual expediency.

The subsequent string of "breathing spaces", though clad in revolutionary jargon, brought about a steady erosion of the ideological component of Soviet foreign policy. In her case study Carole Fink presents the Genoa Conference in 1922 as a daring attempt to negotiate a compromise through the acceptance of ideological differences and the search for accommodation. Ironically, Genoa turned out to be a model of failure of a genuine search for peaceful coexistence. A neat assessment of Moscow's dilemmas in the 1930s leads Teddy Uldricks to the similar conclusion that Soviet foreign policy was indeed motivated primarily by a genuine and desperate search for security.

Richard Debo and Uldricks agree that a review of the initial stages of Soviet foreign policy is essential for detecting missed opportunities in the 1930s, such as the establishment of a common front against Nazism which might have created a solid basis for the Grand Alliance, thus averting the Cold War. The Cold War increasingly emerges as a prolonged process of mutual errors of judgment, most of which derived from the often irrational suspicions prevailing not only in Moscow but also among Western academics and politicians alike. The deterioration of relations in the wake of the Second World War, as Mikhail Narinsky argues on the basis of Soviet archival material, rested on earlier suspicions and mistrust, and led to a situation in which military means became the sole language of diplomacy.

Martin Kitchen offers a survey of Labour's attitude towards the Soviet Union against the background of the looming Cold War. He shows how Bevin, aware of the limitations of British policy in the wake of the Second World War, moulded a sober and realistic relationship with Moscow, demolishing many relics of the past. But by

1947 the USA had taken the lead from the British in confronting the Russians with great power politics. East-West relations were further aggravated by the Americans' conviction of ideological superiority. Indeed, Bruce Kuniholm clearly depicts how Soviet-American rivalry in the Near East superseded the earlier Anglo-Soviet one. Unlike Teddy Uldricks, he believes that while American policy in the region was predominantly dictated by genuine security concerns and aimed at containing the Russians, that of Moscow was expansionist and in flagrant violation of international codes of behaviour.

From a different perspective, Prazmowska relates how the Polish issue came to dominate the meeting at Yalta which symbolizes the "great betrayal" and the emergence of the Cold War. This phenomenon should be viewed in the context of the strategic and military policies pursued by Poland in 1941–43. She contends that the Poles sought to exert disproportional influence, pursuing an illusory conviction that Britain and the United States would prevent the Soviets from taking control of Poland in the event of victory over Germany.

The twentieth century is commonly regarded as the age of "mass participation". Modern governments, sustained by the powerful bureaucratic edifice of civil administration, are compelled to seek legitimization through multiple channels of popular consent. And yet it is hard to deny the prominent role played by the towering figures of this century. Their leadership, often forged by crisis, underlines the supremacy of personality and circumstances.

The absence of archival sources and inside knowledge has diverted historians towards ideology and power politics; in a society where personal contact and back-room politics were and remain a major feature, the human dimension has been ignored. As Alexander Dallin observes, the mechanism of policy making and the relative weight of its executors remain practically unknown. Because of the heavily censored and hagiographic nature of the portraits drawn in the Soviet Union, it was hardly possible to visualize prominent diplomats such as Rakovsky, Maiskii, Krestinskii, Ioffe, Litvinov and Molotov as mortals. Their faces, so far distinguished only by their general contours, have suddenly come to life. Their personal habits, inner thoughts and entourages are brought into focus. Such changes call for striking re-evaluations of the decision-making process.

For many years historians have been blindly clinging to the obsolete totalitarian model of Friederich and Arendt. Besides making a crude and superficial comparison between the Nazi and the Soviet systems, aimed at discrediting the Soviet Union during the Cold War, the model did little to enrich our knowledge of Soviet policy. Sovietologists were often led to produce a subjective evaluation of the motives behind Soviet foreign policy. More often than not such an approach was dictated entirely by preconceived ideas divorced from reality. One of the outstanding features of this collection is the attempt to view the decision-making process through the eyes of leaders and practitioners rather than focusing on ideological, social or economic factors.

Richard Debo, for example, reveals the significance of the intimate friendship between Chicherin and Brockdorff-Rantzau. Their relationship, cultivated in nocturnal sessions at Chicherin's flat in the Commissariat, and nourished by a shared interest in music, literature and culture, transcended national interests or ideological persuasions. These personal insights bring to mind Chicherin's preface to his scholarly book on Mozart written in 1931, in which he defied the newly established practice of alluding to Marx, Engels, Lenin and Stalin. "Mozart," he wrote as an introductory note, "remained throughout my life my best friend and comrade...standing high above world history, beyond its drifts and influence."

The complexities of the decision-making process and the colourful figures behind it are illuminated in Haslam's study. Soviet foreign policy in the crucial late 1930s and in the aftermath of the Second World War is presented as a bone of contention among Litvinov, Molotov and Stalin, rather than the product of a lacklustre hierarchy devoid of any personal initiative. These observations are corroborated by Filitov, who provides further evidence from the Soviet archives on dissent in Moscow over issues such as the outbreak of the war in the Pacific and Roosevelt's proposal for setting up a Supreme War Council.

The inside story is further unravelled in Anatolii Cherniaev's personal reminiscences of the negotiations between Kohl and Gorbachev which led to the reunification of Germany. The proliferation of sources only sharpens controversies and unfolds the intricacy of events for which, in the past, Western historians provided simplified answers and Soviet historians produced dull and dogmatic interpretations. Thus, while Cherniaev credits Gorbachev with a well-orchestrated move towards reunification, Dashichev's eye-witness report depicts the tremendous pressure which forced Gorbachev to concede step by step. Such a discrepancy signals the opening of a diversified and genuine historical dialogue. There is potential for a similar exchange between Viktor Kuvaldin and Carol Saivetz. In Kuvaldin's review of the emergence of "new thinking" in foreign policy his inside information on the Gulf War adds colour to Carole Saivetz's interpretation, which derives from more conventional Western tools.

Another feature which deserves renewed attention is the role played by the various national and ethnic groups in the conduct of

Soviet foreign policy. The axiomatic recognition of the Soviet Union as an indivisible entity led most observers to play down regional and autonomous interests within the various Republics. However, nationalist undercurrents have persisted since the 1920s and are clearly demonstrated by the emergence of an autonomous Ukrainian foreign policy, with distinct attributes, geared towards integration into the emerging bloc of Central European states. The extent to which the Ukraine, under the guidance of Khristian Rakovsky, attempted to assert economic and political independence from the Russians in the 1920s is the subject of a pioneering study by Conte. Yaacov Ro'i shows that it was not global politics but anti-Semitism on the one hand and the activities of Soviet Jewry on the other which were the major factors determining the Soviet demeanour in the Middle East.

I am particularly grateful to Prof. Alexander Oganovich Tchoubarian, Director of the Institute of General History of the Russian Academy of Sciences, for the fruitful collaboration in the mounting of the Moscow conference on the history of Soviet foreign policy in 1992. The research papers presented at the conference served as the backbone of this collection. A special debt of gratitude is owed to Mrs. Deena Leventer for her devotion in the organizational work of the conference and for the meticulous care she and Mrs. Beryl Belsky invested in the editorial work.

Gabriel Gorodetsky
Tel Aviv
July 1993

Part One

# THE GENESIS OF SOVIET FOREIGN POLICY

# 1

# The NEP in Foreign Policy: The Genoa Conference and the Treaty of Rapallo

## CAROLE FINK

One of the most significant events in the early history of Soviet-Western relations took place at the Genoa Conference of 1922. Convened by the Supreme Allied Council to re-establish ties between Soviet Russia and the West, this 34-nation summit conference lasted six weeks but produced no agreement. After only one week, the Soviet and German delegates signed a separate treaty at Rapallo; and after the dismal follow-up conference to Genoa that summer at the Hague, Moscow and the West were perhaps even further apart than before.

Historians of the Genoa Conference have long debated whether both sides were sincere, realistic, or even capable of establishing peace between Soviet Russia and the capitalist world. They have investigated leadership of both sides, their ideological, political and financial structures, and their economic, social, and cultural situations in 1921–22.[1] The unprecedented availability and magnitude of captured German documents, plus the archival sources of North America, Europe and Japan facilitated in producing a balanced multinational perspective. Even with the help of only the printed Soviet sources, it is possible to examine one of the initial and critical episodes in Soviet-Western relations.

The tides of revolution and counter-revolution had ebbed in 1921, and both sides were casting about for alternatives to military and ideological confrontation. Four years after the October Revolution, Soviet Russia, faced at home with internal dissent and a collapsed economy and abroad with diplomatic ostracism and the repression of revolutionary movements, called for a truce with the bourgeois capitalist world. Great Britain was pressed by its own financial, political, and social problems. Convinced of the futility of further efforts to overthrow or exclude the Soviet regime, and intent on revising what it considered an unsatisfactory postwar peace structure, Britain was the first major power to respond to Moscow's overtures. The Anglo-Soviet trade agreement of 16 March 1921 signalled the end of outright antagonism and the search for a new basis of East-West diplomacy.[2]

Both sides were wary of the risks and the costs. Both were led by charismatic, forceful, yet flexible leaders, V. I. Lenin and David Lloyd George, who were flanked at home by vocal opponents on the left and the right. The world's first socialist state and leader of the Comintern, which had repudiated traditional Great Power diplomacy, was about to make overtures to the class enemy. Britain, burdened by imperial responsibilities, heavily in debt to the United States, and bound to European peace treaties, was about to deal with its sworn global opponent.[3]

In 1921, Moscow launched the New Economic Policy and offered concessions to foreign capitalists. Seeking trade and loans, Lenin introduced a series of legal and political reforms to attract Western businessmen and to facilitate Russia's recovery. In the wake of crop failures, famine and epidemics, the Soviet state also appealed for direct aid from the West. Lenin and Georgii Chicherin, the People's Commissar of Foreign Affairs, formulated a policy of peaceful coexistence which included renouncing armed conflict, exploring specific areas of accommodation and establishing a basis for peaceful competition with the capitalist world.[4]

Russians and Westerners have written extensively during the past seven decades on the origins and meaning of the term "coexistence".[5] Some scholars date it back to Brest-Litovsk, and to Lenin's willingness to compromise in order to gain his ends. Seemingly inconsistent with a professed revolutionary regime and with its need and commitment to destabilize Western imperialism, Lenin's policy of coexistence ostensibly stopped the insurrectionist clock, or at least slowed it down.[6]

A precise analysis of this complex policy must await the opening of Soviet archives. In the meantime, one can at least assert the following: coexistence was aimed at winning breathing space and possible economic benefits for the still-precarious Soviet regime. It was a means of promoting trade, credits, diplomatic agreements and the cause of general disarmament. In addition, it served as a valuable propaganda weapon to impress Western liberals and pacifists and to silence right-wing enemies. Indeed, it was an effective tool for balancing Soviet foreign policy between the moderates in the Narkomindel and the ideologues of the Third International.[7]

Peaceful coexistence also had political significance for Lenin in 1922. It seems likely that the selective pursuit of friendly contacts with the West was aimed as much at cementing his personal leadership as preserving the Soviet state. Still attempting to hold the reins of power, the ailing Soviet leader applied the diplomacy of coexistence as a brake against his political rivals. His goal was apparently to dismantle war communism and restructure the military forces, as well as to promote administrative and economic reform.[8]

The West responded to Lenin's overtures with a predictable mixture of fear and political pragmatism. The opponents of the revolution insisted on drawing a clear distinction between the Russian people and the Bolshevik regime; between humanitarian assistance and direct political contacts. The United States, the first to provide massive aid through Herbert Hoover's American Relief Administration, managed its resources independently of Moscow and its former European allies. France, representing over a million dispossessed Russian bondholders, urged a united front of Western capitalists to impose stiff conditions in return for renewed economic ties with Moscow. Lloyd George was the spokesman for the capitalists, workers, and moderate leftist opinion, advocating a complete *détente* with Lenin's Russia, including political ties. Thus the Western camp lined up behind three positions. The proponents of pre-revolutionary Russia, who viewed the Soviet state as a ruined land pitted with menace for all but the most ruthless or witless entrepreneurs, supported Washington. Those governments obliged by their electorate to demonstrate a modicum of interest in the fate of a former pillar of the European system — without jeopardizing basic capitalist principles — adhered to France. Those states persuaded of the necessity of compromise and conciliation backed Great Britain.[9]

Chicherin took the platform on 28 October 1921 to propose the convocation of an international conference which would discuss "opening an opportunity for private initiative and capital to cooperate with the power of the workers in the exploitation of Russia's natural resources".[10] Moscow offered to assume the tsarist debts in return for Allied credits and *de jure* recognition. It stressed its readiness to rejoin the international community, "not as a supplicant, but as an equal".

The Allied response came in January 1922 when the Supreme Council convoked an "urgent" economic and financial conference to meet in Genoa in April. The heads of government of every major state, including Soviet Russia and Germany, were invited. Lloyd George prevailed on the Council to adopt a series of resolutions. The first was a ringing formula for coexistence: "Nations can claim no right to dictate to each other regarding the principles on which they are to regulate their systems of ownership, international economy and government." The sixth resolution proposed a European non-aggression pact. However, resolutions two through five stated the exact price that Russia must pay for Western credits and recognition: full acknowledgement of its debts, complete property restitution, reform of its police, legal system and currency, and repudiation of the propaganda and political activities directed by the Third International against the capitalist world. Four days later the Supreme Council voted to establish a consortium of Western capitalists to coordinate and supervise private investments in Russia.[11]

Lloyd George's daring design, aimed at aiding Britain's ailing export industries and stabilizing his position at home by producing a quick agreement with Moscow, confused and irritated his allies as well as his opponents. France balked at making concessions to Soviet Russia, the United States remained aloof, and Germany, chafing under the Allies' reparation demands, vacillated between following Britain's lead and asserting an independent, pro-Moscow policy; meanwhile, the rest of Europe watched uneasily as the Entente bickered over how to deal with Soviet Russia.[12]

In Moscow, the elaborate preparations for the Genoa Conference and the three-month delay until its opening, proved equally stressful. Unclear whether it would face a united or divided capitalist front, the Soviet government strove to widen its opponents' divisions by making private and public approaches to individual governments while at the same time emitting signals of accommodation. This policy reflected the deep internal split between those hardliners like Trotsky who, expecting nothing from the hostile, feeble capitalists, preached economic autarky, and those pragmatists like Grigorii Sokol'nikov, who favoured the re-establishment of ties with the West. Lenin trod a narrow line, advocating coexistence but also vowing to the metal-workers on 6 March 1922 that there would be no ideological retreats. During the waiting months, there is evidence that "Genoa fever" infected the ordinary Russian as much as the average Briton, German and Swiss: the conference unleashed a combination of hope at the prospect, and fear over the cost, of reconciliation between the capitalist and communist worlds.[13]

The public side of the Genoa Conference, which opened on 9 April 1922, produced a glittering spectacle for the assembled horde of journalists and spectators.[14] But when the two sides finally confronted each other, there was an almost immediate stalemate. Bound by his allies and by the restrictions of his conservative cabinet, Lloyd George presented harsh terms to the Soviet delegation: acknowledgement of all debts and full compensation to dispossessed property owners without reciprocal concessions on loans or recognition. The Soviet negotiators responded by presenting a gigantic bill for the Allied intervention and stalled for time.[15]

Faced by a unified West, Chicherin was apparently persuaded to play his German card. On Easter Sunday the two pariahs, Germany and Russia, signed a treaty at Rapallo, based on a mutual repudiation of debts and claims, the granting of unconditional recognition, the promise of expanded economic relations and continuation of their surreptitious military ties. The Rapallo treaty was a thunderbolt whose reverberations at Genoa and throughout Europe have lasted until today. It threatened the new Poland and the entire East European settlement. A model of bilateralism and reciprocity, it broke the power of the Allies' demands and appeared to represent a striking Soviet victory.[16]

However, having temporarily gained the upper hand, the Russians still needed the West's aid and recognition; but what price were they willing to pay? Testing the waters, Chicherin sent an accommodating signal that he was prepared to continue negotiations.[17] But the division between the pragmatists behind the People's Commissar who were committed to working towards a comprehensive agreement with the West, and the doctrinaires like Adol'f Ioffe and Khristian Rakovsky who were determined to break off relations, had been intensified by Rapallo. Far off in Moscow, a very ill Lenin favoured the Rapallo model and chastised Chicherin's new efforts at *rapprochement*.[18]

To David Lloyd George, fighting the last great struggle of his political career, fell the burden of salvaging an agreement. Like Pitt facing his French opponents in 1797, he was trying to bridge the great gap between ideological enemies and meet Chicherin halfway. All else had failed: the armed intervention had left a legacy of bitterness, ruin and huge Soviet counterclaims; the American policy of hostility and ostracism, and the French and neutrals' policies of indifference and passivity, would be perpetually threatened by another Rapallo. For imperial Britain, Russia's weakness as much as its military might, threatened Europe and the world.[19]

Lloyd George wanted to offer a combination of private and government capital to rehabilitate Russia. Without having any illusions about its crimes and repressiveness, he wanted to recognize Lenin's regime and deal with it directly. The alternatives — a continuing hot or cold war or maintenance of the status quo — were worse. Like Lenin, he recognized the inefficiency of the Bolshevik government, but he preferred it to a regime led by White Army generals or by more doctrinaire radicals. Lloyd George's road to coexistence meant

15

ignoring Rakovsky's taunts and paying serious attention to Chicherin's bargaining. He had a considerable amount of support. Numerous bankers and businessmen were interested in gaining access to their former enterprises in Russia, or exploring new ventures. Western liberal opinion welcomed peace and trade. The European Left applauded aid for Russia and the prospect of increased employment.[20]

Not surprisingly, the post-Rapallo negotiations proved fruitless. Weary and churlish, Lloyd George failed to cajole or bully the Russians or his allies into making any concessions; neither Germany, protecting its own interests, nor the United States, which remained aloof and hostile, helped his flagging crusade. Moreover, the rumours of a Soviet oil concession to British capitalists marred the proceedings.[21] Facing an impending crisis over German reparations, the Allies were forced to close ranks against the Soviets. In fact they had nothing to offer them save vague promises. On orders from Moscow, Chicherin haughtily rejected these, and for good measure condemned capitalist greed, hypocrisy and imperialism. The closing session of the Genoa Conference on 19 May 1922 was the climax of six weeks of dashed hopes; the follow-up meeting at the Hague also ended in failure; and with Lloyd George's fall and Lenin's decline, the "spirit of Genoa" expired.[22]

Western scholars have strongly disagreed over the meaning of the Genoa Conference and the causes of its failure. One view is that the search for conciliation in 1922 represented a temporary, expedient, and ultimately destructive policy by both sides. According to this opinion, the aim of Lenin's policy of coexistence was simply to weaken and divide the Western powers in order to achieve immediate gains. Moscow received its reward at Rapallo, but Germany's pockets were empty and its forms of aid less advantageous than those offered by London or Paris. Due to its shortsightedness and internal divisions, Russia failed to achieve its larger goals of obtaining substantial funds and recognition, ending its diplomatic isolation and attaining disarmament; thereafter, Leninist pliancy gave way to Stalinist inflexibility and to Soviet isolation.

Similarly, Lloyd George, another astute and pragmatic actor with a penchant for ringing phrases, has been accused of shortsightedness. It is claimed that he gambled unsuccessfully with his Genoa policy at hoodwinking France, the United States and the smaller Western powers, keeping the Germans in tow and luring Soviet Russia into a new world order — all for the purpose of securing his own position in power. His failure resulted not only in his own political demise but also in the halt of his chimerical European appeasement policy. For conservative historians, the Genoa Conference has always represented a negative model of the history of East-West relations, a crass and misguided sacrifice of principle; and Rapallo has embodied the potential menace of an aggressive Soviet-German alliance.[23]

The more positive interpretation of Genoa is as a predecessor to Helsinki, and as representing a missed opportunity for long-term stable relations between Soviet Russia and the West on the basis of coexistence.[24] Notwithstanding its revolutionary origins and structure, Soviet Russia had appeared to offer solid concessions and economic, commercial and political accords which were intended to lead to its reintegration into the European system in a stable, if competitive East-West relationship. Behind Lenin stood skilled and articulate pragmatists, such as Leonid Krasin, Nikolai Bukharin, and Sokol'nikov, who were willing to gamble on coexistence.

In the West — despite the adherence to capitalist principles — there was considerable inclination to explore the possibility of long-term *rapprochement* with a former adversary. The growing rightist menace, the mounting rebelliousness in the colonial world, and the increasing power of the United States and Japan, made Lloyd George's conciliatory policy toward Soviet Russia a viable method of preserving and enlarging Europe's influence. Indeed, had Lloyd George's left-centre government survived, it would have led the continent on a different course than that of Baldwin, Chamberlain and Churchill.[25]

Between these two interpretations lies the truth behind the disastrous failure of the first major encounter between Soviet Russia and the West. An unprecedentedly long, acrimonious meeting, Genoa was plagued by technical details, a cumbersome structure, excessive publicity, and stereotyped imagery of friends as well as opponents.[26]

The deeper reality in 1922 was the impact of World War I and the Russian Revolution, with their immense damage to life and property, trade and prosperity. In the Great War, Europe had lost 10 per cent of its population to combat, famine and disease, as well as a considerable amount of its foreign investments. Prices and debts had soared, public reserves and confidence had declined. The general feeling was that the entire region was a "wasteland", with masses of unemployed workers in Britain and Scandinavia, ravaged farmlands in France and Belgium, Poland and Serbia, almost worthless paper currencies in central Europe and acute capital and land hunger in Czechoslovakia and Romania. Although there is no precise way to measure Russia's suffering, Herbert Hoover's relief workers estimated that one half of the country was starving and that it would take half of America's wheat crop for four consecutive years plus one billion dollars to restore normal conditions of production and consumption. Russia's currency base was ruined, its transport system chaotic, many of its industrial workers idle. To be sure, throughout the European continent and within particular countries the scars of war and revolution were evenly distributed among the winners and the losers. In sum, the longing for a return to the world of 1914 was as unrealistic as the hope for quick, comprehensive revision.[27]

There were personal as well as material considerations at the Genoa Conference. The Bolshevik and Allied negotiators of 1922 were temperamentally ill-suited to deal with each other in a conciliatory manner. Moreover, they were forced to mediate among members of their own delegations, communicate with their capitals and assume heroic postures before the world press. The statesmen of the smaller powers, demanding to take part, played a minor, but distracting role.[28] Before and after Rapallo, the Germans pursued a dangerous policy of their own.

An unwieldy summit conference, located in an ailing, politically-charged port city and deliberately placed at a great distance from the major capitals, was an unpromising arena for a reconciliation between the capitalist and communist worlds. Genoa's overloaded cable facilities prevented prompt responses. Only the German delegation went pluckily to Rapallo without checking with Berlin. In addition, the constant surveillance of rival communications and their misinter-pretation, poisoned every element of the negotiations. Remote, but excited public opinion, worked against calm and measured delibera-tion. As the weeks went by and expenses piled up, the home fronts grew more frightened of the costs of an agreement than of the price of breaking off negotiations.

Both sides, while talking of "appeasement" and "coexistence", still heard the sound of the other's gunfire and referred continually to their recent military and ideological battles. Large segments of the Western world were frightened of bolshevism, and the Russians were still scarred by the wars of intervention. Neither Lloyd George's "shop-keeper talk" nor Chicherin's suaveness could conceal the rift that had opened up at Brest-Litovsk. If coexistence demanded renouncing the right to dictate to others one's form of government and system of property ownership, neither side had really given up its faith in ultimate victory.

The faint hopes of the internationalists were also to be sacrificed at Genoa. The League of Nations was excluded except to provide some technical assistance. This blow to the new world organization was understandable, given its unpopularity in London and Moscow as well as in Washington and Berlin. But the negotiators at Genoa were unable to produce a real alternative to the infant organization, only the prospect of more impromptu, inconclusive summits.[29] Indeed, like so many Great Power conferences of the 1920s and 1930s — and, in fact, all the way to Helsinki — the Genoa Conference not only damaged the prestige of a world institution but also ignored the voices of smaller, non-aligned countries.

Finally, the genesis of Soviet-Western diplomacy in the 1920s was firmly embedded in a complex global framework that transcended the rivalry between capitalism and communism. The emerging capitalist powers, Japan and the United States, were each pursuing narrow-minded, nationalistic policies;[30] Europe was divided into victors and vanquished and troubled by reparations and minority questions; the Near East, North Africa and Asia were erupting with nationalism and anti-colonialism. Indeed, Lenin and Chicherin, along with the hard-liners in Moscow, not only recognized the West's troubles and distractions but were all too tempted to exploit them.[31]

Lenin and Lloyd George each tried to use the Genoa Conference to bolster his domestic position by convincing the other to risk peace and cooperation. This episode illustrates the eternal link of domestic politics to the history of Cold War diplomacy. A daring, improvisational and flawed enterprise, the Genoa Conference represented an attempt at negotiation and compromise, an underlying acceptance of ideological differences and the search for areas of accommodation. The Soviet Union subsequently employed the Rapallo model to conclude bilateral agreements with individual Western governments. But, from a multinational perspective Genoa also became a model of failure, because neither side in 1922 was willing or able to desist from exploiting the other's weakness.

NOTES

1. Carole Fink, Axel Frohn and Jürgen Heideking (eds.), *Genoa, Rapallo, and the Reconstruction of Europe in 1922* (Cambridge, 1991) presents the most recent research findings as well as a thorough bibliography of primary and secondary sources.
2. Richard Ullman, *The Anglo-Soviet Accord* (Princeton, 1972).
3. On Lloyd George, see Kenneth O. Morgan, *Consensus and Disunity: The Lloyd Georgian Coalition Government, 1918–1922*, (Oxford, 1979) and Christoph Stamm, *Lloyd George zwischen Innen- und Aussenpolitik: Die britische Deutschlandpolitik 1921–1922* (Cologne, 1977); and on Lenin, E. H. Carr, *The Bolshevik Revolution*, Vol. 3 (Baltimore, 1966) and A. O. Chubarian, *V. I. Lenin i formirovanie sovetskoi vneshnei politiki* (Moscow, 1972).
4. Carr, *The Bolshevik Revolution*, Vol. 3, Ch. 27; I. Linder, "Lenin's Foreign Policy Activity", *International Affairs* 12 (1969), pp. 46–51.
5. See, for example, E. M. Chossudovsky, "Genoa Revisited: Russia and Coexistence", *Foreign Affairs* 50, 3 (April 1972), pp. 554–77; Franklyn Griffiths, *Genoa Plus 51: Changing Soviet Objectives in Europe* (Toronto, 1973).
6. "Two nineteenth century patterns blended in Lenin's mentality: balance of power politics and the primacy of economics in politics", in Louis Fischer, *The Life of Lenin* (New York, 1965), p. 557.

7. Richard K. Debo, "George Chicherin: Soviet Russia's Second Foreign Commissar", Ph.D. diss., University of Nebraska, 1964, p. 213. Cf. E. M. Chossudovsky, "Lenin and Chicherin: The Beginnings of Soviet Foreign Policy and Diplomacy", *Millennium* 3 (Spring 1974), pp. 7–9.

8. A. O. Chubarian, "V. I. Lenin i Genuia", *Istoriia SSSR* 2 (1970), pp. 39–50; also Richard B. Day, *Leon Trotsky and the Politics of Economic Isolation* (Cambridge, 1973).

9. For a review of the contrasting, even contradictory, Western attitudes towards Soviet Russia, see Fink *et al.*, *Genoa, Rapallo, and Reconstruction*.

10. Text in Great Britain, Cmd. 1546; also *Pravda*, 29 Oct. 1921.

11. *Documents on British Foreign Policy*, Vol. 19 (London: HMSO, 1974), pp. 19–34; also documents nos. 8, 13, 16, 19 and 25.

12. Carole Fink, *The Genoa Conference: European Diplomacy, 1921–1922* (Chapel Hill, 1984), pp. 44ff.

13. V. I. Lenin, *Collected Works*, Vol. 33, pp. 143–83; Vol. 45, pp. 409–13, 434, 446–48; also *Quarton Report*, "Interpretation of Recent Political Developments in Soviet Russia", Viborg, Finland, 27 Jan. 1922; US Department of State, 550 E1/40, and V. Buryakov, "Lenin's Diplomacy in Action", *International Affairs* 5 (1972), pp. 93, and Richard B. Day, "Trotsky and Preobrazhensky, The Troubled Unity of the Left Opposition", *Studies in Comparative Communism* 10, 1–2 (Spring–Summer 1977), pp. 69–86.

14. Memorably described in Harry Graf Kessler, *Tagebücher, 1918–1937* (Frankfurt-am-Main, 1961), p. 288.

15. The negotiations can be followed in *Documents on British Foreign Policy*, Vol. 19.

16. There is an immense literature on Rapallo; recent views in Hartmut Pogge von Strandmann, "Rapallo-Strategy in Preventive Diplomacy: New Sources and Interpretations", in Volker Berghahn and Martin Kitchen (eds.), *Germany in the Age of Total War* (London, 1981), and the essay by Peter Krüger in Fink *et al.*, *Genoa, Rapallo, and Reconstruction*.

17. Fink, *Genoa Conference*, p. 187.

18. *Ibid.*, pp. 225–31, 262–64.

19. *Ibid.*, pp. 210–13.

20. See the essay by Andrew Williams in Fink *et al.*, *Genoa, Rapallo, and Reconstruction*.

21. On the oil question, see the essay by A. A. Fursenko in Fink *et al.*, *Genoa, Rapallo, and Reconstruction*.

22. Fink, *Genoa Conference*, pp. 258–302.

23. See the essay by Stephen Schuker in Fink *et al.*, *Genoa, Rapallo, and Reconstruction*, for a strongly negative interpretation.

24. See, for example, George Kennan, *Russia and the West under Lenin and Stalin* (New York, 1961); *La conferenza di Genova e il Trattato di Rapallo (1922) Atti del convegno italo-sovietico* (Rome, 1974); Stephen White, *The Origins of Détente* (Cambridge, 1985).

25. Stephen E. Fritz, "Lloyd George and Peacemaking, 1918–1922", Ph.D. dissertation, University of Kentucky, 1972; Morgan, *Consensus and Disunity*.

26. Carole Fink, "Methods and Results of 20th Century Conference Diplomacy", in Jacques Bariéty and Antoine Fleury (eds.), *Mouvements et Initiatives de Paix dans la Politique Internationale, 1867–1928* (Berne, 1987), pp. 245–58.

27. See the recently opened document by Jacques Seydoux, Director of Political and Commercial Affairs of the French Foreign Ministry, 21 June 1922, Archives of the French Foreign Ministry (Paris), PA-AP Seydoux, Vol. 25.

28. See the essays by Hadler and Adám on the Little Entente, and Fleury on the neutrals, in Fink *et al.*, *Genoa, Rapallo, and Reconstruction*.

29. See the records of meetings of the League's officials who were present at Genoa: League of Nations Archives 40A 20136/20136–84 and "Genoa and the League", 24 May 1922, *ibid.*, Special Circular #184.

30. On the US and Japan, see the essays by Schuker and Ueta in Fink *et al.*, *Genoa, Rapallo, and Reconstruction*.

31. According to a British intelligence report, Chicherin met with Arab and Indian revolutionaries at Genoa: Foreign Office 371 N7227/6003/38; and Lenin recommended that the Third International support insurgents in South Africa: *Collected Works*, Vol. 45, p. 531.

# 2

# G.V. Chicherin:
# A Historical Perspective

## RICHARD K. DEBO

Western historians have generally viewed Georgii Vasil'evich Chicherin in a positive light. Both those who have examined his life and career as a whole and those who have studied narrower portions of it tend to agree that the second Soviet Foreign Commissar was a very able states-man of wit, intelligence and originality.[1] Soviet studies focusing on Chicherin have reached similar conclusions.[2] Many of his con-temporaries were not as complimentary, but then, they had to contend with his industry, intelligence and skill.[3] Chicherin had not been made Foreign Commissar to win accolades from his counterparts abroad or, for that matter, the praise of colleagues and political rivals at home. Even adversaries, such as Richard Child, who represented the United States at the Lausanne Conference and certainly had no affection for Soviet Russia or reason to view Chicherin favourably, were forced to acknowledge Chicherin's talents:

> All Chicherin's weapons are polished. His thrusts flash in the sun. He throws words like javelins. He is ironic, argumentative...He bids for the world's ear and furnishes it with entertainment, brilliant, clever, adroit. He attacks the citadels of his opponents.[4]

This testimony highlights Chicherin's combativeness, but it must be remembered that the 1920s was a tumultuous decade and virtually everyone who held power at the time reflected that turmoil. The Great War traumatized all who passed through it and left its mark, even on our own time.

Chicherin excelled because of an unusual education and superlative linguistic ability. At a time when many Foreign Ministers had little preparation for their office, Chicherin had served two sub-stantially different apprenticeships. The first had been in the tsarist

Foreign Ministry where as a young man, following his graduation from the University of St. Petersburg, he had spent several years reading volumes of documents in the Foreign Ministry archives. As a result, he acquired a deep and lasting knowledge of the policies of Alexander Gorchakov, who had been the Foreign Minister of Alexander II in the years following Russia's defeat in the Crimean War. Gorchakov had had to deal with an international situation in which Russian power was on the decline and hence his ability to influence other powers was limited. He had coped resolutely with the problem, consistently advising the tsar to avoid unnecessary entanglements in Europe, not to antagonize stronger powers, and to seek partial relief from British pressure regarding the Eastern Question by augmenting Russian influence in Central Asia. This would threaten the British in India and, Gorchakov hoped, render them more malleable in Europe. Chicherin would argue successfully for the pursuit of a similar policy in 1919, threatening the newly enlarged British Empire in Asia in order to compel London to end intervention in the Russian Civil War and extend political recognition to the Soviet government in Moscow.[5] The policy actually worked better for Chicherin than for his posthumous mentor. The first appearance of Soviet troops in northern Iran in May 1920 and the opening of negotiations with the Emir of Afghanistan alarmed the British Foreign Office and caused British officials in India to urge Whitehall to negotiate a political settlement with Moscow. This contributed greatly to the conclusion of the Anglo-Soviet trade agreement of 1921.

Chicherin served his second apprenticeship after he left the tsarist Foreign Ministry at the beginning of the twentieth century. This was in the international revolutionary movement among Russian political émigrés in western and central Europe. In exile, Chicherin became a Menshevik and remained so until his return to Russia in early 1918. With the outbreak of the Great War, he adhered to the internationalist faction of the Mensheviks, and from 1916 he followed a line very similar to that of Lenin. During those years he read virtually everything written by the major European Marxists and by 1918 was a prominent, if still secondary figure among proletarian internationalists on the continent. Therefore he possessed the intellectual framework, concepts and vocabulary necessary to be understood in the new Russia which emerged from the revolutions of 1917.

This combination of a knowledge of classical great power politics, together with the ability to express this understanding in the Marxist idiom of his era, made Chicherin unique in revolutionary Russia. Moreover, while multilingualism was not uncommon among Russian revolutionaries, Chicherin stood out even among the great linguists of the early Soviet government. Chicherin could converse in all the major languages of Europe and several of Asia. He routinely dictated his memos to foreign governments in their own languages and then corrected the text before it was transmitted. At both the Genoa and Lausanne conferences he addressed the delegates first in English then provided his own translation into French. In fact, he seems to have been the only major foreign minister of his decade who did not use translators. Robert Hodgson, the keenly observant British agent in Moscow, wrote in 1923 that Chicherin's "knowledge and gifts" were "unique in Soviet Russia and his devotion to the cause and his personal honesty are unquestioned".[6]

Chicherin was not without his idiosyncrasies. He was a perfectionist and what we would call today a "workaholic". Few could keep pace with him, and he required long hours from everyone who worked for him. As he was without family he actually lived in the Foreign Commissariat, and was always available to receive incoming telegrams and radio messages. It is no wonder that Lenin, another workaholic, valued him so much.[7] This industry, however, had a less positive side, because Chicherin was neither efficient nor well organized. His disorganization, in fact, was legendary, and he thought nothing of turning night into day, summoning foreign representatives to late night meetings in the Foreign Commissariat. This was not a problem with Count Ulrich von Brockdorff-Rantzau, the German Ambassador, who had similar work habits, but other foreign representatives did not find Chicherin's conduct of business nearly as satisfactory.

It should be kept in mind, however, that Chicherin had had no training as an administrator. Nothing in his life as a scholar and itinerant revolutionary had equipped him for taking charge of an emergent but rapidly growing bureaucracy. No professional staff of civil servants had greeted him on his arrival at the Foreign Commissariat.[8] Virtually all of the tsarist officials had refused to serve the Soviet government, and Leon Trotsky, the first Foreign Commissar, had not assigned a high priority to the recruitment of new staff before resigning his office in early March 1918. As a result, Chicherin had to build his new commissariat from scratch and it is hardly surprising that efficient organization was not immediately apparent at the Narkomindel.

Chicherin will always be associated in history with his foreign adversaries of the decade from 1918 to 1928. First among these was Lord Curzon, the British Foreign Secretary from 1919 to 1923. The rivalry which developed between these two talented and skillful ministers was extreme. Both used every diplomatic means available to promote the sharply conflicting policies of their governments. Neither yielded anything to the other. The two actually had a great deal in common, as both were great aristocrats in the service of multinational states. The structure of the states was quite different, but the problems presented to those who defended them were quite similar. Had Curzon and Chicherin ever had the opportunity to sit down and dispassionately discuss their common affairs they would quickly have found that they had similar attitudes to the military commanders, economic ministers and proconsuls of their respective regimes. They would also have discovered that they had a similar relationship to their heads of government, Curzon to Lloyd George, and Chicherin to Lenin. Neither Lloyd George nor Lenin was prepared to give his Foreign Secretary/Commissar the latitude each would have wished. Both Lenin and Lloyd George set different priorities from those recommended by their Foreign Ministers.

These similarities would have emerged very quickly from a frank discussion between the two. But, a dialogue of this nature was unthinkable at the time. The two, therefore, engaged in long-distance hostilities. At one point near the end of the negotiation of the Anglo-Soviet Trade Agreement of 1921 Curzon, having just received a particularly venomous communication from Chicherin, declared in a confidential memorandum circulated to the British cabinet:

> With so colossal and finished a liar it is useless to cope. Nor, after my last reply, which I said would be the last of the series, would I propose to do so. The fusillade might go on til the dark-haired among us become grey, the grey-haired white, and white bald.[9]

Curzon in this instance was also venting his frustration with his own colleagues, in particular with Prime Minister Lloyd George who, in opposition to the Foreign Secretary, insisted on pressing ahead with the completion of the trade agreement.

Curzon and the office which he administered, were not particularly devoted to the pursuit of truth in their relations with Chicherin and the Foreign Commissariat. On one occasion in 1920, the Foreign Office, without consulting Curzon, had threatened Soviet Russia with naval reprisals for an allegedly serious incident which Chicherin was easily able to prove had never happened. Taken aback by this revelation, Curzon demanded an explanation from his officials. It proved so unsatisfactory that he commented acidly: "...I think that the Order of Jesuits would derive much pleasure from our explanations".[10]

There was open personal animus in the Curzon-Chicherin relationship. Each genuinely loathed the other. Nor did matters improve when they met briefly at Genoa in April 1922 and then for a longer period at Lausanne later in the year. Chicherin long felt that Curzon had treated him disrespectfully and in Lausanne, when the British Foreign Secretary received him and conducted the entire interview while stretched out on a *chaise longue*, the Foreign Commissar was incensed. Curzon genuinely had a bad back, but a man of his breeding would certainly not have received, say, the French Foreign Minister in this manner. When Chicherin left the meeting he told a reporter that Curzon was mistaken if he believed that his family was of nobler and more ancient lineage than his own. The Chicherin family (originally Cicerini) could trace its roots to the nobility of imperial Rome. Thus, claimed the Soviet Foreign Commissar, his ancestors had sat in the Roman Senate at a time when Curzon's wandered the barren shores of Britain clad only in blue paint.[11]

Behind this personal animosity, however, lay conflicting views of Soviet Russia's place in the post Great War world order. When it became clear in mid-1919 that Soviet Russia would probably not only survive the Civil War but emerge with most of the former empire intact, Chicherin, with the sanction of Lenin and the Politburo, began striving for the restoration of Russia, if not as a great power, at least as a major one and certainly the pre-eminent force in eastern Europe.

This was one of the primary causes of the Soviet-Polish War of 1920. Marshal Pilsudski of Poland had refused to yield hegemony in eastern Europe to Soviet Russia without a struggle. The British would not support Pilsudski's pretensions, but neither would they recognize the claim, made by Chicherin, to Soviet primacy in eastern Europe. As usual, the British supported the emergence of a balance of power in which they reserved for themselves the favourable role of *terens gaudens*. Thus Whitehall, and above all Curzon, expected Soviet Russia to assume the role of a secondary state: stronger than Poland to be sure, but not strong enough to threaten the many British interests in Asia. The failure of the Allied intervention in the Civil War had shown that this objective could not be achieved militarily, but Curzon and the Foreign Office felt that much could be achieved by political means. Soviet Russia, they believed, should be kept at arm's length, relations reduced to a bare minimum, while other states should be encouraged to take a similar course.[12] This infuriated Chicherin, and he sought every possible escape from the isolation which Britain attempted to impose on Moscow. In this he was only partly successful, and during Chicherin's incumbency Soviet Russia never succeeded in achieving the status to which he aspired.

Of course, British hostility was not grounded in Curzon's personal animosity to Chicherin or his policies. Successive foreign secretaries would likewise seek to marginalize Soviet influence in Europe and Asia. In this they were aided initially by the counterproductive policies of the Comintern and, in the NEP period, by the poor performance of the Soviet economy. Ironically, when the Comintern was tamed and rapid industrialization begun, the ferocity of Stalin's dictatorship rendered the Soviet Union even less attractive to London than before. In short, the tragedy of the failure of collective security in the thirties had roots extending back to the inability of the Soviet and Western governments to find more than a *modus vivendi* as a basis for their relationship after the conclusion of the Great War.[13]

In contrast to his hostile relations with Curzon, Chicherin developed a close personal friendship with Count Ulrich von Brockdorff-Rantzau, who served as German Ambassador in Moscow from 1922 until his death in 1928. Both were aristocratic statesmen with similar intellectual interests. They were able to speak frankly with one another on almost any subject. They both represented states which had been defeated in the Great War and, in their view, treated badly by the victorious Allies. They thought in terms of *realpolitik* and ways in which to maximize the reduced power of the states they represented. Both opposed the international system established for Europe by the Versailles treaty. Rantzau had been German Foreign Minister at the time of the Paris Peace Conference and had been summoned to Versailles to receive the document which Wilson, Lloyd George and Clemenceau had formulated. He chose to resign rather than sign the treaty.

Chicherin, for his part, had become fixed in the public mind as a leading opponent of Versailles and the League of Nations. He had missed no opportunity to attack the treaty and mock the League. During Chicherin's stewardship, Soviet Russia would have nothing to do with what he referred to as the "League of Victors". Rantzau deeply appreciated the full-blooded support the Foreign Commissar provided Germany in opposing the Versailles treaty. On one occasion he referred to Chicherin as "nicht nur ein Staatsmann, sondern auch ein Herr" (not only a statesman, but a gentleman, as well).[14]

It should be noted, however, that the basis for substantial political agreement between the two men and their governments, the so-called *Schicksalgemeinschaft* (community of fate), emerged only after the Allied forces had imposed the Versailles treaty on Germany. Although Rantzau, as German Ambassador in Copenhagen during World War I, had long been acquainted with Russian social democrats, he had not always been favourably disposed to them. In his six-month term as German Foreign Minister (until 28 June 1919), he had pursued his government's policy of seeking a more lenient peace from the victorious Allies in return for assisting the Western powers to crush bolshevism in Russia.

It was only after the failure of this approach that Rantzau resigned as Foreign Minister and began promoting closer ties with the revolutionary government in Moscow. Needless to say, Chicherin had scorned Rantzau's policy of seeking accommodation with the Western powers. After the conclusion of the Rapallo treaty in April 1922, the two worked together to further both political and economic cooperation between Russia and Germany in order to increase their governments' freedom to manoeuvre in broader questions of international relations.

These concerns, however, were not the only ones on the agenda. Rantzau's Eastern orientation had to compete with a rapidly developing Western one advocated by the German Foreign Minister Gustav Stresemann after 1923.[15] Furthermore the German army had been conducting its own policy in Russia, frequently at odds with that of Rantzau, who feared the generals would compromise his political objectives through ill-considered agreements with the Red Army. Much of this is known through German documents uncovered after the end of World War II, but the Soviet side now requires detailed study.[16] Just as there was more than one German perspective on the development of Soviet-German relations, there were numerous Soviet ones as well. The intrusive Comintern and the Red Army had their own objectives and these must be studied in the future, together with other influences on Soviet-German relations which have not yet come to light.

A number of other questions need to be studied more closely. Uppermost, is the process by which Soviet foreign policy was formulated in the 1920s. Until he fell ill, Lenin appears to have supervised Chicherin's day-to-day conduct of foreign relations. Who, if anyone, assumed this role in the immediate aftermath of Lenin's illness? How did this change with time, and especially after Lenin's death? To whom did Chicherin report and in what manner? What other agencies and/or individuals were heard at the same time? Western historians have long assumed that the power struggle following Lenin's illness had a negative impact on Soviet foreign policy. Do Soviet sources confirm this? If so, what was the effect of this struggle on Soviet policy, for example, in the Ruhr crisis of early 1923, and the near revolutionary circumstances in Germany later that year? Similarly we need to look more closely at the evolution of Soviet reaction to the stabilization of Germany following the end of the great inflation and the adoption of the Dawes Plan. There must have been several views on this process as well as on Stresemann's move toward *rapprochement* with the Western powers and the application for German membership in the League of Nations.

Another area requiring further study is the emergent influence of

Joseph Stalin on Soviet foreign policy.[17] As a leading member of the Bolshevik Central Committee and Politburo, Stalin had long had an interest in certain areas of foreign policy and, after 1919 at any rate, did not hesitate to express his views on those which concerned him. In the last eighteen months of the Civil War he intervened time and again to promote policies which he considered necessary or desirable. But there must have been a qualitative change in his ability to influence foreign policy, first after assuming the post of General Secretary and then following Lenin's serious illness. At what point did the Narkomindel begin to respond directly to Stalin's initiatives and what form did this response take? Chicherin and Stalin did not get along particularly well prior to 1923. Did relations simply continue to deteriorate or was there some period between 1923 and 1926 when the two worked better together than before? By 1926 we know that Chicherin was complaining bitterly of Stalin's interference in the conduct of foreign policy, but this knowledge is based only on very limited sources. Are there Narkomindel documents which provide a full exposition of Chicherin's views and how they developed over time? Do they, or other sources, show how Chicherin was eased out of office after 1928? When Chicherin finally resigned in 1930 Litvinov, not surprisingly, declared that this would not result in any significant change of policy. At what point did a change of policy take place and how in fact was Litvinov installed as the actual head of the Foreign Commissariat? All these and many other questions require urgent attention in the years to come.

## NOTES

1. Louis Fischer, *The Soviets in World Affairs: A History of the Relations between the Soviet Union and the Rest of the World, 1917–1929*, 2 Vols. (New York, 1930); E. H. Carr, *A History of Soviet Russia*, 10 Vols. (New York, 1951–1979); George Kennan, *Russia and the West under Lenin and Stalin* (Boston, 1961), are classic works in the field. More recent interpretations are offered by Teddy J. Uldricks, *Diplomacy and Ideology. The Origins of Soviet Foreign Relations 1917–1930* (London, 1979); Timothy Edward O'Connor, *Diplomacy and Revolution. G. V. Chicherin and Soviet Foreign Affairs, 1918–1930* (Iowa, 1988); Richard K. Debo, *Survival and Consolidation: The Foreign Policy of Soviet Russia, 1918–1921* (Montreal/Kingston, 1992).
2. A. O. Chubarian, *Brestskii mir* (Moscow, 1964); A. O. Chubarian, *V. I. Lenin i formirovanie sovetskoi vneshei politiki* (Moscow, 1972); I. L. Gorokhov, I. Zamiatin, I. Zemskov, *G. V. Chicherin: Diplomat leninskoi shkoly* (Moscow, 1966); S. V. Zarnitskii and A. N. Sergeev, *Chicherin* (Moscow, 1980); Yelena Belevich and Vladimir Sokolov, "Foreign Affairs Commissar Georgy Chicherin", *International Affairs* 3 (1991), pp. 90–99.
3. See for example David R. Francis, *Russia from the American Embassy* (New York, 1921); Karl Helfferich, *Der Weltkrieg*, 3 Vols. (Berlin, 1922); R. H. Bruce Lockhart, *British Agent* (London, 1933); Joseph Noulens, *Mon ambassade en Russie soviétique 1917–1919* (Paris, 1933); W. J. Oudendyk, *Ways and Byways in Diplomacy* (London, 1939).

4. Richard W. Child, *A Diplomat Looks at Europe* (New York, 1925).
5. G. V. Chicherin, *Stat'i i rechi po voprosam mezhdunarodnoi politiki* (Moscow, 1961), pp. 86–98.
6. *Documents on British Foreign Policy, 1919–1939*, First series, XXV, p. 45.
7. V. I. Lenin, *Leninskii sbornik* XXXVI, pp. 54–55.
8. See Debo, *Revolution and Survival: The Foreign Policy of Soviet Russia, 1917–1918* (Toronto, 1979), pp. 19–20, 88–89.
9. Public Record Office, Foreign Office (FO) 371/6853/N.1997/5/38.
10. FO 371/3981/1089/193046.
11. *New York Times*, 8 July 1936, p. 19.
12. See Debo, *Survival and Consolidation*; Richard H. Ullman, *The Anglo-Soviet Accord* (Princeton, 1972); and Stephen White, *Britain and the Bolshevik Revolution: A Study in the Politics of Diplomacy 1920–1924* (New York, 1980).
13. On Anglo-Soviet relations in the twenties, see Gabriel Gorodetsky, *The Precarious Truce: Anglo-Soviet Relations, 1924–1927* (Cambridge, 1977) and White, *Britain and the Bolshevik Revolution*.
14. Papers of Brockdorff-Rantzau, German Foreign Office documents, microfilm copy 9101/225129.
15. See Kurt Rosenbaum, *Community of Fate. German-Soviet Diplomatic Relations 1922–1928* (Syracuse, 1965).
16. A start has already been made. See Sergei Gorlov, "Soviet-German Military Cooperation, 1920–1933", *International Affairs* 7 (1990), pp. 95–113.
17. For an earlier study, see Robert C. Tucker, "The Emergence of Stalin's Foreign Policy", *Slavic Review* 36 (Dec. 1977), pp. 563–89.

# 3

# The Formulation
# of Soviet Foreign Policy:
# Ideology and *Realpolitik*

## GABRIEL GORODETSKY

At first glance, the initial decade of Soviet diplomacy appears rather impressive. In spite of the limited arsenal at its disposal, the revolutionary regime was able to exploit the rivalry amongst the major European powers and repel attempts to suppress the revolution by military, diplomatic and economic means. By the beginning of 1924, the Soviet government had gained *de jure* recognition from the major European countries and had even succeeded in attracting foreign capital on a small scale. However, these accomplishments were marred by persisting fears of renewed intervention, as well as by frustration at the revolution's failure to extend beyond the borders of Russia.

The first decade of the Russian Revolution was characterized by a dynamic re-evaluation of foreign policy. The Bolsheviks faced a tremendous challenge in their attempts to reconcile two contradictory factors: the axiomatic need to spread the revolution and the prosaic need to guarantee survival within recognized borders. The difficulties were overcome initially through the adoption of Trotsky's theory of permanent revolution. The concept rested on the assumption that revolution in Russia, the weak link in the chain of capitalism, would not be secured until the threat of imperialist intervention was removed by a revolution in the industrialized countries of the West. The establishment of socialism in economically backward Russia depended, therefore, on technical and economic support from successful revolutions in such countries.[1]

As long as the belief in an imminent revolution persisted, the Bolsheviks refrained from formulating principles of foreign policy.

Trotsky viewed his position as Commissar for Foreign Affairs with contempt. He saw little significance in establishing diplomatic relations with capitalist regimes whose fate, he believed, had already been determined. "The victorious revolution," he claimed, "would not bother seeking recognition from the representatives of capitalist diplomacy." In a fiery speech to the astounded employees of the newly formed Foreign Commissariat, he announced his intention to publish the secret treaties with the imperialist governments, print revolutionary pamphlets, and then "close shop" and dismiss them.[2] In 1926, British Foreign Office officials noted with satisfaction the rise of the "strong, stern, silent" Stalin as the unchallenged leader of the Party. "It is not surprising," they commented, "that the defeat of the fanatic Bolshevik opposition indicates a foreign policy which utilizes 'national tools'."[3]

The gap between Trotsky's pronouncements and the impression of the British Foreign Office reflects the change which Soviet foreign policy had undergone during the first decade of the revolution. The initial supposition that foreign relations and official recognition would be superfluous in a world shattered by revolution, was replaced, particularly from 1924 onwards, by a sober-minded evaluation of the need to reach a *modus vivendi* with the outside world. And yet, even after the setback to the world revolution and the failure of the capitalist regimes to crush the Bolshevik regime by force, class antagonism remained a principal element in the formulation of Soviet foreign policy. Throughout the 1920s it was assumed that reconciliation between the two political systems was virtually unattainable as long as the capitalist world was determined to mount a crusade against the Soviet Union.[4]

Indeed normalization was rarely presented as an ultimate goal, but rather as "breathing space" tactics.[5] These tactics were endorsed by Lenin and employed successfully in the drawing up of the Peace Decree, the Treaty of Brest-Litovsk and the Treaty of Rapallo. The continuity between Lenin's tenets and their incremental realization by Stalin is all too obvious. The Soviet leadership was gradually drifting towards a more traditional image in its foreign policy.

The Bolshevik leadership was generally in agreement with the idea that appropriate conditions had been created for economic integration with Western Europe. It may well be argued that the mutual suspicion, which led to the collapse of the symbiosis of the 1920s, was a major factor in the gradual but steady decline towards the Cold War in the international arena, as well as in the search for alternate economic solutions such as collectivization. On the domestic scene, Aleksei Rykov, chairman of the Council of People's Commissars, Lev

Kamenev, member of the ruling triumvirate from 1924, and Grigorii Sokol'nikov, the Treasury Commissar, persisted in their efforts to expand trade with the Western European countries. Georgii Chicherin, Trotsky's successor as Commissar for Foreign Affairs, declared:

> There may be differences of opinion as to the duration of the capitalist system, but at present the capitalist system exists, so that a *modus vivendi* must be found in order that our socialist states and the capitalist states may coexist peacefully and in normal relations with one another. This is a necessity in the interest of all.[6]

Stalin, whose statements on foreign policy were few prior to the death of Lenin, took a similar position:

> Some comrades who participated in the October Revolution were convinced that the socialist revolution in Russia would only be successful if it sparked a massive revolutionary uprising in the West. The course of events contradicts this assumption. It is a fact that the Russian Revolution, which did not win the support of the Western proletariat and which has remained surrounded by hostile capitalist regimes, continues to exist.[7]

The leadership had by no means abandoned its belief in a proletarian revolution. On the contrary, world revolution continued to be regarded as inevitable. The NEP and the new diplomacy were conceived as temporary measures. Indeed, throughout the 1920s even the moderate Bolsheviks reverted to radical positions when revolutionary opportunities presented themselves. The militant stance taken during the political upheavals in Germany in 1921 and 1923 stands out in particular. In 1921, in what became known as Red March, Grigorii Zinov'ev, the president of the Comintern and subsequently a member of the ruling triumvirate, openly incited the German communists to participate in the struggle. There is considerable evidence of Lenin's support for this effort, which was at variance with the tenets of the new moderate policy which he himself had recently initiated. The revival of revolutionary opportunities in Germany in 1923 created a strong wave of expectations. Trotsky preached direct support for the German Communist party. Bukharin reverted to the concept of revolutionary war in *Pravda*. Revolutionary momentum reached its peak with overt Soviet support for the rebellion in Hamburg in October 1923. However, the complete collapse of the uprising seriously undermined the assumption that the security of the Soviet Union depended exclusively upon a proletarian revolution in Europe.[8]

Frustration over the failure of the revolutions in central and eastern Europe, and the unanticipated *de jure* recognition by Italy, Great Britain and France, persuaded the Bolshevik leadership that the intermediate "breathing space" tactics would have to be extended. However, the tacit admission of even partial and temporary political stability posed a contradiction in a regime which presented itself as dynamic and internationalist. Desperate attempts were made by the Bolsheviks in the first decade to adhere to their revolutionary principles through the adoption of a dual foreign policy. This dualism was manifested in the attempt to achieve national security by fostering diplomatic relations with the West, while simultaneously encouraging subversion and revolutionary activities when conditions seemed propitious.

The overwhelming tendency in both Western and Soviet his-toriography has been to overlook the dualism of Soviet foreign policy by avoiding the examination of revolution and *realpolitik* under the same spotlight. This chapter will outline briefly the interplay between the two components and identify the circumstances in which an internal hierarchy, establishing clear priorities, was constituted.

In the 1920s, relations with Britain tested the dual concept under-lying Soviet policy making: the need to preserve the Soviet leadership's status as the vanguard of world revolution without sacrificing national interests. The point of convergence between the Comintern's policy and Soviet diplomacy occurred in Britain shortly after the hesitant *de jure* recognition of the Soviet Union by the first Labour government in 1924. However, MacDonald's dislike of communism and his political weakness hampered any genuine improvement in relations.

The pressing economic exigencies and fear of renewed intervention resulted in a search for alternative methods for realizing foreign policy goals. This was especially true after the fall of the Labour government in November 1924, when the issue of Labour's association with communism, exemplified by the Anglo-Soviet treaties and the "Zinov'ev letter", had dominated the election campaign.[9] Extraordinary efforts were directed towards gaining diplomatic advantages from the fraternal ties established with various British workers' movements, particularly with the Trades Union Congress (TUC). These steps were taken despite the clear realization that such opportunism weakened the revolutionary drive in Britain and undermined the position of the Communist party there.

The ineffectiveness of this unconventional diplomacy was striking. With hindsight, it is difficult to grasp the extraordinary Soviet expectation that the trade unions would succeed in forcing the Conservative government to adopt a benign policy towards the Soviet Union. The clue to understanding these expectations lies in Russia's experiences between 1918 and 1920. It should be borne in mind that in 1924 the Soviet leadership tended to draw on the recent Leninist heritage, rather than either the Tsarist doctrines of foreign policy (as is often suggested) or Marxist theory which had never established a *modus operandi* for foreign affairs.

While the British government had led the intervention in the Civil War, the British Left had consistently opposed the dispatch of troops and munitions to Poland in 1920. In 1918, workers' action councils had begun to appear spontaneously in various places in Britain. Under the slogan "Hands off Russia", they engaged in propaganda to end British military intervention in Russia.

In mid-1919, the movement's centre of gravity shifted to a national level, following cooperation between the Labour party and the TUC. The government was pressed to "immediately take appropriate steps to return British forces from Russia". With the advance of the Red Army towards Warsaw in August 1920, the British government weighed the possibility of intervention and prepared to arm Poland. An action council was instantly set up aimed at forestalling the government. The adoption of the Russian revolutionary concept of *council* (soviet) attracted undue attention in Moscow. In a memorable episode British longshoremen refused to load the *Jolly George* with weapons bound for Danzig.[10]

At this stage the ambivalent Russian position on "revolution and diplomacy" had already emerged. Kamenev was present in Britain during the time of creation of the action council and held discussions with Lloyd George in an attempt to bring about *de facto* recognition of the Soviet Union. While Kamenev was the strongest ideological critic of its organization, he was also aware of the council's great diplomatic potential. In his messages to Lenin and Chicherin (which the British intercepted and deciphered), he noted his frequent contacts with the council and "the importance of the British labour organizations, which prevent war against the Soviet Union by confronting their government". In another message, Kamenev expressed amazement at the fact "that the workers stand by us, support Russian interests at all costs, under all circumstances, regardless of the issue at hand".[11]

Researchers are still divided over whether the council's pressure was the decisive factor in the government's decision not to renew the intervention, or whether the labour movement would have, in fact, resorted to "direct political action". The Russians, however, attributed the removal of the threat of military intervention to the efforts of the trade unions.

The theoretical foundations for tighter collaboration with trade unions abroad was introduced at the Eleventh Party Congress and at the Fourth Comintern Congress in 1922 through the adoption of "united front" tactics. These tactics permitted the establishment of alliances with non-communist organizations but limited them strictly to cooperation with the rank-and-file; political agreements with the higher echelons were ruled out.[12]

The deviation from the orthodox ideological position was accelerated in 1924 when a united front was created from above with the leaders of the TUC. Marxist acrobatics were employed to justify the front on the grounds that the prominent leaders of the trade unions, now serving as ministers in MacDonald's government, were replaced by militant leaders in the TUC who were even aligned to the Communist party. The tactics were approved by the Fifth Congress of the Comintern and the Third of the Profintern (the International Congress of Trade Unions) in early 1924. Zinov'ev now reluctantly admitted the ascendancy of an "era of stabilization of capitalism" which was characterized by a regrouping of the European capitalist states; he advocated a reorientation in the activities of the communist parties and the front organizations in defence of Russia, which represented the peak of world revolution.[13]

The encounter between the representatives of the trade unions of both countries took place during the Anglo-Soviet conference, which was convened in London in the spring and summer of 1924 to iron out outstanding economic issues. The Soviet delegation to the conference was led by Mikhail Tomskii, the president of the All-Union Central Council of Trade Unions (AUCCTU) and a member of the Politburo. A reception held by the TUC in honour of the Soviet delegates turned into a miniature conference in which "a very cordial and frank exchange of opinions occurred"; all present realized "the necessity of direct contact between the two movements" but no concrete proposals were made in that direction.[14] The fraternal feelings of solidarity acquired particular significance when it was realized during the arduous negotiations that the Labour government was reluctant to proceed beyond *de jure* recognition.[15]

The collaboration took on a more institutionalized and organized form as a result of the fall of the Labour government in November 1924. The Conservative government returned to power determined to bring an end to Labour's flirtation with Russia.[16]

In November 1924 a TUC delegation paid a reciprocal visit to Moscow. From the moment the delegation set foot in the Soviet Union it became apparent that the Russians were seeking an effective alternative to their deteriorating diplomatic status in Britain. This was clearly reflected in Zinov'ev's survey of the international scene to the Sixth Trade Union Congress at which the British delegates were present. Zinov'ev foresaw an improvement in the situation not through the "art of the Red diplomats" or the "strength of the Red Army", but through the mobilization of support of the world proletariat based on the very general terms of "struggle against reaction and capitalism".[17]

Zinov'ev was not uttering empty slogans; his speech accurately reflected the views of the Politburo, which had adopted the "unity" policy as a means of thwarting the belligerent designs of the British government.[18] Indeed, the visit was concluded with an agreement in principle between the trade union movements of both countries to form a permanent joint committee.[19] In order to conceal Soviet opportunist tendencies, the future alliance was cloaked in revolutionary phraseology. It was often argued that under certain circumstances the collaboration might have become a turning-point in the history of the international labour movement.[20]

The ambiguity of the Russian position resulted in the creation in April 1925 of an amorphous Anglo-Russian Joint Advisory Committee (ARJAC), with the ill-defined intention to "weld closer the friendly relations" between the trade union movements of the two countries through the promotion of cooperation "as advisable", the initiation of discussions as "necessary...from time to time", and the extension of joint contacts and development of mutual aid "as opportunities were provided".[21]

The Russians undoubtedly hoped that this ambiguity would allow them to present the committee as a revolutionary organization, while at the same time enabling them to use it for diplomatic purposes. The latter aspirations were kept alive by Tomskii, the Trade Union Council president, while the revolutionary ones, relegated to second place, were pursued by Lozovskii, the General Secretary of the Profintern.

By the autumn of 1925 the conservative wing of the TUC, headed by Ernest Bevin and Walter Citrine, had resumed leadership of the TUC. Their motives for cooperation were now strictly economic: to ease unemployment by opening Russian markets for British goods. Some representatives, such as Walter Thomas, Minister for the Colonies, expressed their determination "to fight Moscow's unsatisfactory methods to the bitter end".[22]

It soon dawned on the Russians that their expectations from the still incipient committee had been set too high. The vague nature of the cooperation had a serious disadvantage: it allowed the British partners to abstain from either militant or diplomatic activity during a crisis. The Soviet approach was fundamentally anachronistic. Just as they had exaggerated the threat of renewed British military intervention, so too they tended to overestimate the assistance they would receive from the workers' organizations. The latent tensions in the dual policy, and the pressing need to establish priorities, became the focus of a bitter debate launched by the Trotskyite opposition, which demanded the dismantling of the partnership at the Fourteenth Congress of the

Communist Party in December 1925.[23]

The disenchantment with the TUC as a revolutionary body was demonstrated during the sixth plenum of the Executive Committee of the Comintern (IKKI) and the fourth session of the Profintern in early 1926. The resolutions, though lauding the *rapprochement* between the trade unions of the two countries, nonetheless expressed strong scepticism about the success of such a policy, given the "state of insufficient development" of the left wing in England.[24] Consequently, the Russians retained only those functions of the joint committee which promised to facilitate trade between the two countries. They lowered their expectations further after the arrest of the entire leadership of the lilliputian British Communist party in October 1925.[25]

The diminishing interest in ARJAC was matched by intensive moves to improve Anglo-Soviet relations through the conventional diplomatic channels. These approaches evoked some response at the beginning of 1926, when considerable pressure was exerted on the Foreign Office by economic circles in Britain, to create the proper conditions for the opening of the Russian market to British goods. "A hint of the glad eye towards Russia," Austen Chamberlain, the Secretary of State for Foreign Affairs, informed the cabinet, "might be useful at home and abroad." He promptly declared in Parliament that the Franco-Soviet negotiations, then in progress, might "facilitate the renewal of negotiations with Britain".[26] Germany's determination not to sacrifice its ally in the East for the sake of gaining a new one in the West also contributed to the thaw in Anglo-Soviet relations.[27]

It was, however, the Russian involvement in the British General Strike of May 1926, an inevitable outcome of the dual policy, that halted the *rapprochement*. The Russians tended to belittle the importance of the approaching dispute in the British mining industry. Zinov'ev's eagerness to instil hope in the British proletariat by emphasizing the uneven stabilization and overall deterioration of world capitalism was checked by his own cautious estimate that even if the revolution followed the quickest route, it was expected only within "3–4–5 years". This guarded optimism, however, was dampened by Bukharin, who stated that the situation appeared to be unrevolutionary. Even the militant Lozovskii proposed restrained slogans calling for "a more practical, concrete approach to the masses, and the implementation of united front tactics". Rather than intervene more actively in the dispute, the Russians allowed this hopeless outlook to dictate a fatalist policy of "letting the events show the results".[28] The unequivocal verdict in Moscow was that strikes of solidarity with the miners, let alone a general strike in Britain, were unlikely.[29] Indeed, the prospects of a prolonged struggle there seemed so unreal that in

Russia itself there were no consultations with trade union leaders, even with leaders of the miners, to plan assistance to their British brethren.[30]

As relations deteriorated, the Russians could not afford to abandon the joint committee at that time since this would have been tantamount to accepting the criticism aired by the Leningrad and left opposition during the Fourteenth Congress. A more substantial reason was recognition of the diplomatic potential of the cooperation, the importance of which had increased as a result of the dramatic decline in the diplomatic position of the Soviet Union during that period. The powerful die-hards among the conservatives demanded the severance of relations. The Locarno treaty, inspired by Britain, weakened the Rapallo treaty and threatened to further isolate the Soviet Union. It also paved the way for the entry of Germany into the League of Nations, which the Russians regarded as the spearhead of the crusade against the Soviet Union. "The so-called League of Nations," declared Chicherin, "is, in fact, a convenient disguise for offensives against the country of workers-peasants, whenever capitalist policy does not wish, or more correctly, is not able, to renew intervention." However, the expedient views of Tomskii, who held the balance of power in the Politburo, prevailed. He continued to advocate maintaining the collaboration, even if it involved "hanging to the devil's horns or approaching the Pope in Rome".

The Russian assessment concerning the situation in Britain was to be completely discredited by subsequent events. On 1 May, as a result of the termination of the agreement with the government and the refusal of the owners and the miners to withdraw their demands, the miners found themselves locked out. A special conference of trade union executives which was already in session placed the authority for conducting a national stoppage in the hands of the General Council of the TUC. The date was set for 3 May, to allow for hasty preparations, but also to enable the General Council, which was averse to taking such a course, to reach a negotiated settlement with the government. This, however, proved to be unexpectedly difficult because of the cabinet's confidence in its ability to handle the situation with the help of the strike-breaking machinery meticulously prepared by W. Joynson-Hicks, the Home Secretary.[31]

The danger inherent in the double-edged united front tactics was revealed with the TUC's decision to launch a general strike on 1 May 1926. This threw the Russians into a state of perplexity. No commentary was issued, while the unprecedented step was taken of withholding publication of all major daily newspapers so long as negotiations were still in progress. In the meantime, there was feverish activity behind the scenes in an attempt to establish a concerted attitude towards the strike. This was particularly difficult as the Russians could neither "unreservedly approve" the policy of the General Council, which had been the target for continuous abuse, nor remain "mere onlookers, mere observers of the greatest historical events".[32] Yet by the time the strike entered its first day hardly any signs of hesitancy could be detected. The Soviet regime, which purported to lead world revolution, could only wholeheartedly support it. A special meeting of the executive bureau of the Profintern, which was convened on 4 May, spent minimal time on self-incrimination. Crude attempts were made to conceal the Russians' embarrassment and create the impression that the revolutionary events were inevitable. This campaign was so successfully executed that only a month later Stalin, turning a blind eye to his own failing, made an uncontested accusation that the strike had taken the General Council by "complete surprise".[33]

The demonstration of a united façade and the support for the miners led observers to dramatize the spontaneous enthusiasm of the Russians, who "hung on the telegraph wire waiting with tense impatience for every tiny item of news".[34] However, it was not until 6 May that all the executive committees of the soviets passed resolutions in support of the strike, following the lead given by the government.[35] Heartfelt jubilation was manifested mostly in lower echelons, where Party members were not acquainted with the animosity which had penetrated the relations of the Russian trade unions with their British counterparts.[36] Thus, despite their conversion, the Russians remained highly doubtful about the outcome of the strike so long as the General Council remained in control. Even Zinov'ev's exhilaration about the arrival of a "new era in the English and world workers' movement" was diluted by awareness of the "acute danger from the right-wing leaders of both the trade union movement and Labour". He expressed doubts about the ability of such leaders to transfer the strike to the "political realm".[37] It was clear that the Russians did not expect the strike to develop into a full-scale revolution. And yet they could not possibly turn their backs on a class struggle of such magnitude even if their expectations of it were limited. On the other hand, utmost precautions were taken to disclaim direct interference by the Soviet government in the conflict; this would be more than likely to strain Anglo-Soviet relations. Support of the strike was therefore initially explained as discharging the debt of the Russian proletariat to the British workers for their help during the intervention. The organization of assistance was assigned to the Profintern, a non-governmental institution.[38]

The TUC's rejection of the "red gold" from Moscow, shook the foundations of the collaboration with the British trade unionists. Once the news of the unconditional surrender of the TUC reached Moscow, the General Council was criticized for its "disastrous and treacherous" conduct of the strike, as contrasted with the masses, who provided "an example of how to lead such a gigantic strike".[39] With Lozovskii in full control, and the Trotskyite opposition launching its major onslaught on Stalin, the diplomatic considerations behind the collaboration policy seem to have fallen into temporary neglect. Stalin, who had anticipated the opposition's censure of the opportunist motives behind the collaboration, now gave official cachet to Lozovskii's prolific criticisms of the TUC.[40] In the Politburo the opposition was forestalled by the majority's declaration that the left wing of the General Council was "as much responsible" as the right wing for the "shameful collapse of the strike".[41]

Once the opposition was defeated Stalin gave his seal of approval to the continued cultivation of solidarity with the TUC, with the clear intent to take advantage of it as an instrument of diplomacy. As if oblivious to the criticism of the leadership of the TUC, the Executive Committee of the Comintern openly stated that ARJAC could be counted upon to play a "momentous role in the struggle against all attempts at intervention directed against the USSR".[42] At the same time, the Comintern and the Profintern reserved the right to engage in an unbridled, penetrating criticism of their partners. This criticism in turn embittered relations with the TUC at a time when its support was vital in preventing the severance of relations.

The duality could no longer be maintained. Soviet involvement in the strike and maintenance of a revolutionary stance undermined Moscow's diplomatic standing. This intolerable state of affairs led to the first reappraisal of the dual policy. The change was reflected in feverish diplomatic efforts to improve relations with Britain. In the autumn of 1926, the seriously ill Leonid Krasin, who enjoyed a reputation as a seasoned diplomat, was rushed to London in a last-ditch attempt to avert a crisis. However, these emergency measures were taken too late and were insufficient to prevent a chain of diplomatic defeats during 1927. In Germany, the Western orientation was revived. In April of that year, the Chinese police, acting on British initiative, raided the offices of the Soviet delegation to Peking, and Chiang Kai-Shek's Kuomintang forces slaughtered communists. In May, the British government raided Arcos, the offices of the Soviet trade delegation in London. Claiming to have found incriminating documents proving Soviet subversion, it broke off diplomatic ties with the Soviet Union. Simultaneously, the door slammed shut on the policy of solidarity when the TUC abandoned the Anglo-Russian Joint Committee. In June, the Soviet Ambassador to Poland was murdered and a month later, the leftist Kuomintang regime in Hankow broke off relations with the Chinese Communist party. In September, economic talks between France and the Soviet Union reached an impasse and Khristian Rakovsky, the Soviet Ambassador to France, was declared *persona non grata.*[43]

This gloomy year produced an atmosphere of pessimism and suspicion in Moscow, which at times bordered on paranoia, and produced fears that a new intervention against the Soviet Union was imminent. Even if one accepts the claim of some scholars that Stalin was merely utilizing the "war scare" to curb internal opposition and to prepare the population for the sacrifices demanded by collectivization and industrialization, its invocation was essentially an admission of the failure of the dual policy.[44]

The series of diplomatic and ideological setbacks at the end of the first decade dictated an urgent reassessment of priorities. The illusion of unconditional support from the world proletariat had been shattered beyond repair. On the face of it the Comintern had adopted a militant line, proclaiming the end of the stabilization of capitalism and discerning the revival of revolutionary opportunities in the West. United front tactics were abandoned and replaced by militant slogans on class struggle. However, after thoroughly sovietizing the shaky communist movement in Europe, the Comintern of the 1930s no longer resembled the Comintern of the first decade. Militancy was no more than a form of lip-service paid to ideology. The decision to carry out collectivization and industrialization through the exploitation of internal resources was finally taken in the wake of the severance of relations with Britain, and the failure to obtain foreign investments. What became known as the "third revolution", necessitated adoption of a diplomatic approach. Given the reality of capitalist encirclement and fears of renewed intervention, the removal of the external threat was a *sine qua non* for the achievement of "socialism in one country". Soviet diplomacy gradually came to resemble that of its Western counterparts and even enjoyed the prestige reserved for diplomacy in other regimes. Wide-scale purges were conducted in the Narkomindel hierarchy. Chicherin was recognized as pursuing a double-edged policy. For a decade he had dictated a policy whose hallmark was the attempt to bring about the stabilization of the Soviet Union by forging links with Germany while driving a wedge between Germany and Britain (toward the latter, he had developed a personal rancour). This policy seemed to him to be the only possible way to renew revolutionary opportunities. Opposite him stood Maxim Litvinov, his deputy, who consistently preached conventional policy and integration within the European system. His frequent appearances at sessions of the League of Nations after 1927 symbolized the sharp turn in Soviet foreign policy.

The lessons drawn in the Soviet hierarchy from the abandonment of the "dual policy" had serious consequences for policy in the 1930s. Thus, for example, the sectarianism and isolation of the communist movement during the years 1928 to 1934 partly explain the position taken by the German Communist party in the elections which saw Hitler's rise to power. Soviet fears and disappointments in foreign relations at the end of the first decade stemmed from the utter failure of its attempt to conduct a revolutionary policy and *realpolitik* simultaneously. The decision in favour of survival and security, and the sacrifice of the international revolutionary movement was a severe defeat for the remnant of the Bolshevik left, which had consistently stood for doctrinaire positions.

From its incipience, Soviet foreign policy was characterized by a gradual but consistent retreat from unbending hostility to the capitalist regimes and by a concomitant advance towards peaceful coexistence based on mutual expediency. This at first appeared to be tactical, and thus temporary. However, the NEP, which forms the subject of this chapter, turned out to be the first in a series of "breathing spaces" which have been clad in a variety of ideological guises: socialism in one country, the Popular Front, the Grand Alliance, the Thaw, *détente,* and most recently, glasnost. The prolongation of these "transitional" periods has represented a steady and consistent erosion of the ideological dimension of Soviet foreign policy.

NOTES

1.  Isaac Deutscher, *The Prophet Armed: Trotsky: 1879–1921* (Oxford, 1979), Chs. 8 and 9.
2.  L. Trotsky, *Moia zhizn'*, Vol. II (Berlin, 1930), pp. 62–63.
3.  Minutes, Public Record Office (PRO), Foreign Office (FO) 371/11779 N319 and N560/53/38, 27 Jan. and 11 Feb. 1926.
4.  The best overall survey of Soviet foreign policy in the 1920s is still Teddy J. Uldricks, "Russia and Europe: Diplomacy, Revolution, and Economic Development in the 1920s", *The International History Review* 1, 1 (1979).
5.  Although Lenin did ocassionally refer to a possible lasting truce with the capitalist world he was usually careful to use the tactical term *peredyshka* (breathing space) and very rarely used *mirnoe sosushchestvovanie* (peaceful coexistence) which has a long-term connotation. Historians now writing about Genoa tend to use these terms interchangeably.
6.  Quoted in E. H. Carr, *The Bolshevik Revolution 1917–1923*, Vol. 3 (London, 1966), p. 166.
7.  Iosif Stalin, *Sochineniia*, Vol. 8 (Moscow, 1948), pp. 118–20.

8. An adequate treatment of these episodes can be found in E. H. Carr, *The Bolshevik Revolution, 1917–1923*, Vol. 3, (London, 1953) and W. T. Angress, *Stillborn Revolution: The Communist Bid for Power in Germany, 1921–1923* (Princeton, 1963).

9. G. Gorodetsky, "The Other 'Zinoviev Letters': New Light on the Mismanagement of the Affair", *Slavic and Soviet Series* 1, 3 (1976).

10. L. J. Macfarlane, "'Hands off Russia' — British Labour and the Russo-Polish War 1920", *Past and Present* 38 (1968).

11. R. H. Ullman, *Anglo-Soviet Relations, 1917–1921*, Vol. 3 (Princeton, 1961) and *The Anglo-Soviet Accord* (Princeton, 1972), Chs. 4–6.

12. See J. Degras, "United Front Tactics in the Comintern, 1921–1928", in D. Footman (ed.), *International Communism, St. Antony's Papers* 9 (London, 1960).

13. *Piatyi vsemirnyi kongress Kommunisticheskogo Internatsionala, stenograficheskii otchet*, Vol. II (Moscow, 1925), pp. 33–34 and 66.

14. *Report of Proceedings at the 56th Annual Trades Union Congress* (London, 1924), p. 244.

15. The first suggestions to that effect were made in *Trud*, 20 April 1924. They were also incorporated in the resolutions of the seventh congress of Soviet railwaymen and miners: *Trud*, 22 April 1924.

16. On the formulation of the Conservative party's policy, see PRO, Cabinet Papers 23/49 60(24)9, 19 Nov. 1924. The Soviet reaction is best expressed by Chicherin, writing under the pseudonym of Sharonov, in *Izvestiia*, 30 Dec. 1924.

17. *VI-oi sezd professional'nykh soiuzov, 1924, stenograficheskii otchet* (Moscow, 1924), pp. 17–37. On the Soviet expectations from the delegation, see also *Pravda, Izvestiia* and *Trud*, 11 Nov. 1924.

18. Reported in *Pravda*, 19 Nov. 1924.

19. *VI-oi sezd*, pp. 386–89. See also *Report of 57th Annual Trades Union Congress* (London, 1925), pp. 295–96.

20. See, for instance, D. Manuil'skii, General Secretary of the Comintern, in *International Press Correspondence (INPRECOR)*, 4 Dec. 1924.

21. TUC Archives, typed record of inaugural meeting of ARJAC, 6–8 April 1925, B 114 9/8/7.

22. TUC Archives, *Minutes of the General Council, 1924–25*, 23 June 1925, p. 118.

23. *XIV sezd Vsesoiuznoi kommunisticheskoi partii (b), stenograficheskii otchet* (Moscow, 1926), pp. 987–88.

24. *VI-oi rasshirennyi plenum ispolkoma Kominterna, stenograficheskii otchet* (Moscow-Leningrad, 1927), pp. 42–43 and "Rezoliutsii", pp. 21–22 and 44–45. *Chetvertaia sessiia tsentral'nogo soveta Krasnogo internatsionala profsoiuzov, otchet* (Moscow/Leningrad, 1927), p. 31.

25. CPGB's report to Orgburo of IKKI in *INPRECORR*, 13 Jan. 1926. See also the proceedings of the meeting of IKKI on 20 Jan. 1926 in *Otchet ispolkoma Kominterna (aprel' 1925–ianvar' 1926)*, Vol. 6, pp. 141–43.

26. Minutes by Chamberlain, 6 Feb. 1926, FO 371/11786 N644/387/38, and *Parliamentary Debates. House of Commons*, Vol. 191, col. 1017, 10 Feb. 1926.

27. British Ambassador in Berlin on conversations with Stresemann, 1,6 and 9 April 1926, FO 371/11791 N1498/1555, 1593/718/38.

28. A. Ioffe in *Mirovoe khoziaistvo i mirovaia politika* 3 (1926), pp. 121–22.

29. *VI-oi rasshirennyi plenum IKKI*, pp. 201–2; *VI-aia sessiia Profinterna*, Vol. 3, p. 33. On the changing outlook, see leader in *Pravda*, 29 Jan. 1926 and Petrovskii, the Comintern's representative in Britain, in *Pravda*, 7 Feb. 1926.

30. A. Lozovskii admitted this in sharp exchanges with Akulov, leader of the Ukrainian miners, in *VII-oi sezd professional'nykh soiuzov SSSR. Stenograficheskii otchet* (Moscow, 1927), p. 324.

31. Accounts of the events in the Miners Federation of Great Britain, *Annual Volume of Proceedings for the Year 1926* (London, 1927), pp. 204–6.

32. A. Andreev, *Anglo-russkii komitet* (Moscow/Leningrad, 1927), p. 21.

33. *Mezhdunarodnoe rabochee dvizhenie*, (1926), pp. 18–19: meeting of executive bureau of Profintern, 13 May 1926 and leaders in *Trud* and *Pravda*, 5 May 1926. Stalin in *Sochineniia*, Vol. 8 (Moscow, 1948), p. 160. L. Trotsky, in *My Life* (London, 1930), p. 450, was enraged by the "cynical distortion of fact" in the press.

34. L. Fischer, *The Soviets in World Affairs, 1917–1929*, Vol. II (Princeton, 1951), p. 626.
35. *Krasnyi internatsional profsoiuzov*, 7 (1926), p. 19.
36. For instance, the Leningrad trade union organization still praised the General Council for its "high level organization and leadership" after the Russian aid had been rejected, see TUC Archives, letter to Citrine, 11 May 1926, B 132 13/7/23.
37. G. Zinov'ev, "Velikie sobytiia v Anglii", *Pravda*, 5 May 1926.
38. See leaders in *Ekonomicheskaia zhizn'* and *Pravda*, 5 May 1926, and Lozovskii in *Trud* and *Izvestiia*, 6 and 8 May 1926, respectively.
39. *Mezhdunarodnoe rabochee dvizhenie*, 20 (1926): meeting of the executive bureau of Profintern on 13 May 1926; see also a savage attack on the General Council by Radek, "Tragediia mass i fars pravykh vozhdei", *Pravda*, 13 May 1926.
40. Trotsky Archives, declaration to Politburo meeting, 3 and 6 June 1926, T-2986, and "Vseobshchaia stachka, general'nyi sovet i nasha politika", 18 May 1926, T-2985.
41. An account of the meeting in Bukharin's speech to party activists in Moscow, on 8 June 1926, reported in *Pravda* and *Izvestiia*, 26 June 1926.
42. *Puti mirovoi revoliutsii. VII-oi rasshirennyi plenum ispolnitel'nogo komiteta Kommunisticheskogo Internatsionala* Vol. II (Moscow/Leningrad, 1927), p. 182 and Molotov in *XV-aia konferentsiia VKP(b)*, (Moscow/Leningrad, 1927), p. 669.
43. See Uldricks, "Russia and Europe", pp. 72–75.
44. J. P. Sontag, "The Soviet War Scare of 1926–27", *The Russian Review* 1 (1975).

# 4

# The Foreign Policy of the Soviet Ukraine and Its Domestic Implications, 1919–1923

## FRANCIS CONTE

In his unpublished notes "Rakovsky in the Ukraine", Trotsky admitted that in its early years, the Bolshevik regime was not certain about how Ukrainian diplomacy should be incorporated in Soviet diplomacy. "We did not hurry to accomplish this," he commented, "because no one knew what shape international relations would take, and no one could say whether it would be beneficial for the Ukraine to link its fate with that of Russia."[1]

It was Lenin who made the decision to grant the new Ukraine a certain level of independence in its foreign policy in order to gain international recognition for the Ukrainian government. It was thus necessary for the Ukraine to have at least the appearance of an independent entity. Lenin further hoped that such a move would serve to counteract efforts of Ukrainian governments-in-exile, which still claimed to be the sole legal representatives of the Ukraine. Lenin appointed Khristian Rakovsky as the Commissar for Foreign Affairs of the Soviet Ukraine — a post which he occupied from January 1919 to August 1923, simultaneously with that of Chairman of the Soviet of People's Commissars of the Ukraine and member of the Politburo of the Ukrainian Central Committee. In the hands of Rakovsky, the "myth" of independent Ukrainian diplomacy became a reality.

Prior to 1917 Rakovsky was known in the European socialist movement as a militant internationalist, undisputed leader of the Socialist party of Romania and secretary of the Federation of Socialist Parties in the Balkans. When the victorious uprising of October 1917 in

Petrograd ignited powerful revolutionary activity on the entire territory of the former tsarist empire, Rakovsky anticipated that it would have inevitable reverberations in Romania, as had been the case after the Revolution of 1905. It was then that he decided to link his fate with that of the Bolshevik Revolution, and to join forces with its leaders, although he shared neither Lenin's theoretical views, nor his operational principles.

Lenin was primarily concerned with promoting the international revolution. He understood very well that the fate of the Russian Revolution depended to a large extent on the support of the European proletariat. Rakovsky's transition to bolshevism was thus highly valued by Lenin.

Throughout the Civil War, Rakovsky's main task was to fortify Soviet authority in the Ukraine, and to impose his own government and administration. Hence, he created the Ukrainian Army as a vanguard and "conscience" of the proletariat in the struggle for freedom on revolutionary fronts — both domestic and foreign.[2] In March 1919, at the Second Congress of the Ukrainian Soviets, the constitution of the Ukrainian SSR was ratified: it established officially, for the first time, close economic and military union between the Soviet Ukraine and Soviet Russia (RSFSR) "in order to pursue the struggle until the triumph of the world communist revolution".[3]

Relations between the Ukraine and Russia became more clearly defined after the signing of the important Treaty on Economic and Military Cooperation in December 1920. The RSFSR was represented by Lenin and the Commissar for Foreign Affairs, Georgii Chicherin, and the Ukraine by Rakovsky. The primary objective of this agreement was to ensure that the future development of the two republics would be determined by the mutual interests of workers and peasants.[4] The emphasis laid on the deep community of revolutionary interests of the Ukrainian and Russian peoples undermined Ukrainian independence. However, Lenin did include one phrase on the right of the Soviet Ukraine to self-determination, in order to counter any accusations of Russian imperialism. "The Soviet Ukrainian Republic does not bear a single obligation in relation to anyone as a result of the fact that the territory of the Soviet Ukraine belonged at one time to the Russian Empire," he declared.[5]

In accordance with the terms of this treaty, the two governments agreed to unite their Commissariats of Military and Naval Affairs, Foreign Trade, Finance, Information, Posts and Telegraph.[6] Lenin carried out this union under the banner of "proletarian solidarity", but he consented to the establishment of a Ukrainian Commissariat of Foreign Affairs. This was duly executed by a decree of the Ukrainian

Central Committee on 16 March 1920.

The Bolsheviks exploited the "independence" of Ukrainian diplomacy in ending the Soviet-Polish war in the summer of 1920. At the outset of the negotiations, the Russian delegation asked the Polish government to empower its representatives to negotiate with the Soviet Ukraine as well. In an attempt to gain time, Chicherin sent a telegram to the head of the Soviet delegation, Danishevskii, on 16 August — when Soviet troops were still advancing toward Warsaw. He introduced the Ukrainian representatives as the "delegation of the independent Ukrainian Soviet Republic, which is not part of the Russian Republic".[7] Indeed, before entering into negotiations with the Russian and Ukrainian delegations, the Poles had to produce a special mandate signed by their government empowering them to participate. This was a diplomatic success in itself, since it was tantamount to the acknowledgement of an independent Soviet Ukraine, and officially distanced them from their erstwhile ally Simon Petlyura. Indeed, the representatives of the Soviet Ukrainian government, Emmanuil Kviring and Iurii Kotsiubinskii, signed the Treaty of Riga on 18 March 1921, together with the Russian representative, Adol'f Ioffe.

In the following years, Rakovsky tried to assert the independence of his government's diplomacy and to exercise international influence. Between 1920 and 1923, the Ukrainian Republic signed several official treaties with Germany, Austria, Poland, Czechoslovakia, Italy and Lithuania.[8] However, these primarily reflected Soviet Russia's relations with Western Europe, as well as the beginning of political, diplomatic and economic confrontation between the two blocs.

The official line of Ukrainian diplomacy was described by V. I. Yakovlev, Deputy Commissar for Foreign Affairs of the Ukrainian Republic, in an interview with *Izvestiia* in August 1922:

> As regards foreign policy, the Ukraine must have the same concerns as Russia, since it is, like the Ukraine, a proletarian state. The Ukraine has an independent foreign policy, where her specific interests are concerned. But in matters of political and economic interests, common to all other republics, the Russian and Ukrainian commissariats for foreign affairs work as a joint federal body.[9]

The two commissariats were run by very different personalities. Although both Chicherin and Rakovsky had joined the Bolshevik party only after its victory in Russia in October 1917, they acquired different degrees of political influence. Unlike Chicherin, Rakovsky sought to enhance his power; he was a member of the Central Committee, the Central Executive Committee and its Presidium, as well as leader of the Ukrainian Communist party. In contrast, Chicherin was never made a member of the RSP(b) Central Committee and did not share any political responsibilities. Although Rakovsky greatly valued Chicherin's diplomatic gifts, he scorned his lack of political courage. "Every time Georgii Vasil'evich pulls his handkerchief out of his pocket," he commented, "he has to send a report to the Politburo."[10]

Toward the end of 1921, Rakovsky expressed his deep-seated conviction of the need for the Ukraine to be granted real autonomy. In a report to the Sixth Conference of the Ukrainian Communist party on 10 October 1921, the anniversary of the Russian Revolution, he declared: "we must give more independence to Ukrainian organizations, especially those which are already united, for the simple reason that the other organizations are [already] independent".[11] Lenin understood clearly the meaning of Rakovsky's words and the new direction he was going to impart to relations between Kharkov and Moscow, as he admitted wryly a few months later:

> The Ukraine is an independent republic, we all agree on that. But...sometimes...let me see, how could I phrase it? Sometimes she tries to get around us, and we shall have to put this right. Over there, the people in charge are cunning, and, I would not go so far as to say their Central Committee deceives us, but somehow it keeps itself at a distance.[12]

Lenin's reproach was precipitated by a decision of the Ukrainian government concerning foreign trade. It was also, however, a direct response to Rakovsky's efforts to appoint Ukrainian diplomatic representatives abroad.

Early in January 1922, Rakovsky persuaded the Ukrainian Economic Council to pass a motion which would invalidate in the Ukraine trade agreements entered into by the RSFSR.[13] Two months later, the head of a British trade delegation to the Ukraine, reported to the Foreign Office that "the Ukrainian government seems set on gaining full control over its commissariats, as in the case of the Commissariat for Trade, which is no longer a branch of the Moscow one".[14]

In his report to the Sixth Conference of the Ukrainian Communist party, Rakovsky stated his intention of demarcating Russian and Ukrainian spheres of influence. Poland, Czechoslovakia, Bulgaria, Turkey, and Austria were to be under Ukrainian influence, while everything else would go to Russia. This attempt was recognized by an agreement signed early in 1922 by Rakovsky and Leonid Krasin, the Russian Commissar for Foreign Trade. Thus, the representative for Ukrainian foreign trade in Turkey was appointed as chairman of the Joint Ukraine-RSFSR Mission. There is little doubt that between early 1922 and July 1923, when the constitution of the Soviet Union came into effect and Rakovsky was dismissed as head of the Ukrainian Republic, the Kharkov government assumed increasing responsibilities.

The relationship between the Kharkov regime and representatives of the American Relief Organization during the difficult period of the 1921 famine, illustrates the degree of Ukrainian autonomy achieved under Rakovsky. In 1921, famine hit the whole of southern Russia, along the Volga Valley. Toward the end of 1921, governments in several West European countries and in the United States had become concerned about the situation and had decided to offer their help to the starving population.

The largest volume of aid came from the American Relief Administration (ARA), run by Herbert Hoover. This organization alone fed 1,132,660 people in 1922. Yet, in spite of the grim circumstances, Rakovsky showed his determination to defend his principle of national independence. Late in 1921, representatives of the American Relief Administration arrived in Kharkov. They had just signed an agreement in Riga with the Soviet Russian government and wanted it endorsed by the Ukrainian government. Rakovsky categorically refused to do so on the grounds that the Russian government's deeds and treaties were not binding on the Ukraine. In spite of the Americans' insistence that "they came to the Ukraine, not for politics, but to feed the starving", Rakovsky demanded the inclusion of a statement that "the Ukrainian Soviet Republic has no connection with the Treaty of Riga and its conditions are not binding on it...".[15]

Moscow could do little and Rakovsky's obstinacy frequently overcame foreign reluctance to recognize the independent status of the Ukraine. He would show the same determination when it came to the question of establishing separate Ukrainian embassies and legations abroad. In April 1920, Rakovsky dispatched his first diplomatic representative, M. Levitskii, to Prague. Although Levitskii established himself there, the Czechoslovak Republic had recognized neither Soviet Russia nor the Ukraine, and he was able to present his credentials only two years later when the two countries signed an interim treaty.[16] Early in 1921, Vladimir Aussem was appointed Ukrainian envoy in Berlin, while his brother, Otto Aussem, was appointed as representative of the Ukrainian Commissariat for National Education, first in Berlin, and later in Prague. In the autumn of 1921, a third Ukrainian diplomat, A. Shumskii, was appointed as permanent representative to Poland.

The Ukrainian diplomats were very active. The first treaties signed independently by the Soviet Ukrainian Republic were with Lithuania on 14 February 1921, with Latvia on 3 August 1921, and with Estonia on 25 November of the same year. Separate negotiations were conducted with Poland, Czechoslovakia, Turkey, Italy, France, Germany and Great Britain.

In an interview given to *Izvestiia* on 13 August 1922, Deputy Foreign Minister Yakovlev declared that one of the most pressing problems facing the Ukrainian Commissariat for Foreign Affairs was that of the Ukrainian émigré community. The government's objective was to reduce the influence enjoyed by nationalist groups claiming to represent the Ukrainian national government:

> These improvised Ukrainian national republics which, for the last two years, have not controlled a single square meter of Ukrainian territory, were until recently represented in many European countries. To put an end to the claims of these adventurers was no mean task, but because both sides, especially the Western European countries, had to re-establish economic relations with the Ukrainian Soviet Republic, they concluded treaties with us. This is how Petlyura's illegal government and his representatives ceased to be recognized.[17]

Naturally, both the Russian and the Ukrainian governments were very concerned about counter-revolutionary agitation. By 1922, however, the émigré groups were in a sorry financial state — a fact Rakovsky used to his benefit.[18] He decided to weaken the power of these movements by coming to terms with some of them and gaining their support. He selected the two most influential groups: one based in Vienna, under the leadership of Iu. Kotsiubiskii, head of the Ukrainian Soviet Mission in Vienna; the other run from Paris by Markotun, the chairman of the Ukrainian National Committee. Rakovsky's greatest success was with Markotun, who agreed to act as liaison between Kharkov and the French and German governments. In return for Markotun's services, and in view of its acceptance of the Soviet regime as the only power to represent the Ukraine, the Ukrainian National Committee "was allowed to become an officially recognized party and an ally of the Soviets".[19]

In London, the *Times* uneasily remarked that a close look at some parts of the letters exchanged between Markotun and Rakovsky revealed that the French government had made no objection to this new development, and that, even if it were realized only in part, the French were likely to become involved in the activities of the Soviet Ukrainian Republic.[20] Markotun, apparently on Rakovsky's instructions, opened talks with both the French and the German governments. Rakovsky believed that competition between the two great European powers could only "lower the rate of interest" they would ask in exchange for economic aid. According to a report of the British SIS on Markotun's negotiations in the summer of 1922:

> The Germans want to use the "White" Ukrainians who are well disposed towards them to bring about an understanding between the Ukraine and Germany. This would make it possible for anti-Bolshevik Ukrainians to take an active part in German plans for rebuilding the Ukraine under a Soviet regime.[21]

In December 1922, France and the Ukraine began negotiations on setting up a joint French-Polish-Ukrainian trade company. However, major obstacles to the development of trade between French and Ukrainian commercial firms remained. France was short of capital and could not provide the Ukraine with a long-term loan. Moreover, the high exchange rate of the franc in relation to German, Czechoslovak and Austrian currencies, made competition very difficult on the Ukrainian market.[22]

From 1920 to 1924, the Ukraine and France discussed the possibility of allowing French industrialists to regain the role they had played in Ukrainian industry before 1917. In the meantime, the Ukrainians had established diplomatic and economic ties with other European countries, especially with Britain and Germany. Close relations developed between Germany and the Ukraine on the basis of a common desire to cooperate in military affairs. The Ukraine had reached agreements similar to those signed by Moscow with Germany. In order to circumvent the ban on German armament stipulated in the Treaty of Versailles, the Russians had permitted German pilots to train on Russian soil in exchange for the supply of German military equipment. German engineers would also reorganize production in Soviet weapons factories. As the British consul to Chernovitz observed:

> Many German officers are employed by the army, the air force, and some technical departments in Kiev. Most of them stayed on after German troops left the country, but there is a steady trickle of Germans coming in and they always find employment.[23]

Rakovsky also decided to draw up a separate economic agreement with Germany, as he later tried to do with Britain.[24] The draft treaty bore some similarities to the Rapallo treaty signed by Germany and Soviet Russia on 16 April 1922. A zealous promoter of a German-Soviet *rapprochement,* Rakovsky was nonetheless determined to adapt it to the Ukraine's specific needs.[25]

The reason for the failure to reach a final agreement lay in differences between Litvinov, the Russian delegate, and representatives of the independent republics. Litvinov regarded the separate negotiations as a mere device for an extension of the privileges of the Rapallo treaty to the independent republics, while the delegates from these republics, the Ukrainian representative in particular, sought a genuine accord.

Rakovsky's attempts to assert economic and political independence from the Russians were an unexpected source of embarrassment for Litvinov. The Ukrainians insisted on receiving the 400 million marks which they had claimed from Germany after the occupation, in spite of a clause in the Rapallo treaty stipulating that the dispute between them had ended.[26]. In a telegram to Moscow, Litvinov denounced the move as a "plot", and Chicherin was rushed to Berlin. The Ukrainian representative was formally warned by the Russians that he was in no way entitled to conclude a separate treaty with Germany, and that the Russian delegate was sole spokesman in those negotiations.[27] If it had not been for this intervention, Rakovsky had intended to exploit the reparations demanded for the German occupation of the Ukraine and its requisitions in 1918, as a basis for future economic transactions between the two countries.

The shortage of credit also led Rakovsky to seek a trade agreement with Britain similar to the one signed by the Russians in March 1921. Diplomatic and economic negotiations between the two countries began in January 1922, when a British trade mission under Major Dunlop arrived in Kharkov, and lasted for nearly two months. Dunlop formed the following impression of Rakovsky:

> I am told that when Lenin and Trotsky disagreed last year, Rakovsky chose to side with the latter. Nowadays, he seems to carry out Moscow's instructions quite faithfully, although he is ultimately supposed to seek his own benefit.[28]

Dunlop, however, stressed that "the Ukrainian government seems determined to exercise full control over its Comissariats",[29] and that the leader of the Soviet Ukraine asserted his independence on foreign policy issues.

In order to remedy the ailing economy, Rakovsky advocated seeking external help through trade concessions to foreign firms.[30] Major Dunlop subsequently wrote:

> In answer to my question whether the previous owners had any chances of re-opening their factories, [Rakovsky] said it was merely a matter of agreeing on terms. He added that any such agreement had to be negotiated with the Ukraine, because the authorities of this country regard themselves in no way bound by decisions made in Moscow. He gave me his permission to quote his words officially.[31]

The Kharkov authorities and the British delegation also examined the question of credits and undertook to remedy the shortage of capital by setting up an Anglo-Ukrainian merchant bank.

The development of these economic relations further highlighted Rakovsky's autonomy from Moscow in the area of foreign affairs. Thus, in May 1923, when Lord Curzon threatened to cancel the trade treaty concluded two years earlier by Great Britain and Soviet Russia, Rakovsky sent a conciliatory telegram to London. While noting the "sense of anxiety" that had filled the Ukrainian masses when they heard of the harsh British plans against the RSFSR, "an ally of the

Ukrainian Soviet Republic", and warning that the British stand endangered the strong economic relations that had developed between the Ukraine and Britain, he nonetheless expressed his hope that a speedy solution could be found to the misunderstandings between Britain and Russia.[32]

Relations between the Ukraine and the outside world continued to improve until July 1923. Commercial ties with Poland, Italy and Britain, in particular, were expanded. Already, in August 1922, the Deputy Commissar for Foreign Affairs declared that the Ukrainian government had received a large response to its policy of granting concessions to foreign firms — especially from German settlers and large Czechoslovak enterprises.[33] In June 1923, the Central Committee of the Ukrainian Communist party put an official seal on this policy: a decree was issued requiring foreign companies to obtain permission to open offices or branches in the Ukraine from the Concessions Committee run by the Ukrainian Economic Council. Any prior agreement signed in Moscow was declared invalid and the various firms and trusts concerned had to reapply to the Ukrainian Economic Council for ratification. This was the last independent Ukrainian measure. A month later Stalin suddenly forced Rakovsky to step down.

Rakovsky's resignation was a direct consequence of his long opposition to Stalin, dating back to the time when the latter had been Commissar for Nationalities and head of the Bolshevik bureaucracy. In July 1923, Rakovsky was condemned to "diplomatic exile", where he would prove his skill throughout the 1920s. His departure ended Ukrainian attempts to pursue an independent foreign policy.

NOTES

1. L. Trotsky, *Rakovsky in the Ukraine*, dossier bMS. Russ. 13, Trotsky Archives, Houghton Library, Harvard University.
2. Khristian Rakovsky, "The Soul of Victory", *Communist International* (English edition), 1921, pp. 60-64.
3. *Istoriia sovetskoi konstitutsii v dokumentakh, 1917–1956* (Moscow, 1957), pp. 207–8.
4. See E. H. Carr, *The Bolshevik Revolution, 1917–1923*, Vol. 1 (London, 1964), p. 386 and Iu. Borys, *The Russian Communist Party and the Sovietisation of the Ukraine* (Stockholm, 1960), pp. 285–86.
5. *Sbornik deistvuiushchikh dogovorov, soglashenii i konventsii, zakliuchennykh RSFSR s inostrannymi gosudarstvami* (Petrograd, 1921) I, 8, pp. 15–16.
6. Khristian Rakovskii, *Novyi etap v sovetskom soiuznom stroitel'stve* (Kharkov, 1923), p. 17.
7. The full text of this telegram appeared in the Ukrainian émigré periodical published in Vienna, *Vpered*, 5 Sept. 1920.
8. The history of these treaties, which are the external evidence of a profound change, has been covered at length; see, for instance, V. Markus, *L'Ukraine soviétique dans les relations internationales, 1917–1923* (Paris, 1959).
9. *Izvestiia*, 13 Aug. 1922; *Russian Information and Review*, 15 Sept. 1922.

10. Louis Fischer, Notes on his conversations with Rakovsky, Saratov, April 1929.
11. *Biulleten' Vseukrainskoï Konferentsii KP(b)U* (Kharkov, 1921), p. 12.
12. V. I. Lenin, Speech delivered at the Eleventh Congress of the KPR(b), 27 March 1922, *Works* (English edition), Vol. 33, p. 298.
13. *Kommunist* (Kharkov), 29 Jan. 1922.
14. "Ukrainian-British Trade Collaboration": Conversation with Major Dunlop of the Foreign Office, 8 March 1922, Foreign Office (FO) 371/8165.
15. H. H. Fisher, *The Famine in Soviet Russia* (New York, 1927), pp. 248–50.
16. Rakovsky signed the new agreement on 19 Jan. 1922.
17. *Izvestiia*, 13 Aug. 1922.
18. Communication of SIS, No. 775, "Ukrainian Groups Abroad", 13 July 1922, FO 371/8165.
19. Communication of SIS, Section 1, "Agreement between Ukrainian National Committee in Paris and Ukrainian Soviet of People's Commissars", 24 June 1922, FO 371/8165.
20. *The Times* (London), 5 June 1922.
21. Communication of SIS, Section 1, 24 June 1922, FO 371/8165.
22. "Les Concessions en URSS", *Europe Nouvelle*, 19 June 1926.
23. "Military and Economic Cooperation between Germany and the Ukraine", 7 Sept. 1922, FO 371/8165.
24. *Izvestiia*, 13 Aug. 1922.
25. Louis Fischer, *op. cit.*
26. *Rote Fahne*, No. 249, 31 March 1922.
27. Chicherin to Berlin, *Lokal Anzeiger*, No. 254, 1 June 1922.
28. Dunlop to Foreign Office, 8 March 1922, FO 371/8165.
29. *Ibid.*
30. See *Dokumenty vneshnei politiki*, Vol. VII, p. 700.
31. "Ukrainian-British Trade Collaboration", FO 371/8165.
32. *Dokumenty vneshnei politiki*, Vol. VI, p. 312.
33. *Izvestiia*, 13 Aug. 1922.

# 5

# Litvinov, Stalin
# and the Road Not Taken

## JONATHAN HASLAM

Two facts about Litvinov taken together have always seemed something of a paradox. First, he was the most pro-Western of all Soviet statesmen and consistently so, through the best and worst of times, both in and out of power. Second, he survived the two phases of Stalin's xenophobic terror (1937–39 and 1948), and died of natural causes in 1951 after receiving the finest medical treatment at the Kremlin's disposal. Symbolic of his values was the photo he kept on his desk. In contrast to his close friend and fellow pro-Westerner Boris Shtein, who had a photograph of Stalin (for insurance), Litvinov kept one of Roosevelt.[1] Yet he doubted his chances of survival during the height of the terror to the extent that he slept with a loaded pistol under his pillow and stayed up fully dressed until three in the morning playing incessant rounds of bridge with his family, for fear of being taken in his pyjamas.[2] There was in him at one and the same time a cool self-assurance about his value to Stalin, side by side with an acute awareness of the precariousness of his own position, and not least that of his family, under such a fickle dictator. Indeed, according to his widow Ivy, "One day [after his dismissal in 1939] he called up Beria...to ask why the number of security cars prowling around our green fence had lately been doubled. 'You don't know your own worth, Maxim Maximovich', said Beria. 'I do,' quipped Maxim, 'but I'm not sure if others do'."[3]

Behind these contradictions lies the half-hidden and as yet untold story of the curious personal relationship between Stalin and Litvinov. But, beyond that, there also emerge Stalin's own ambivalence and deep-seated doubts in matters of foreign policy: the need always "to keep a stone up one's sleeve".[4] Hence the entire Litvinov story offers a fascinating view of Stalin's conduct of foreign relations and opens up many key questions in the history of those relations during his dictatorship.

After the October Revolution, Litvinov and Stalin found themselves on common ground. In stark contrast to their comrades in the leadership, neither held out much hope for the prospects of revolution elsewhere in Europe. During the fierce debate on peace with Germany early in 1918 (when Litvinov was still in London) Stalin alone stood to the right of Lenin, arguing that "there is no revolutionary movement in the West, there are no facts but only a potential, and we cannot count on a potential".[5] Stalin was no more optimistic about prospects in Germany in 1923[6] or even during the Great Depression.[7] Litvinov was equally pessimistic. "The prospect of world revolution disappeared on November 11, 1918," he told journalist Louis Fischer.[8] And while his superior, Commissar for Foreign Affairs Chicherin — along with the bulk of the leadership — favoured supporting wars of national liberation against British imperialism during the 1920s, Litvinov preferred a deal with Britain.[9] His essentially statist and conservative orientation in international relations was shared with Stalin, as was the bleak realism that contrasted sharply with the ultimate romanticism of men like Trotsky, Chicherin or even, unlikely as it may seem, the dull bureaucrat Molotov.

In these circumstances, the ascents of Litvinov and Stalin were closely intertwined. For all the differences in temperament and outlook that separated them, both men were to varying degrees authoritarian; both pragmatists rather than visionaries; both plain and devoid of the self-conscious flamboyancy evident in the manner of the middle and upper class revolutionaries. Differences existed none the less. Litvinov was pre-eminently formed by the educative, bitter-sweet experience of "emigration" in Britain, where his future wife met and married him — "a Pickwickian figure in goldrimmed pincenez, always trailing a walking stick behind him in his two clasped hands and looking wistfully into the window of Swanziger's Viennese bakery".[10] In contrast, the brutal and ruthless Stalin was formed largely by the uniformly bitter and confining experience of "internal exile", which had narrowed his vision and furthered his ignorance, not to say deep suspicion, of the outside world.

Inevitably, therefore, there remained a tension in the relationship. The collaboration which grew from the time of Litvinov's *de facto* supremacy at the Commissariat of Foreign Affairs in 1928 (formalized two years later) and which reached its peak when Stalin accepted Litvinov's trenchant logic in favour of the collective containment of Nazi Germany, turned out to be only conditional — a meeting of interests that converged and ultimately diverged as a result of conflicting dynamics.[11]

Litvinov's influence rested in part on the fact that Stalin — at least until 1939 and intermittently thereafter — was content to take advice on the conduct of foreign policy and delegate operational control to others: a wise precaution considering his ignorance of such matters and his overriding and unsettling preoccupation with economic reconstruction at home and with the "enemy within". The trouble was that Litvinov was not the only, and at times not even the dominant, influence in such matters. Stalin tended to diffuse responsibility and power among subordinates who mistrusted one another; this was one means of retaining exclusive and ultimate control. Litvinov's chief rival and opponent (once Chicherin was safely out of the way and Deputy Commissar Karakhan had been sent off as *polpred* to Turkey) was the Chairman of the Council of People's Commissars, Molotov. Litvinov and Molotov hated one another. Just as Litvinov had fought his case against Chicherin in the Politburo in the 1920s,[12] so too he fought against Molotov (and later Zhdanov) in the 1930s. Litvinov was not a member of the Politburo, but this did not deter him from attending sessions or from openly expressing his disagreement with or even contempt for Molotov, who was a full voting member. On more than one occasion he could be heard yelling "*durak!*" (fool) down the phone at Molotov.[13]

Litvinov had an unusual rapport with Stalin, but this understanding was more than once jeopardized by Stalin's irresistible urge to bet on more than one horse in each race. Moreover, although Stalin shared much with Litvinov, he had a good deal more in common with Molotov who, since Lenin's last days, had thrown in his lot with Stalin. Like Stalin, Molotov had suffered internal exile; like Stalin he had an enormous capacity for hard and dreary work which, in his case, partly compensated for a lack of intellectual ability. He was brusque, if not brutal, with subordinates. Where he differed from Stalin (and especially Litvinov) was in his Bolshevik fundamentalism, his belief in world revolution, and his genuine commitment to the future of socialism, though not a socialism of a kind that we would recognize in the West.

Until recently it was assumed that Molotov was merely his master's voice. But this is now known to be untrue. Gromyko reveals that not only did "much depend upon Molotov" in "the resolution of concrete questions of relations with other countries", but that "Molotov exerted a noticeable influence upon Stalin".[14] "I would say," Khrushchev recalled, "that he was the only person in the Politburo who opposed Stalin on this or that question for a second time." And in Zhukov's opinion, Molotov "exerted serious influence over Stalin, particularly in questions of foreign policy in which Stalin, until the war, considered him competent". When attacked by Stalin, "Molotov by no means always remained silent". Indeed, "at times it reached the point where Stalin raised his voice and even lost all self-control, and Molotov, smiling, rose from behind the table and held firm to his point of view".[15]

It is in light of this evidence that one ought to view the secret overtures made to Nazi Germany in 1933, 1935 and 1937.[16] It was primarily from Molotov that Stalin received the arguments in favour of a *rapprochement* with Germany. It is striking and entirely consistent with this fact that the circular sent out to embassies abroad on Litvinov's dismissal on 3 May 1939, should refer explicitly to "the serious conflict between the Chairman of the People's Council of Commissars, Comrade Molotov, and the People's Commissar for Foreign Affairs, Comrade Litvinov".[17] It was Molotov who returned from Berlin in November 1940 convinced that Hitler was not about to attack the Soviet Union.[18] And it was Molotov who, some years later, had a major row with Litvinov in the back of a car (which the hapless Gromyko was driving), after he had asserted that Britain and France had pushed Hitler into attacking the Soviet Union in 1941.[19]

Although it did not take much to convince Stalin that potential and actual allies were plotting against him, Molotov (and Zhdanov) did play a significant role in the dismissal of Litvinov from the Foreign Commissariat at a critical moment in the country's fortunes. Litvinov's ouster meant the rejection of collaboration with the Western democracies on any terms other than those that explicitly sanctioned the expansion of Soviet influence, and with it military power, into Eastern Europe. Stalin rejected the multilateral and collective security approach to international relations in favour of spheres of influence (a euphemism for military and ideological domination).

Molotov's reinforcement of Stalin's worst suspicions continued to be effective even after the blunders of 1939–41; he remained Foreign Commissar and became First Deputy Chairman to Stalin's chairmanship of the Council of Ministers. Thus, even after the Soviet Union entered into alliance with Britain following the German invasion of 22 June 1941, Stalin continued to suspect collusion between London and Berlin. In the late autumn of 1942, prior to the establishment of a second front in Europe, Stalin sent a telegram to Ambassador Ivan Maiskii indicating that he believed Churchill was heading not only for a peace settlement but for an alliance with Germany against the USSR.[20] The situation caused Litvinov, now *polpred* in Washington, to seriously debate with his wife the option of defecting to the United

States.[21] After being instructed to return to Moscow and having made the decision to do so (his children and grandchild were still there), Litvinov complained to Under Secretary of State Sumner Welles on 7 May 1943:

> ...that the very confidential and apparently influential relationship which he had enjoyed with Stalin until 1939 was non-existent today. He said that his successor as Foreign Commissar had removed from the Foreign Commissariat every important official who had any experience with the outside world and any personal knowledge of the United States or of the Western democracies.

He would attempt to persuade Stalin of his point of view, favouring multilateral postwar collaboration, on his return to Moscow.[22]

Litvinov had drawn the correct conclusion that the option of genuine postwar inter-Allied collaboration had been dashed against the rocks of Kremlin paranoia. The only cooperation Stalin and Molotov envisaged was that which permitted the Soviet Union to grab all the territory that it sought and which did not rule out continued directives for the conduct of class war by fraternal communist parties in Allied countries (now Zhdanov's rather than Molotov's sphere of operations). This much became clear to Litvinov on his return to Moscow, and Stalin refused to be persuaded by him. Litvinov was given the post of Deputy Commissar for Foreign Affairs, but in practice his influence on policy was negligible. As the Red Army advanced into Central Europe, communist-dominated regimes were established in its wake and political freedoms that had sprouted were crushed under its heel. The option of a multilateral and interdependent approach to world order was brusquely cast aside in favour of a unilateral solution to the Soviet Union's security problems; and side by side with this, the ideological arm — epitomized in the condemnation of US Communist party leader Earl Browder in April 1945 for moving towards dissolving the party — was clumsily reactivated precisely two years after the dissolution of the Comintern.

Litvinov was approached by the Western correspondent C. Sulzberger at the May Day parade on Red Square, while standing in the crowd rather than sitting with the diplomats. Asked why he had not been given a seat, he said he had been, "But I prefer it down here with the masses". According to Sulzberger:

> His pale, ugly face looked thoughtful and sad; none of the exuberation of a magnificent triumph. He never once looked up at Stalin and his lieutenants standing atop Lenin's tomb. He just stared out at the long rows of cannon and marching troops.[23]

East-West relations were already drifting towards conflict and there was little Litvinov could do about it, except perhaps speak out. On 23

May 1946, he told US Ambassador Bedell Smith:

> ...toward the end of the War and directly afterwards I had hoped for real international cooperation, but wrong decisions have been made and of the two paths which might have been taken, the wrong one has been chosen. I now feel that the best that can be hoped for is a prolonged truce.[24]

Increasingly frustrated, Litvinov finally threw caution to the winds. With the Cold War under way and Litvinov now almost seventy years of age, he agreed, on 18 June 1946, to see CBS correspondent Richard Hottelet. Hottelet was startled by his outspoken remarks: "There has been a return in Russia to the outmoded concept of security in terms of territory — the more you've got the safer you are." What would happen if the West conceded positions to Moscow? "It would lead to the West being faced, after a more or less short time, with the next series of demands." What lay behind this policy? "As far as I am concerned, the root cause is the ideological conception prevailing here, that conflict between the communist and capitalist worlds is inevitable."[25] Precisely one month later Litvinov was dismissed from his post.[26] The *Sunday Times* correspondent Alexander Werth saw him at a reception on 23 February 1947. Litvinov told Werth:

> ...he was extremely unhappy about the way the Cold War was getting worse and worse every day. By the end of the war, he said, Russia had had the choice of two policies: one was to "cash in on the goodwill she had accumulated during the war in Britain and the United States". But *they* [Stalin and Molotov] had, unfortunately, chosen the other policy. Not believing that "goodwill" could constitute the *lasting* basis for any kind of policy, they had decided that "security" was what mattered most of all, and they had therefore grabbed all they could while the going was good — meaning the whole of Eastern Europe and parts of Central Europe.[27]

He spoke equally frankly to the British diplomat Frank Roberts, warning him of a fundamental decision taken in the Kremlin that "precluded the development of friendly relations on the basis of our joint war effort", and asserting "that this decision made increasing suspicion and friction inevitable". Roberts subsequently reported: "When I have suggested to him that the Soviet rulers in the Kremlin could not want war, Litvinov has agreed but has usually added: 'Neither did Hitler, but events became too strong for those who should control them, if they have set a wrong course'."[28] In private, Litvinov insisted that Russia had won the war but lost the peace. As to what the West — "we" — should do about it, his constant refrain was "you've got to bully the bully".[29]

Stalin had these exchanges recorded — evidently through microphones hidden in Litvinov's office and doubtless also his home and dacha.[30] "Complete treachery", was Molotov's description of these conversations.[31] Litvinov was dismissed from his post, yet Stalin still kept him alive. Indeed, he continued to dine in the Kremlin with his former colleagues. And before he died in December 1951 he had, according to his widow Ivy, "round-the-clock nurses...weekly consultations by the first [best] heart specialists in the country... antibiotics...sedatives...at last the oxygen tent".[32] The ever-cautious gambler Stalin evidently wished to retain the one figure who could speedily strike a deal for true coexistence with the West, even as he moved the country ever more certainly into a collision with the United States and the NATO alliance now formed against it. This is what Litvinov believed to be the explanation of his own survival.[33]

Throughout his long career Litvinov's approach epitomized one option in Soviet foreign policy: *rapprochement* with the capitalist world and normalization of the revolution in its external aspects. This required the explicit abandonment of the goal of world revolution and the Leninist heritage. Stalin, although never a true ideologue in the manner of Lenin, Trotsky, or even Molotov and Zhdanov, found common cause with this Westernizer only to the extent that Moscow's security dilemma from 1933–39 and 1941–45 required someone of Litvinov's talents and inclination to open the road to limited collaboration. Stalin was ideological only in the negative sense: his rejection of Western values and of the Western path of development. For all Stalin's native sense of caution — which ultimately kept Litvinov alive — the strains of paranoia in his personality blended with the rejectionist elements in Bolshevik ideology, prompting him to block the road not taken to the West.

NOTES

1. Interview with Litvinov's daughter, Tat'iana.
2. *Ibid.*
3. Ivy Litvinov Papers (Hoover Institution, Stanford), Box 9.
4. A phrase used by Stalin and conveyed verbatim by Krestinskii (then Deputy Commissar for Foreign Affairs) to Boris Shtein (*polpred* in Finland in the early thirties). Shtein in turn passed this on to Z. Sheinis, Litvinov's biographer: Sheinis, "Srazheniia u golubogo ozera", *Oktiabr'* 8 (1967).
5. Minutes of a session of the Central Committee, 11[24] January 1918: *The Bolsheviks and the October Revolution: Central Committee Minutes of the Russian Social Democratic Labour Party (Bolsheviks) August 1917–February 1918* (London, 1974), p. 177.
6. E. H. Carr, *The Interregnum 1923–1924* (London, 1965), pp. 202–3.
7. Carr, *Twilight of Comintern 1930–35* (London, 1982), Chs. 1–5.
8. L. Fischer, *Men and Politics: An Autobiography* (London, 1941), pp. 124.
9. *Ibid.*, p. 125.
10. Ivy Litvinov Papers, Box 7.
11. See Haslam, *The Soviet Union and the Struggle for Collective Security in Europe, 1933–39* (London/New York, 1985).

12. See Mikoian's recollections in 1968: "Diplomat Leninskoi shkoly" preface to Z. Sheinis, *Maksim Maksimovich Litvinov: revoliutsioner, diplomat, chelovek* (Moscow, 1989) p. 3. For Litvinov's later battles within the Politburo: Sheinis, p. 257.
13. Interview with Tat'iana Litvinov.
14. A. Gromyko, *Pamiatnoe*, Vol. 2, 2nd ed. (Moscow, 1990), p. 427.
15. Quoted in Haslam, *The Soviet Union and the Threat from the East, 1933–41: Moscow, Tokyo and the Prelude to the Pacific War* (London, 1992), p. 17. Also, see V. Erofeev, "Desyat' let v sekretariate Narkomindela", *Mezhdunarodnaia zhizn'* (Sept. 1991), p. 114.
16. See Haslam, *The Soviet Union and the Struggle*, pp. 22, 86 and 127, respectively. For recent information on the approaches which, to the author's mind remains inconclusive, see N. Abramov and L. Bezymenskii, "Osobaia missiia Davida Kandelaki", *Voprosy istorii* 4–5 (1991), pp. 144–56.
17. Quoted from the archives in V. Sokolov, "Narkomindel Maksim Litvinov", *Mezhdunarodnaia zhizn'* (April 1991), p. 119.
18. D. Volkogonov, *Triumf i tragediia: Politicheskii portret I. V. Stalina*, Vol. 2, part 1 (Moscow, 1989), pp. 64, 67. For some of the documentation on the visit see "Nakanune: Peregovory V. M. Molotova v Berline v noiabre 1940 goda", *Mezhdunarodnaia zhizn'* (Aug. 1991), pp. 104–19. Also, we have Zhukov's testimony in K. Simonov, "K biografii G. Zhukova", *Marshal Zhukov: Kakim my ego pomnim* (Moscow, 1988) p. 97.
19. Gromyko, *Pamiatnoe*, p. 423.
20. "All of us in Moscow have gained the impression that Churchill is holding to a course leading to the defeat of the USSR in order then to come to terms with the Germany of Hitler or Bruning at the expense of our country", Stalin (Moscow) to Maiskii (London), 19 October 1942, in *Sovetsko-angliiskie otnosheniia vo vremia velikoi otechestvennoi voiny 1941–1945*, Vol. 1, doc. 147 (Moscow, 1983).
21. From Ivy Litvinov's papers. See also J. Carswell, *The Exile: A Life of Ivy Litvinov* (London, 1983), p. 155.
22. Memorandum to Under Secretary of State Welles, 7 May 1943, in *Foreign Relations of the United States*, 1943, Vol. III (Washington, 1963), p. 522.
23. Diary entry for 1 May 1945, C. Sulzberger, *A Long Row of Candles: Memoirs and Diaries (1934–1954)* (New York, 1969) p. 258.
24. Smith (Moscow) to Secretary of State (Washington), 24 May 1946, National Archives, US Department of State, 761.00/5-2446.
25. *Washington Post*, 21 Jan. 1952.
26. Sheinis, *Maksim Maksimovich Litvinov*, p. 422.
27. Alexander Werth, *Russia at War 1941–45* (London, 1964), pp. 838–39.
28. Roberts (Moscow) to Bevin (London), 6 Sept. 1946, Public Record Office, Foreign Office 371/56731. This information was coded "green" (top secret) when it arrived, in order not to damage Litvinov.
29. *Ibid.*, p. 97.
30. Testimony of Molotov in *Sto sorok besed s Molotovym — Iz dnevnika F. Chueva* (Moscow, 1991), p. 96.
31. *Ibid.*, p. 97.
32. Ivy Litvinov Papers, Box 3.
33. Interview with Tat'iana Litvinov.

Part Two

# THE SECOND WORLD WAR
# AND THE GRAND ALLIANCE

# 6

# Soviet Security Policy in the 1930s

## TEDDY J. ULDRICKS

The nature and objectives of Soviet foreign policy from December 1933 to August 1939 have been the subject of sustained controversy. During the 1930s the USSR presented itself publicly as the champion of collective security against aggression. The broad contours of this policy are well known — Soviet membership in the League of Nations, Foreign Commissar Litvinov's eloquent pleas at Geneva for joint resistance to aggression, security pacts with France and Czecho-slovakia, and the anti-fascist, Popular Front line in the Comintern. Subsequently, officially sanctioned Soviet scholars have been unani-mous, at least until 1987, in characterizing the Collective Security policy as a sincere attempt to cooperate with Great Britain, France and other powers to deter or, if necessary, defeat German aggression. Collective Security, they contend, was pursued with determination and without deviation, not merely as a stratagem in pursuit of Russian national interests, but as a matter of high moral principle.[1] In contrast to this image of Soviet sincerity and high-mindedness, the traditional Soviet view condemns Britain, France and the United States for their unprincipled failure to ally with the USSR against the menace of fascist aggression. The Western democracies are accused of facilitating Hitler's rise to power and the construction of the Nazi war machine, as well as seeking deliberately to foment a Russo-German war.[2]

This picture of the Soviet Union as the leader of a moral crusade against fascism and war was rejected by some Western political leaders at the time and it has since been attacked by a number of non-Soviet historians. Many officials of the British Foreign Office and of the Conservative party, as well as Prime Minister Neville Chamberlain himself, saw Soviet Collective Security policy as a duplicitous attempt to divide Britain and France from Germany, provoke war and revolution and pave the way for Soviet expansion. More recently, one school of Western historians has argued that an alliance with the Western democracies against Nazi Germany was never the real aim of

Soviet policy in the 1930s. The whole Collective Security campaign, together with the Popular Front line, they contend, was no more than an elaborate courtship ritual directed at Hitler. In their view, the real foreign policy of the USSR is not to be found in the impassioned speeches of Litvinov at Geneva, but rather in the covert contacts with Berlin by Karl Radek, David Kandelaki, Sergei Bessonov and others. In this light, the Nazi-Soviet Pact is seen not as a regrettable alternative necessitated by the failure of the Collective Security campaign, but as the ultimate achievement of the real aim of that campaign.[3]

Neither of these views — the Soviet Union as champion of an anti-fascist moral crusade or the USSR as Hitler's secret suitor — adequately deal with the full range of available evidence concerning Soviet policy in the 1930s. The interpretation espoused by, or imposed on, all official Soviet historians before the advent of perestroika has a number of weaknesses. The alleged moral and ideological bases of the Collective Security policy are suspect. That policy did not manifest consistent opposition, either to aggression and fascism in general, or to Nazism and the Third Reich specifically. In regard to aggression, the policy of the USSR toward Japanese expansionism in the Far East was ambivalent at best. Soviet policy in that arena contained both measures of resistance to Japanese aggression and elements of appeasement of Tokyo. The USSR shipped considerable military aid to Nationalist China, but refused to sign a mutual assistance pact with Nanking; it massively reinforced the Sino-Soviet border, but also sold the Chinese Eastern Railway to Japan.[4] Similarly, the positive relationship between the USSR and Mussolini's Italy belies the notion of consistent anti-fascism on the part of the Kremlin. Moscow responded slowly to the Italian invasion of Ethiopia, hoping to avoid a confrontation with Rome which would wreck the prospect of uniting the European powers against German aggression. The USSR did eventually support a comprehensive economic boycott against the Italian war effort, but when that measure failed to materialize, the Soviet Union actually increased its oil shipments to Italy.[5] The most recent detailed study of Italo-Soviet relations in this period suggests that Moscow labored hard to preserve its cooperative association with Rome and abandoned that relationship only when it felt constrained to make a choice between Britain and Italy as potential collaborators against the menace of Germany and Japan.[6]

Furthermore, the behaviour of the Soviet Union toward Germany did not evidence an entirely principled and consistent anti-fascism. Many Western scholars and, more recently, a number of Soviet historians as well, have contended that Stalin and his closest associates, at first, badly misunderstood the significance of German fascism. The sectarian course pursued by Soviet diplomacy and Comintern policy from 1928 to 1933, therefore, contributed materially to the rise of Hitler. Moreover, the USSR initially sought to continue the Rapallo tradition of Russo-German cooperation, even with the Nazi regime. For example, a month after Hitler assumed the Chancellorship, Deputy Foreign Commissar Nikolai Krestinskii wrote to his Ambassador in Berlin, Lev Khinchuk:

> We want the present government to keep to a friendly position in relations with us. We are counting on this — that the Hitler government is dictated by the necessity of not breaking with us and, at least, maintaining previous relations...In order that Hitler and his entourage appreciate the necessity of an appropriate public declaration on relations with us it is necessary that they see the restraint on our part in waiting for such a declaration.[7]

It was not a morally or ideologically based aversion to fascism, but the rejection of Soviet overtures by Berlin, which caused the Soviet Union to abandon the Rapallo orientation and launch the anti-German Collective Security campaign. The Politburo did not authorize the new Collective Security strategy until 20 December 1933.[8] Once begun, that campaign was subject to a number of deviations and ambiguities. Publicly, the USSR expended a great deal of effort in attempts to reinvigorate the collective anti-aggression mechanism of the League of Nations, to construct a regional security pact in Eastern Europe, to negotiate anti-German bilateral defence pacts with the non-fascist powers and to encourage, through the Comintern, the election of governments in the Western democracies committed to opposing Nazi expansionism. Even at the height of the Collective Security campaign, however, Moscow was anxious not to alienate Berlin. At a meeting with Anthony Eden on 29 March 1935, Stalin told the British Foreign Secretary that he preferred an East European security agreement which included Germany. "We do not wish to encircle anyone," Stalin added.[9]

Moreover, there is evidence of another, seemingly contradictory policy operating secretly beneath the highly visible initiatives of the Collective Security campaign. Most importantly, on several occasions Stalin may have used non-diplomatic personnel, as well as some of his regularly accredited representatives, to transmit covert overtures for a *rapprochement* with the Third Reich. As early as October of 1933 an operative who claimed to represent Stalin and Molotov, and who may have been Karl Radek, contacted the German embassy in Moscow on several occasions to reassure the Germans that the USSR was not implacably hostile to the Third Reich.[10] Radek further assured the Germans in January of 1934 that "nothing will happen that will permanently block our way to a common policy with Germany".[11] According to the German documents, David Kandelaki, the Soviet trade representative in Berlin, introduced the possibility of a political *rapprochement* into trade negotiations between June and November 1935, and again between December 1936 and February 1937.[12] Similarly, the German documents depict the Soviet embassy counsellor in Berlin, Sergei Bessonov, attempting to restore a Rapallo-style political accord in Russo-German relations, in talks which took place in December 1935 and May–July 1937.[13] These approaches constitute an extremely sensitive subject which historians in Russia have only recently begun to discuss.[14] For all of these reasons, it seems that the traditional image in Soviet historiography of a USSR committed un-equivocally and as a matter of principle to an anti-fascist, anti-aggression Collective Security policy must be rejected.

At the same time, the radically different interpretation advanced by Gerhard Weinberg, Robert C. Tucker, Jiri Hochman and others — that Collective Security was only a mask for Stalin's alleged preference for alliance with Hitler — is not adequately supported by the available evidence, either. They contend that the Radek, Kandelaki and Bessonov missions demonstrate a pro-German orientation at the core of Soviet foreign policy. The problem with this contention is that three unofficial and tentative feelers can scarcely tip the scales against the weight of the Collective Security campaign pursued with vigour from late 1933 to 1939. This interpretation suggests that the USSR expended virtually all of its vast political and diplomatic efforts during the 1930s in pursuit of objectives which, in reality, it did not actually seek to achieve, while it devoted only negligible resources to obtaining Stalin's supposedly real goal — a pact with Hitler. Despite this imbalance, Weinberg has suggested that whenever a regime simultaneously pursues two opposite policies, one in public and the other in secret, the latter must invariably be the "real" policy while the former can be nothing but an attempt to gain leverage in pursuit of the latter. The problem with this line of argument is that, in the absence of definitive documentary evidence, a number of other equally plausible ex-planations of this dual policy phenomenon can be advanced. One such alternative hypothesis will be developed below. Moreover, the German scholar, Ingeborg Fleischhauer, has argued recently that the Radek-Kandelaki-Bessonov contacts cannot even be con-sidered serious attempts by Moscow to pursue an alliance with Germany.[15] Instead, she claims that the Nazi-Soviet Pact had its origins in the persistent efforts of German diplomats who urged a Russo-German entente upon both Stalin and Hitler. Similarly, the British scholar Geoffrey Roberts suggests that the Radek-Kandelaki-Bessonov contacts were aimed at cultivating ties with non-Nazi elements in the German élite, rather than at reaching agreement with Hitler.[16]

Those who see the Collective Security policy as a ruse also lean heavily on the testimony of a few defectors and dissidents. For example, Leon Helfand, who defected from the Soviet embassy in Rome in the summer of 1940, told the British diplomat Neville Butler that "Stalin had been nibbling for an agreement with Hitler since 1933". According to Helfand, only Hitler's continued rejection of Soviet feelers caused Moscow to negotiate seriously with the Western powers.[17] The problem with this account and similar assertions by Walter Krivitskii, Vladimir Petrov and Evgenii Gnedin, is that they constitute speculative interpretations by lower level functionaries who had no direct access to the Kremlin policy-making process and who too often relied on the gossip of other functionaries. Moreover, as defectors or dissidents, these men had entirely rejected the Stalinist system. They were, therefore, ready to believe the worst about every aspect of it. They knew that Stalin was a consummately evil man, so they assumed that he must have conducted an unstintingly evil foreign policy — that is, an attempt to collaborate with Hitler.

Some of the critics of the Collective Security strategy have suggested that the Great Purges of the 1930s provide further evidence for their view that Stalin always preferred a deal with Hitler over an agreement with the Western democracies. As they see it, the Purges were, at least in part, motivated by the need to destroy the ideologically principled, militantly anti-fascist Old Bolshevik cadres as a prerequisite to concluding a cynical alliance with Hitler.[18] This approach fails to take into account the paradox that, if Stalin intended the Purges to prepare the way for the Nazi-Soviet Pact, he killed the wrong people. In the Narkomindel, for example, many of the strongest proponents of the traditional Rapallo orientation fell victim, while numerous supporters of cooperation with the Western democracies survived. In fact, since the main result of the terror was to decimate the Soviet élite and thereby weaken the USSR, the Purges made the USSR a less desirable potential ally for either Hitler or the West. Thus, the Purges make no sense in terms of any foreign policy.[19]

Another problem with the Weinberg-Tucker-Hochman thesis is that it is based almost entirely on German documents. That, of course, is the fault of the former Soviet government which did not publish many of the most important Narkomindel and Kremlin papers, and which issued others in a tendentious form.[20] The recent publication of the far from adequate two volume document collection, God krizisa (The Year of Crisis), demonstrates the danger of interpreting Soviet policy entirely through the prism of Auswärtiges Amt records.

A comparison of the strikingly different Soviet and German versions of the famous Merekalov-Weizsäcker conversation of 17 April 1939 is a case in point. Weizsäcker's much quoted memorandum pictured the Soviet Ambassador as arguing boldly for a broad political *rapprochement* between Soviet Russia and the Third Reich. In contrast, Merekalov's report characterized his remarks to Weizsäcker as focused strictly on the problem of securing the fulfillment of previously negotiated Soviet orders from firms in German-occupied Czecho-slovakia. Hitler had reassured Moscow that its contracts with Czech businesses would be honoured, but, Merekalov protested, General Franz Barckhausen of the German occupation force was preventing deliveries of Czech goods to the USSR. Merekalov insisted that these barriers be removed at once and that Czech shipments, particularly from the Škoda arms works, be permitted to reach the Soviet Union without further hindrance. Contrary to Weizsäcker's version, there is no indication in the Soviet Ambassador's telegram that he launched a sweeping initiative, or even dropped a subtle hint, for a *rapproche-ment* with Germany. In fact, according to Merekalov, it was Weizsäcker who broached political topics by referring to the harmful effect of purported military negotiations between Britain, France and the Soviet Union, and by stating his government's desire to further develop relations with the USSR despite the political differences between Moscow and Berlin.

Ingeborg Fleischhauer's hypothesis, that a cadre of pro-Rapallo German diplomats was attempting to persuade both Moscow and its own government to restore amicable Russo-German relations, may also explain some of the discrepancies between Merekalov's and Weizsäcker's versions of their conversation of 17 April. Perhaps, in preparing their memoranda, Rapallo-oriented German diplomats on occasion may have put words into the mouths of their Soviet colleagues, just as they may also have failed to record their own unauthorized initiatives for a Russo-German entente. Given this enormous discrepancy between the two versions of the Merekalov-Weizsäcker conversation, it is scarcely prudent to base sweeping conclusions about the character of Soviet foreign policy on either document.[21]

In order to construct a clearer and more balanced assessment of Soviet foreign policy in the 1930s, it is necessary to review the underlying goal of that policy. Stalin was motivated neither by a comprehensive anti-fascist impulse, nor by a pacifistic aversion to war; neither by admiration or loathing of Hitler, nor by any really operative desire to foment foreign revolutions. While he was not averse to territorial acquisitions, gaining additional lands was not his central objective, either. Rather, perceiving that the Soviet Union existed in an extremely hostile environment, Stalin's principal objective was to preserve the country's national security. He had explained the security thrust of Soviet foreign policy in this era in his speech to the 17th Party Congress in 1934:

> We never had any orientation towards Germany, nor have we any orientation towards Poland and France. Our orientation in the past and our orientation at the present time is towards the USSR and towards the USSR alone.[22]

Stalin shared the view of Lenin and the other old Bolsheviks who had ruled the Soviet state in the 1920s that the USSR existed precariously amid an ever-threatening imperialist encirclement. The rise of Hitler and the rearmament of Germany, combined with the emergence of Japanese expansionism in the Far East, only made a bad situation worse. The siege mentality which created the war scare of 1927 now had a much more serious threat on which to feed.

From the time of the Bolshevik Revolution and continuing through-out the 1920s, the Soviet leadership had feared most of all the formation of a mighty coalition of imperialist powers linking London, Paris, Berlin, Washington, and perhaps also Tokyo, in a great crusade to crush the communist experiment in Russia. Even though Allied intervention in the Russian Civil War had been quite limited in scope and ultimately aborted, the fear of a renewed, and this time more powerful, anti-Bolshevik crusade continued to plague the Kremlin.[23] In the absence of world revolution, Lenin suggested, only a skillful strategy of keeping the imperialist states divided against themselves could prevent a renewed anti-Soviet onslaught. It was further assumed in Moscow that Great Britain, the apparent linchpin of the capitalist system, was the centre of all efforts to renew military intervention against the USSR. Germany replaced England as the presumptive main enemy only after Hitler had made unmistakably clear his implacable hostility to the Soviet Union. Even then, the fear of an imperialist coalition remained strong in Moscow.

These considerations help to account for the ambiguities of the Collective Security campaign. In the first place, the initiation of that campaign did not signify a lack of Soviet interest in re-establishing an amicable relationship with Berlin, nor did it indicate a fixed intent to oppose the Nazi regime because of its ideological repulsiveness or evil nature. No less an apostle of Collective Security than Litvinov himself publicly proclaimed that Soviet estrangement from the Third Reich had nothing to do with ideology and that Russo-German relations could be rebuilt if the security interests of the USSR were respected by the Reich.

> We certainly have our own opinion about the German regime. We certainly are sympathetic toward the suffering of our comrades [in the KPD]; but you can reproach us Marxists least of all for permitting our sympathies to rule our policy. All the world knows that we can and do maintain good relations with capitalist governments of any regime including Fascist. We do not interfere in the internal affairs of Germany or of any other countries, and our relations with her are determined not by her domestic but by her foreign policy.[24]

It seems significant in this context that in his impassioned speeches at Geneva for peace and against international lawlessness, Litvinov seldom attacked Germany by name, preferring instead to condemn "aggression" in general.

Secondly, the Soviet Union was not quite as bold a champion of Collective Security as is sometimes alleged. Of course, the policy of appeasement followed by Britain and France, and the policy of relative isolation pursued by the United States, left the leadership of the anti-Nazi struggle to the USSR by default. Yet, the Soviet leaders were anxious not to outstrip the Western democracies in the struggle against German (or Japanese) aggression. They feared isolation or, worse still, the awful prospect of being manoeuvred into a war with Germany and/or Japan, while the Western powers sat on the sidelines. Even Litvinov, the strongest proponent of East-West cooperation, feared "...that England and France would like to prod Germany to take action against the East...that they would like to direct aggression exclusively against us...".[25] Stalin's strong suspicions in this regard help to account for the escalation of Soviet demands for greater specificity and higher levels of military commitment from the West just when, in the months after Munich, London and Paris had begun to abandon the policy of appeasement.[26] Calls for measures against indirect aggression and for troop transit rights in East Europe need not be seen as deliberate roadblocks to East-West cooperation against Hitler, but rather as a prudent military safeguard and a test of Western sincerity.

Thirdly, the existence of disagreement within the Soviet élite over foreign policy and its implementation does not, in itself, cast doubt on the genuineness of Collective Security. Several scholars, including Jonathan Haslam and Vitalii Kulish, have cited evidence that some of Stalin's entourage, especially Molotov and Malenkov, had substantial doubts about the possibility of cooperating with the Western democracies against Hitler.[27] Some commentators, such as Evgenii Gnedin and Abdurakhman Avtorkhanov, have concluded that such doubts, or even opposition to the Collective Security line, must mean that it was never really accepted by Stalin at all and was therefore never the real policy of the USSR.[28] However, the existence of policy debates seems entirely unexceptional. Only those still holding to the largely discredited theory of totalitarianism would expect to find lock-step unanimity throughout the Soviet élite on such a complex and dangerous issue. Yet, it also seems impossible, given what we know of Stalin's style of governing, that Litvinov and Molotov could have operated two entirely contradictory foreign policy lines at the same time. Even if, on further investigation, the Radek-Kandelaki-Bessonov contacts do turn out to have been serious attempts at Russo-German *rapprochement* (and that is still a debatable question), it is highly unlikely that these gambits were elements of a foreign policy separate from and antithetical to the Collective Security line. Nikolai Abramov and Lev Bezymensky, broaching the subject of the Kandelaki initiatives for the first time in any Soviet publication, argue (based on unpublished diplomatic and Politburo documents) that the Soviet trade representative's gambits in Berlin represented part of a coherent, overall security policy based on the hope that pro-Rapallo elements of the German élite might be able to soften the strongly anti-Soviet policy pursued by Hitler and Ribbentrop.[29]

There was only one foreign policy line, both before and after 1933 and, for that matter, after August 1939. That line included the assumption of hostility from all of the imperialist powers and, therefore, the need to keep them divided. It mandated a balance of power policy which motivated the USSR to make common cause with Germany against a perceived British threat before the rise of Hitler, and thereafter to seek Anglo-French cooperation against an even more menacing Third Reich. Throughout the decade, suspicion of all imperialist powers and a desperate search for security remained constant. Stalin may be faulted for a great many mistakes in attempting to carry out the Collective Security line, but the line itself seems indisputably genuine.

## NOTES

1. For example, *Istoriia vneshnei politiki SSSR*, Vol. II, *1917–1945gg.* (Moscow, 1986), Chs. X and XI.
2. This line of analysis was established in 1949 in the pamphlet *Falsificators of History (An Historical Note)* (Moscow, 1949), and followed rigorously by all subsequent Soviet commentators until the late 1980s. For further discussion of this subject, see Teddy J. Uldricks, "Evolving Soviet Views of the Nazi-Soviet Pact", in Richard Frucht (ed.), *Labyrinth of Nationalism/Complexities of Diplomacy* (Columbus, 1992), pp. 331–60.
3. Important examples of this view include Gerhard Weinberg, *The Foreign Policy of Hitler's Germany*, Vol. I, *Diplomatic Revolution in Europe, 1933–1936* and Vol. II, *Starting World War II, 1937–1939* (Chicago, 1980); Robert C. Tucker, *Stalin in Power: The Revolution from Above, 1928–1941* (New York, 1990), Chs. 10–21; and Jiri Hochman, *The Soviet Union and the Failure of Collective Security* (Ithaca, 1984).
4. See Jonathan Haslam, "Soviet Aid to China and Japan's Place in Moscow's Foreign Policy, 1937–1939", in Ian Nish (ed.), *Some Aspects of Sino-Japanese Relations in the 1930s* (London, 1982) and A. M. Dubinskii, *Sovetsko-kitaiskie otnosheniia v period Iapono-kitaiskoi voiny, 1937–1939* (Moscow, 1980), Ch. II.

5. See Michael Seidman, "Maksim Litvinov: Commissar of Contradiction", *Journal of Contemporary History* 23, 2 (April 1988), pp. 233–37 and Jonathan Haslam, *The Soviet Union and the Struggle for Collective Security, 1933–39* (New York, 1984), Ch. V.
6. J. Calvitt Clarke, III, *Russia and Italy against Hitler: The Bolshevik-Fascist Rapprochement of the 1930s* (New York, 1991), p. 193.
7. Krestinskii to Khinchuk, 23 Feb. 1933, quoted in I. F. Maksimychev, *Diplomatiia mira protiv diplomatii voiny: Ocherk Sovetsko-germanskikh diplomaticheskikh otnoshenii v 1933–1939* (Moscow, 1981), p. 28.
8. V. Ia. Sipols, *Vneshniaia politika Sovetskogo Soiuza 1933–1935* (Moscow, 1980), p. 150.
9. *Dokumenty vneshnei politiki SSSR*, Vol. XVIII, doc. 148.
10. See *Documents on German Foreign Policy* (*DGFP*), Series C, Vol. I, No. 477, and Vol. II, No. 24. Evgenii Gnedin, *Iz istorii otnoshenii mezhdu SSSR i fashistskoi Germaniei: Dokumenty i sovremennye kommentarii* (New York, 1977), pp. 22–23, identifies this anonymous operative as Radek.
11. *DGFP*, Series C, Vol. II, doc. 173.
12. *DGFP*, Series C, Vol. IV, docs. 211, 383, 386–87, 439 and 453, and Vol. VI, docs. 183 and 195.
13. *DGFP*, Series C, Vol. IV, docs. 453 and 472, and Vol. V, doc. 312. Also see J. W. Brügel (ed.), *Stalin und Hitler: Pakt gegen Europa* (Vienna, 1973), p. 38.
14. Lev Bezymenskii and Nikolai Abramov, "Osobaia missiia Davida Kandelaki", *Voprosy istorii* 4–5 (1991) pp. 144–56.
15. Ingeborg Fleischhauer, *Der Pakt: Hitler, Stalin und die Initiative der deutschen Diplomatie, 1938–1939* (Frankfurt, 1990), pp. 10–19.
16. Geoffrey Roberts, *The Unholy Alliance: Stalin's Pact with Hitler* (London, 1989), Ch. V.
17. Helfand-Butler talk of 13 Sept. 1940, Public Record Office, N6758/30/38.
18. For example, Vernon V. Aspaturian, *Process and Power in Soviet Foreign Policy* (Boston, 1971), pp. 628–30 and Robert C. Tucker, "Stalin, Bukharin and History as Conspiracy", in Tucker and Stephen Cohen, *The Great Purge Trial* (New York, 1956), p. xxxvi.
19. See Teddy J. Uldricks, *Diplomacy and Ideology: The Origins of Soviet Foreign Relations* (London, 1979), pp. 181–84.
20. Aleksandr Nekrich, *Otreshis' ot strakha: vospominaniia istorika* (London, 1979), pp. 139–40.
21. Compare *God krizisa, 1938–1939: Dokumenty i materialy, 29 sentiabria 1938g.–31 maia 1939g.*, Vol. I (Moscow, 1990), p. 389, with the German version in Raymond J. Sontag and James S. Beddie (eds.), *Nazi-Soviet Relations: Documents from the Archives of the German Foreign Office As Released by the Department of State* (Washington, 1948), pp. 1–2. This discrepancy is analyzed in Geoffrey Roberts' forthcoming article, "Infamous Encounter? The Merekalov-Weizsäcker Meeting of 17 April 1939", in *The Historical Journal* (Dec. 1992).
22. I. V. Stalin, *Works* (Moscow, 1955), Vol. XIII, pp. 308–9.
23. See Teddy J. Uldricks, "Russia and Europe: Diplomacy, Revolution and Economic Development in the 1920s", *International History Review* I, 1 (Jan. 1979), pp. 55–83.
24. M. M. Litvinov, *Vneshniaia politika SSSR* (Moscow, 1935), p. 70.
25. *Soviet Peace Efforts on the Eve of World War II* (Moscow, 1976), Part I, doc. 7.
26. See, for example, the demand published in the 11 May 1939 issue of *Izvestiia* for a mutual defence pact — the terms of which were equal and reciprocal.
27. Jonathan Haslam has argued that, "the struggle for collective security had to be fought at home as well as abroad": Haslam, *The Soviet Union and the Struggle for Collective Security*, p. 5. Also see V. M. Kulish, "U poroga voiny", *Komsomol'skaia pravda*, 24 Aug. 1988, p. 3, and Paul D. Raymond, "Conflict and Consensus in Soviet Foreign Policy, 1933–1939", Ph.D. diss. (Pennsylvania State University, 1979).
28. E. Gnedin, *Iz istorii otnoshenii mezhdu SSSR i fashistskoi Germaniei: Dokumenty i sovremennye kommentarii* (New York, 1977), pp. 7–8 and Abdurakhman Avtorkhanov, "Behind the Scenes of the Molotov-Ribbentrop Pact", in *Kontinent 2* (Garden City, 1977), pp. 85–102.
29. Bezymenskii and Abramov, "Osobaia missiia Davida Kandelaki", pp. 144–56.

# 7

# The Secret Protocols of 1939 as a Problem of Soviet Historiography

## LEV BEZYMENSKY

The well-known dictum according to which mankind bids farewell to its past with a smile, is not universally applicable. In fact, the process of burying the past often stirs up contrary emotions. Such was the case following the acknowledgement by the Soviet Union of the existence of Secret Protocols, supplementary to the Soviet-German Pact. In these secret agreements, signed on 23 August and 28 September 1939, Germany and Russia partitioned Poland between them and delineated spheres of influence in Eastern Europe.

Paradoxically, these so-called Secret Protocols were never secret. Shortly after their signature, the Americans were notified of their existence through a German source.[1] This information was later relayed to the British government.[2] Even in Berlin where officials of the Foreign Ministry had pledged to keep the matter confidential,[3] it took only a few weeks for the content of the Protocols to become known to German representatives in the Baltics. However, they never became common knowledge. After 22 June 1941 the German government had little interest in exposing its agreement with the "Jewish-Bolshevik" USSR, while Britain and the USA were reluctant to harm the fragile coalition.

When these considerations lost their relevance, events began taking a different course. The Soviet historians Iu. N. Zoria and N. S. Lebedeva revealed in 1989 that their government had anticipated such a change immediately following the war.[4] While preparing for the Nuremberg trials, Soviet officials included the Pact of 1939 in a list of topics which they did not want raised. This list, officially endorsed by Molotov (undoubtedly in consultation with Stalin), was submitted to the Allies and agreed upon, together with the Allies' own list of "forbidden topics". All the same, discussion of the Pact and Protocols at Nuremberg could not be averted.

The events which unfolded in March 1946 at Nuremberg could

justifiably be viewed as one of the first signals of the Cold War. While officially Western representatives adhered to the list and supported demands by the head of the Soviet prosecution that testimony regarding the Protocols be dismissed, Rudolf Hess's attorney, Alfred Seidel, certified that he had received pertinent documents from American sources. In 1948 the US Department of State published the text of the Protocols in a collection entitled *Nazi-Soviet Relations 1939–1941*. The Soviets dismissed the documents as forgeries in a pamphlet entitled *Falsificators of History (An Historical Note)*.[5]

It was at this point that the official Soviet position, and consequently that of Soviet historiography towards the Protocols was formulated. The refusal to acknowledge the existence of these documents was a logical corollary of Stalinist diplomacy. The Protocols undermined the socialist foundations of Soviet foreign policy: first, because the agreements between the USSR and Germany exemplified a classic case of imperialist division of spheres of interest; and second, because they represented an imperialist means of resolving territorial disputes at the expense of a third, smaller, country. It was precisely for these reasons that no reference to them was made in fundamental Soviet works such as *A History of Diplomacy, A History of Soviet Foreign Policy, The History of the CPSU, The History of the Great Patriotic War of the Soviet People 1941–1945* or *The History of the Second World War 1939–1945*. Andrei Gromyko, who supervised the publication of *Foreign Policy Documents of the USSR*, chose to cancel the entire series in order to avoid publishing the volume dealing with 1939.[6] Subsequent volumes, such as *The Struggle of the USSR for Peace on the Eve of World War II* (1971) and *Documents and Materials Relating to the Eve of World War II* (1981), were organized topically rather than chronologically and all material relating to Soviet-German relations during that period was omitted from these works.

It became so habitual to deny the existence of the Protocols that Molotov insisted, even in private conversations after his retirement, that there had been no secret agreements, or at least that "he had no recollection of them".[7] Gromyko, held firmly to this view in an interview with *Der Spiegel* as late as April 1989.[8]

For the Soviet establishment, the issue of the Protocols became a matter of principle. The non-existence of the Protocols confirmed the infallibility of Soviet foreign policy and its consistent anti-fascist character, as well as the reputation of Western historiographers as "falsifiers".

Soviet historians, however, found themselves in a very difficult position: adhering to the official line on the documents obliged them to compromise themselves in the eyes of the entire international community of historians. They were prepared to accept the arguments of their Western colleagues in private but unwilling do so in print until the era of glasnost.

The revision of Soviet society's attitude towards its own past has proceeded in accordance with specific domestic priorities. Having begun with a reassessment of Stalin's repression and his personality *per se*, this process tended to embrace a constantly expanding range of questions, mostly relating to foreign policy. The Protocols would have been low on the priority list had it not been for two factors. The first was connected with the necessity to resolve certain issues in Soviet-Polish relations. The events of 1939 remained an open wound for the Polish public as long as the Poles could not obtain from their Soviet partner convincing, or at least well-documented, responses to questions concerning the Soviet role in the early stages of World War II and in the wake of its invasion of Poland. At a meeting with Jaruzielski in 1987, Gorbachev yielded to Polish pressure to create a joint Soviet-Polish commission made up of historians, which was to submit to the leaders of both countries its conclusions concerning the so-called "blank pages" of history. These included the Polish-Soviet war of 1920, the fate of the leadership of the Polish Communist party during the repressions of the 1930s, the events of 1939, the Warsaw uprising, and finally, the Katyn massacre. The issue of the Protocols, although not high on the agenda, did emerge during the commission's deliberations. For the Soviet side, it was much more difficult to comply with the legitimate claims of the Polish representatives concerning some of the other points, especially Katyn, because the KGB, the Prosecutor's Office and the Soviet Ministry of Foreign Affairs refused point blank to provide any information.

The second catalyst for bringing the Protocols to the forefront of the revision process was the transformation that was taking place in the Soviet Baltic republics. The upsurge of national self-awareness and unequivocal demands for secession from the USSR affected a broad spectrum of the public in Lithuania, Latvia and Estonia, including historians, who turned out to be much more open in their interpretation of the facts than their colleagues in Moscow. The popular fronts which emerged in these republics demanded in their political programs that the secret agreements of 1939 be repealed.

It should be pointed out that, whereas the considerations regarding Poland played a positive role in urging the Soviet leadership to revise its attitude towards the Protocols, pressure from the Baltics created exactly the opposite effect. The Politburo of the CPSU Central Committee at that time obstinately believed that any move toward recognizing the existence of these Protocols would serve the interests of secessionists, and so it was not inclined to revise its stand. Thus the Protocols became a domestic affair — a bone of contention between reformers and conservatives in the CPSU.

The years 1985–1988 were therefore marked by an unprecedented gap between the work of historians and the official line of the CPSU. In academic discussions many Soviet historians found ways to refer to the Protocols within the context of the events of 1939, albeit as one variant. At the very least they attempted to reject the charge of falsification. Demands to continue and intensify archival research in connection with the Protocols were increasingly voiced at various conferences devoted to the approaching 50th anniversary of the beginning of World War II. The official position, however, was little affected. The pronouncements made in *Pravda* on 1 September 1988 by the head of the Historical and Diplomatic Directorate of the Soviet Ministry of Foreign Affairs, Feliks Kovalev, and the leading Soviet historian of the period, Prof. Oleg Rzheshevskii, were highly indicative: "Western historians and political scientists used to insist that in addition to the Pact, 'secret protocols' had been ostensibly signed...". The authors went on to repeat the well-known argument that the original texts of the Protocols had never been found — only "extremely contradictory" versions of the copies. At the same time, articles had appeared in the journal *Voprosy istorii*, as well as in the Soviet press (by Mikhail Semiriaga, Iurii Afanas'ev and Vyacheslav Dashichev), which made direct references to the Protocols.[9]

However, the attitude of the Soviet Party and State leadership towards the Protocols underwent considerable change in the postwar years, as indicated by official documents and unofficial information. A long and thorny path was trod — from outright denial of their existence to recognition and solemn denunciation.

The first effort to revise the traditional position occurred during the "thaw" of the late 1950s. Il'ia Zemskov, initially chief of the Diplomatic History Department of the Ministry of Foreign Affairs and later Deputy Minister, can be considered the initiator of this attempt. He was well acquainted with international publications on the subject and cautiously pointed out to Gromyko that the official position on the Protocols contradicted irrefutable facts. Gromyko remained un-moved.[10] Until the end of the 1980s the question was never discussed openly.

The onset of the Gorbachev era brought a turnabout in the approach to the Protocols. The necessity of formulating a definite position became apparent to Gorbachev during one of his meetings with Jaruzielski in 1987. The Soviet leader decided to delegate responsibility for re-examining the official position on the Protocols to various departments of the Central Committee and the Foreign Ministry: the Historical and Diplomatic Directorate of the Foreign Ministry, headed by Kovalev, and the Ideological Department, which was under the general supervision of Politburo member and Central Committee Secretary Aleksandr Yakovlev, the International Department, headed by Anatolii Dobrynin, and the Department for Relations with Socialist Countries of the Central Committee under Vadim Medvedev.[11]

Progress was very slow. A draft of the commission's recommendations was ready only in December 1987. It contained a historical survey of the issue and discussed the range of possible positions: maintaining the status quo, partial admittance of the existence of the documents, and outright acknowledgement. A special memorandum containing the recommendations and signed by Eduard Shevardnadze and the members of the commission was forwarded to the Central Committee of the Communist party.[12] However, it came up for discussion only on 5 May 1988, the eve of Gorbachev's visit to Poland.

During the session, the official speaker for the Foreign Ministry, Deputy Foreign Minister Leonid Il'ichev, and G. L. Smirnov, Director of the Institute of Marxism-Leninism, reminded their colleagues that there was exhaustive evidence that the Protocols did exist. Nonetheless, Gromyko, then Politburo member and Chairman of the USSR Supreme Soviet, evaded the topic with a vague observation that "one must have a point of view" on the matter. He added that "from the historical perspective, it is necessary to tell the truth", but did not elaborate any further. There is now documented evidence that on at least two occasions (in 1975 and 1979), Gromyko was shown originals of the Protocols which were preserved in the special archival 6th Section of the General Department. Viktor Chebrikov (then head of the KGB and a Politburo member) categorically opposed revealing the existence of the Protocols, because "it would serve no purpose" and because there were no legal grounds for it. Gorbachev was sceptical too, reasserting that the originals had not been found. No resolution was reached.[13]

Thus Gorbachev's behaviour in Poland was predictable. During his visit in June 1988 he disappointed the Poles by adhering to the official line on the Protocols. In fact, a hardening of this position was evident in the writing of one of the advocates of the "new thinking", Valentin Falin. In August 1988 he reverted to using the term "falsification" in his discussion of the Protocols.

The creation of new supreme bodies of power, primarily, the Congress of People's Deputies and the first elections in March 1989, provided a new outlet for the expression of public opinion. This time the "Baltic factor" came into play. As early as the first Congress in June

1989, the Baltic deputies raised the question of Soviet-German agreements and the Secret Protocols. In accordance with a proposal by the Estonian delegate E. Lippmaa, a commission for political and legal assessment of the Soviet-German Pact of 23 August 1939 was created on 2 June. It was headed by Aleksandr Yakovlev.[14]

The commission consisted of 26 members — ten were from the Baltic Republics; three were professional historians. Iurii Afanas'ev, Rector of the Historical Archives Institute, Valentin Falin, Chief of the International Department, and Estonian People's Deputy Edgar Savisaar, were appointed as Yakovlev's assistants. The commission held six plenary sessions and four seminars of experts over a period of seven months; 172 unpublished documents from the Foreign Ministry and expert reports of historians and legal advisers were sent to the commission at its request. Information was also received from the German Foreign Ministry.[15]

A major difficulty arose already at the first session. The delegates of the three Baltic republics were pursuing an urgent political objective, prompted by the upcoming 50th anniversary of the Ribbentrop-Molotov Pact. This rendered their arguments (as well as those of Afanas'ev, who took their side) mostly political and highly emotional. The opposing wing was represented by Ukrainian Foreign Minister Kravets, who firmly adhered to the "Gromyko line". Yakovlev, Falin and Georgii Arbatov, Director of the Institute of the USA and Canada, took a different approach: they deemed it necessary to make a detailed analysis of the historical context of those years and of the causes that led to the signing of the Pact. However, their opponents viewed this as an attempt to "rehabilitate" the Stalinist leadership.

The impasse proved impossible to resolve even after experts had been called in. Latvia, Lithuania and Estonia sent their own specialists who took a radical position. The Moscow team (of which the author was a member) split into "traditionalists" who adhered to previous official interpretations, and "radicals" who demanded a revision of those interpretations. However, none of the experts — not even those who were most conservative in interpreting the causes which had led to the signing of the Pact — questioned the existence of the Secret Protocols and/or the authenticity of the German copies.

In August 1989 a crisis emerged in the work of the commission. The radical group led by Afanas'ev demanded publication of at least interim results by 23 August, but no authorization was obtained from Gorbachev or the chairman of the commission. The idea was opposed outright by conservative Politburo members Egor Ligachev, Vladimir Kryuchkov and Mikhail Solomentsev.[16] Subsequently, several members of the commission leaked the preliminary text of the draft resolution to the international press (the text contained acknowl-edgement of the existence of the Protocols), thus subjecting their chairman to criticism at a press conference. The commission now faced real danger of disintegration. However, Yakovlev managed to keep the commission intact. It was decided that he would make a "personal statement" which would not demand approval of the commission or the Politburo; the only requirement was that a draft resolution be prepared and presented to the Congress, with a brief explanatory note. These documents were ready by 4 November; the report was presented on 23 December.[17]

Yakovlev had no illusions about the situation. He warned the members of the commission that they should not expect support for the radical ideas of Afanas'ev and his Baltic colleagues in the Congress. In fact, even his own cautious and balanced address incensed the legislators. On 23 December the conservative majority of the Congress firmly rejected the proposal to denounce the Pact of 1939 and annul the Protocols. However, the following day Yakovlev persuaded the delegates to reconsider by producing for them a document confirming the existence of the originals.

The document consisted primarily of a statement compiled in April 1946 by two employees of Molotov's secretariat, D. V. Smirnov and B. F. Podtserob, which confirmed the existence of eight original agreements, including the Secret Protocols of August 23 and September 28, 1939:

> We, the undersigned, Deputy Head of Comrade V. M. Molotov's Secretariat, D. V. Smirnov, and Senior Assistant to the USSR Minister of Foreign Affairs, B. F. Podtserob, on this day, the former handed over and the latter received the following documents of the Special Archives of the USSR Ministry for Foreign Affairs:
>
> 1.  *Documents on Germany*
>
> 1. The original of the Secret Additional Protocol of August 23, 1939 (in Russian and German), plus three copies of the said protocol.
> 2. The original of the official commentary on the Secret Additional Protocol of August 23, 1939 (in Russian and German), plus two copies of the said commentary.
> 3. The original of the Confidential Protocol of September 28, 1939 (in Russian and German), plus two copies of the said protocol.
> 4. The original of the Secret Additional Protocol of September 28, 1939 ("On Polish Propaganda") (in Russian and German), plus two copies of the said protocol.
> 5. The original of the Secret Additional Protocol of September 28, 1939 ("On Lithuania") (in Russian and German), plus two copies of the said protocol.
> 6. The original of the Secret Protocol of January 10, 1939 concerning a part of Lithuania's territory (in Russian and German).

7. The original of the additional Protocol between the USSR and Germany of October 4, 1939 (concerning the border) (in Russian and German).
8. The original of the Protocol — description of the location of the USSR state border and the state border of Germany (two volumes in Russian and German).[18]

The pages which followed contained a description of additional documents unrelated to the Protocols. The last page bore their signatures and was dated "April 1946".

The Smirnov-Podtserob document requires some explanation. First, how should one interpret the fact that the documents listed were handed over from one Molotov functionary to another? The answer is that after 1939, Molotov had two offices. He retained the post of Chairman of the Soviet of People's Commissars after he became the People's Commissar for Foreign Affairs. Hence, he preserved his office and secretariat in the Kremlin. His other office was in the building of the People's Commissariat for Foreign Affairs. This situation did not change after Stalin took over the post of Chairman of the Soviet of People's Commissars in 1941, on the eve of the war. Thus, one of Molotov's secretariats was located in the Kremlin and headed by I. Lapshev. Smirnov became Lapshev's assistant after the war. The other secretariat was in the building of the People's Commissariat of Foreign Affairs (later the Ministry of Foreign Affairs) and was headed by Podtserob, a career diplomat who subsequently occupied a number of ambassadorial posts.

The act was signed, therefore, by the representatives of two secretariats — Smirnov removed the documents from the "special archive" of one office and handed them over to Podtserob of the other office, which indicates that Molotov wanted to have the originals under his personal control. The copies of the Secret Protocols contained in the above file had been certified by one V. Panin, whose position was not stated.[19] A comparison of these copies with those from Ribbentrop's archives provide, perhaps, the most important revelations:

1. The copies from the German and the Soviet archives were not carbon copies: the layout of the text differs, but the content is absolutely identical.
2. Panin's text and the German one were typed on the same typewriter which evidently belonged to Molotov's secretariat and was used for typing the most important documents.
3. Suspicions (raised also by Gorbachev) of the authenticity of the Pact and Protocols based on the argument that Molotov's signature had been written in Latin script in the German version proved to be

unfounded. Molotov signed the Russian original in Cyrillic script, but presumably when it came to signing the German text (of both the Pact and the Protocols), he decided to demonstrate his university education. Ribbentrop signed both versions in Latin script.

4. The author has been able to have Panin's signature authenticated by the official's family.

It should be added that all these conclusions apply not only to the Secret Additional Protocol of 23 August 1939, but also to other secret protocols signed during Ribbentrop's second visit to Moscow on 27–29 September and dated 28 September of the same year.

Thus ended the most important and, so it was believed, final chapter in the history of the Protocols. Their existence was officially acknowledged and their content condemned by the highest legislative body — the Congress of People's Deputies of the USSR. However, events which occurred in October 1992 (already following the disintegration of the USSR) were even more dramatic.

As has been noted, the main argument of those who questioned the existence of the Protocols was the fact that the originals had not been produced. This argument was repeatedly used by Gorbachev, even after initiating the policy of perestroika (including at sessions of the Politburo in 1988 and 1989, and in his public appearances). Yakovlev's commission also resigned itself to the absence of the originals because it managed to deal with the problem on the basis of persuasive circumstantial evidence alone.

However history is subject to frequent and unexpected turns — one of which occurred at the end of 1992. During the sorting of certain documents of the "Kremlin" (also known as the "President's") archive, which were to be transferred and made available to researchers, two sealed envelopes containing the original versions of the Secret Protocols were discovered.[20] This find, which was made public on 29 October 1992 compels us to view all the events described above in a different light.[21] While, in the final analysis, it does not contribute anything new, it exemplifies one of the deeply-rooted features of Soviet conduct: the formulation of policy based on conscious lies. This harsh judgement derives from an examination of the contents of the two envelopes, numbered 34 and 35, which leads to the following conclusions:

1. The originals of the additional Protocols of 23 August and 28 September 1939, were at Molotov's disposal from 1939 to 1952.

2. In December 1952, they were transferred to the General Department of the Central Committee of the CPSU, more precisely, to its 6th Sector, where the most secret documents of the Politburo

were kept, including those preserved in special files stamped *osobaia papka* (special file) and *zakrytyi konvert* (sealed envelope). It was the latter, the most secret classification, which was given to the Protocols (file 34) and maps accompanying the Protocols with the signatures of Stalin and Ribbentrop (file 35).

3. Copies were made from these originals twice — in 1975 and 1979 — and sent to the Ministry of Foreign Affairs in the name of Zemskov for forwarding to Gromyko.

4. The last time the envelopes were opened was on 10 April 1987 in accordance with a directive of Valerii Boldin, Chief of the General Department of the Central Committee. Boldin later resealed the envelopes and ordered that they be kept under close watch in the 6th Sector. If Boldin ever showed the contents of the envelopes to anyone, it was never registered in the files.

It is thus apparent that the upper echelons of the Soviet leadership which succeeded Stalin — at least from 1975 onwards — knew that the originals did exist. The question of whether Gorbachev had personal knowledge about the originals still remains open. He himself denies it, but the claims of some that it is inconceivable that Boldin did not discuss such an important issue as the contents of envelopes nos. 34 and 35 with the General Secretary are equally credible.

The diplomatic aspects of the Molotov-Ribbentrop Pact are not within the scope of this chapter, although it is a topic which has constituted a focus of debate in Soviet historical literature over recent years and one which requires special study. These discussions can and must continue. However, at least one question has finally been resolved conclusively: The long-standing "accursed problem" of Soviet historiography concerning the existence of secret agreements has been removed from the agenda. Now Soviet historians can unashamedly look their colleagues in the eyes — and continue their common work on documentary studies in this extremely important chapter of European history — Soviet foreign policy in the pre-war period.

## NOTES

1. Hans v. Herwarth, *Zwischen Hitler und Stalin* (Berlin, 1985), p. 193 and Charles Bohlen, *Witness to History* (New York, 1973), pp. 70–83.
2. Public Record Office, Foreign Office 371/23686.
3. Politisches Archiv Bonn, Büro RAM, F 11/9939.
4. Iu. N. Zoria and N. S. Lebedeva, *Mezhdunarodnaia zhizn'* 9 (1989).
5. *Falsificators of History (An Historical Note)* (Moscow, 1949).
6. The volume was finally prepared and published by the Ministry of Foreign Affairs (*Mezhdunardonaia otnosheniia*) in 1992.
7. *Sto sorok besed s Molotovym — Iz dnevnika F. Chueva* (Moscow, 1991), p. 20.
8. *Der Spiegel* 17 (1989).
9. *Voprosy istorii* 6 (1989).
10. Gromyko reportedly told Zemskov: "Anyway, nobody will be able to expose us."
11. Based on information from the personal archive of Vadim Medvedev.
12. From discussions with V. Medvedev in October 1992. Such was the established practice at that time. A departmental note was submitted to the Central Committee and discussed by the Secretariat or the Politburo.
13. From discussions with Medvedev and Alexandrov.
14. *Second Congress of People's Deputies of the USSR*, Moscow 1990, Vol. IV, p. 255.
15. Information from the personal archives of V. A. Alexandrov and the author.
16. According to Yakovlev, he was supported in the Politburo only by Shevardnadze. Only after Yakovlev threatened to resign from the post of chairman of the commission did Gorbachev consent to his making a speech before the Congress (from a conversation with Yakovlev, Feb. 1992). As for Gorbachev, he realized the necessity of rejecting the traditional position only after the demonstrations which took place in Aug. 1989 (from discussions with Gorbachev's personal assistant, Anatolii Cherniaev).
17. *Second Congress of People's Deputies of the USSR*, Moscow 1990, Vol. IV, p. 255.
18. Published in *Vestnik MID SSSR* 4 (1990) without the stamp of the USSR Foreign Ministry Archives. Attached to the file were the TASS messages on the discussion of the question of the Protocols at the Nuremberg Trials. The original document is located in the Arkhiv vneshnei politiki Rossiiskoi Federatsii, delo 600/700, list 17.
19. V. I. Panin was Deputy Head of Molotov's secretariat in the Council of Ministers until 1941. He was succeeded after his death in 1941 by Smirnov.
20. General Department, Sector VI, Central Committee of the CPSU, fond 3, opis' 64, delo 675-a.
21. Press conference with Rudolf Pekhoia, Dmitrii Volkogonov and Aleksandr Yakovlev.

# 8

# Poland Between East and West – The Politics of a Government-in-Exile

## ANITA J. PRAZMOWSKA

It is ironic that the very man whom present day Poles consider to have been the *éminence gris* in the British Foreign Office and a malign influence on all decisions concerning Polish matters, foresaw one of the key areas of weakness of the government-in-exile. Commenting upon the establishment of the Polish government in France, Lewis Namier wrote in November 1939:

> Emigré governments are essentially weak because they depend on strangers, are therefore amenable to foreign influence and can be made into instruments of a foreign policy. In the best interest of Poland and of her future, even the appearance of such developments should be avoided...such exploitation comes to an émigré government in a most seductive form: by their being treated as fully and exclusively representative of their country.[1]

By November 1943 the Polish government-in-exile had done everything against which Lewis Namier had cautioned. It had come to depend exclusively on British and American support, and had placed all its resources, primarily manpower, at the disposal of the British, who were either using or proposing to use them on fronts which were of little direct relevance to Poland. Finally, the exile government had endeavoured to convince itself that the future of Poland depended entirely on its own cooperation with those very Allies. In reality, its policies for the restoration of Poland had been reduced to one option only: dependence on Britain to place it in power in liberated Poland and to defend its new, and also hopefully enlarged, borders.

The result was that by 1943, the British viewed Polish aspirations and territorial demands as a mere obstacle to obtaining full Soviet cooperation. The symbolic turning point when the government-in-exile seems to have lost its political independence and influence (for there was no specific crisis or incident which tipped the scales), occurred at the Tehran Conference. In Tehran, Churchill repeatedly sought to neutralize Poland as a potential impediment to British-Soviet relations, demonstrating not only that Polish territorial demands were not going to be defended, but also that he would use his influence to induce the exile government to accommodate Soviet needs.

During discussions on 28 November, Churchill proposed that future frontiers be defined. It was left to Stalin to enquire whether "it would be without Polish participation". Churchill assured him that "they could go to the Poles later".[2] Both men were referring to the Polish government-in-exile which had taken up residence in London. These exchanges suggest an agreement to sidestep that government when making decisions relating to Poland. At the same meeting the principle of redrawing Polish boundaries further west was accepted. During the session between Stalin, Churchill and Roosevelt on 30 November, Stalin made a distinction between the aspirations of the Polish public and those of the government-in-exile. Roosevelt and Churchill eagerly sought a compromise acceptable to Stalin. They therefore accepted Molotov's assertion that the September 1939 line corresponded to the Curzon line and that Lvov should be included in the territory of the Soviet Union. According to the minutes of the proceedings, Churchill stated:

> ...that the Poles would be wise to take our advice. They were getting a country 300 miles square and [he said] that he was not prepared to make a great squawk about Lvov and (turning to Marshal Stalin) he added that he did not think that we were very far off in principle.[3]

In spite of growing doubts as to whether their efforts would be rewarded, the Poles henceforth sought to increase their role in the Allied military effort. By December 1943 the Polish government-in-exile had approximately 100,000 men in the three services, fighting or undergoing training in the West. These numbers were to increase during the remaining years of the war. Nevertheless, the government's political influence was to remain negligible. It could be argued that the influence of the Polish government was to decrease irreversibly after Stalin and Churchill's Tehran Conference agreement on the Polish question.

As victory appeared certain, following the Soviet summer offensives against Germany, Poland was reduced to a mere object in Allied negotiations; and with Soviet victories in the east, the Allies distanced themselves increasingly from the Polish-Soviet impasse. This chapter argues that, for the Poles, the political advantages of military cooperation with the Allies were dubious from the outset. The following issues will be addressed: What were the political objectives of the Polish government-in-exile? What were the implications of Poland's military contribution during the period prior to the Tehran Conference? How did the above two issues affect the course of Polish-British and Polish-Soviet relations?

The establishment of an exile government in Paris at the end of September 1939 implied not merely a transfer of power from the previous government trapped in Romania, but more importantly, a change in its composition and leadership. During the early days of the war, General Władysław Sikorski was identified by some French military and diplomatic personalities as a preferred leader of any Polish legions which might be raised in France, and possibly even of an exile administration. He and like minded pro-French Poles were assisted in leaving Poland and making their way to France by the then French Ambassador Leon Noël.[4] It is unclear whether the French aim from the outset had been to aid in the creation of an exile government in Paris.[5] Nevertheless, when the Poles, under the leadership of Juliusz Łukasiewicz, made arrangements for the nomination of a new government, the French did interfere in order to influence its composition. They vetoed the appointment of Wieniawa Długoszowski, a leading Pilsudskiite, to the Presidency,[6] insisting instead on the weak and indecisive Władysław Raczkiewicz. Inevitably, Sikorski became the Prime Minister and the opposition was temporarily routed. In addition, Sikorski assumed control over the Ministry of War and Ministry of Justice.[7]

The most important decision made by the Poles even before the outbreak of the war was that Poland should continue to be seen fighting even if its territory was occupied. Thus the departure of political and military leaders in the wake of defeat in September was not a disorganized exodus but a move to Allied territories, where a government-in-exile could continue to coordinate fighting and participate in all negotiations concerning postwar settlements.[8] This decision constrained the exile government's manoeuvrability. From the start it was dependent upon the Allied war effort. Although the government-in-exile would have preferred to have had its own autonomous sphere of military action, one which would have highlighted the Polish contribution to the war and confirmed the Allies' need of Poland, such an opportunity did not arise. The dependence on Allied strategic planning also imposed severe restrictions on Polish political freedom.

The government therefore faced several serious problems. First, it was wholly dependent on the Allies in all military matters and unable to assert its independence politically. At the same time, the visibility of its military contribution was a critical factor in securing it a place at the negotiating table, and ultimately restoring Poland to its pre-September 1939 borders. The second problem was how and when to try to resume the direct military struggle to liberate Polish territory. After the fall of Poland, the country's troops were deployed in remote war zones. This would hamper their ability to return to Poland in time for the crucial battle for territorial liberation. Leaders of the government-in-exile were aware that allies could easily become former allies once hostilities ended.

From the outset the Polish government was limited in its choice of partners. After the implementation of the Ribbentrop-Molotov Pact the Soviet Union became an arch-enemy. Although Sikorski was able to impose upon the exile government cooperation with the Soviet Union, after the German attack on Russia he continued to encounter strong opposition to this policy. At the same time, neither Britain nor the United States was willing to support the Poles in their anti-Soviet policy.

On 30 December 1939, Sikorski wrote that the government's primary objective was to establish and then increase its influence upon the Allies in order that a compromise peace not be signed with the enemy at Poland's expense.[9] This influence and commitment could only be secured if Poland was an active military partner. The creation of an army therefore became a means of gaining Allied commitment to the Polish cause. This explains Polish demands for inclusion in the Supreme War Council and the Executive War Council, both of which were rejected. It also explains why the government sought to deploy Polish units in a variety of battle zones. On 21 February 1940, the Chief of Staff argued the case for sending Polish units to fight in Finland:

> Polish units in Finland will be real proof of the fact that Poland exists and continues to fight with the Allies. I stress that in my understanding this is not a case of prestige but one that is very important and fundamental to Poland.[10]

From within the ranks of the military (which were highly politicized in the Polish tradition), Sikorski faced opposition to his determination that the newly formed army in France should go into battle on the Western front. He rejected the proposal of his own Chief of Staff, General Alexander Kędzior, made public in April 1940, that the army's strength be preserved for the vital battle on Polish territories. Sikorski insisted that only joint military participation in the Allied war effort could guarantee the Allies' commitment to Poland.[11] In response to this wave of dissent among Polish officers, Sikorski ordered a wholesale purge of agitators and their incarceration in a penal camp.[12]

The collapse of France in June 1940 dashed hopes that the war might end quickly. Moreover, it shattered any illusion that Polish participation could be confined to the European front. Dependence on military cooperation with Britain meant that the war had to be seen from the British perspective, as a global conflict. Reluctantly, the Poles joined in the fight against Italy, which they had considered, until that time, to be a friend.[13]

With an eye to future involvement in the Balkan area, the Sikorski government had been trying to maintain a neutral position in relation to Italy after the German attack on France. On several occasions the Polish government-in-exile had discussed the problem of Italy. Most ministers believed that the Polish and Italian nation were united in friendship and that Italy could thus be treated as a weak link of the Axis.[14] The dilemma came to a head when in October 1940 the British proposed to use the Polish Carpathian Brigade in the defence of Egypt. The Italian declaration of war in June 1940 meant that there was a possibility of military conflict between Allied troops in the Suez region and Italian troops from Ethiopia and Eritreia. Not until Sikorski qualified his earlier statement on the subject to mean that Polish troops could be used against Italian ones, was the Carpathian Brigade re-equipped by the British in December 1940.[15]

The Poles also tried to resolve the dilemma concerning France, which they shared with the British, by maintaining diplomatic relations with the Vichy government[16] while, at the same time, according De Gaulle limited recognition.[17] On 30 June 1940 the government's ministerial committee approved basic principles of its future foreign policy. It defined the restoration of France to its position as a European power as one of its main aims. Good relations were thus to be maintained with the present French government so that "in the event of the defeat of Germany, France would have a say in matters relating to political issues concerning postwar Europe".[18]

Undoubtedly Sikorski's most difficult and controversial decision concerned the re-establishment of diplomatic relations with the Soviet Union. His reasons for taking this politically risky move were complex. Sikorski had earlier become aware of limits on the expansion of Polish units following the disappointing response to the recruiting effort in Canada and the United States. Moreover, only some 30,000 men were evacuated to Britain after the defeat of France. While still in France, Sikorski had contended with opponents of his policy of direct and unqualified military support for the Allied war effort. He was therefore irreversibly committed now to making a maximum contribution to the war. His thinking inevitably moved in the direction of gaining access to Poles imprisoned and trapped on Soviet territory. It has been estimated that the Soviet authorities had deported 1,250,000 Poles into the Soviet interior after the occupation of the Polish eastern regions.

Of these, 180,000 were prisoners of war and were incarcerated in military and penal camps, and in prisons.[19]

Earlier discreet efforts to obtain access to Polish soldiers imprisoned in the Soviet Union had not been successful. One such attempt was made in December 1939, with the Turkish government acting as intermediary.[20] Subsequently, a governmental crisis was sparked by Sikorski's communication to the British Foreign Secretary of 19 June 1940 which included, among signs of his willingness to consider establishing relations with the Soviet Union, a suggestion that a Polish "semi-official counsellor" be attached to the staff of Sir Stafford Cripps, the British Ambassador in Moscow.[21] The object of this exercise was clearly to re-establish contact with Poles in the Soviet Union. The so-called June crisis caused by this communication forced Sikorski to withdraw his proposal and abandon his efforts to pursue communication with the Soviet authorities.

In the summer of 1941, Sikorski was convinced that in spite of the fact that the USSR had refused to renounce the territorial adjustments made in September 1939, there was no choice but to sign an agreement with the Soviets. Since the British government was determined to forge ahead in its cooperation with the Soviet Union, reaching an accommodation with the Soviets would, Sikorski reckoned, allow the government-in-exile to remain in the Allied camp and to have a say in matters concerning its future.[22] As Sikorski explained in a message to the underground leadership in Poland on 26 June 1941, British and American support for the Polish cause could only be maintained if the Poles aligned themselves with the policy of drawing the Soviet Union into the anti-German bloc.[23] The earlier crisis had weakened the opposition and he was now able to get the decision approved by the government.

Mistrust of Britain did play a role in Sikorski's considerations. His chief of counter-intelligence, Colonel Leon Mitkiewicz, on several occasions cautioned against excessive reliance on British goodwill.[24] He was not alone in his concerns. Sikorski's Minister for Foreign Affairs, August Zaleski, believed that Britain should participate in guaranteeing Poland's territorial agreements with the Soviet Union.[25] While Sikorski rejected these arguments, he was not entirely free from anxiety about British policies towards Eastern Europe. He therefore maintained that by being associated with Britain's policy of *rapprochement* towards the Soviet Union, Poland would deter discussions and compromises at its own expense. The formation of Polish units in the Soviet Union would open up new opportunities for direct military involvement in the liberation of Poland. This point was frequently and forcefully made by Sikorski to the Commander-in-Chief of the Polish army in Russia, General Władysław Anders.

A military agreement was concluded between the USSR and the Polish government-in-exile in London on 14 August. Polish citizens released by the Soviet authorities from prison and from labour and resettlement camps in accordance with the agreement, were now being enlisted into Polish units being formed on Russian territory. These were to be used on the Eastern front, but also to bolster the continuing build-up of forces already fighting under British command in North Africa, and with the British Air Force. Nevertheless, even during this early period of successful cooperation between the Poles and the Soviet authorities, serious disquiet was caused by the failure to ascertain the whereabouts of some officers. During the first meeting which took place between Anders and General Zhukov on 1 October 1941, the Soviet authorities admitted to holding only 1,658 Polish officers.[26] This number was suspiciously low. Henceforth, Polish military and political representatives in the Soviet Union and the government-in-exile in London would endeavour to ascertain the whereabouts of approximately 40,000 missing men.

Cooperation with Britain remained, nevertheless, the main plank of Sikorski's policy. He thus informed General Anders, on 1 September 1941:

> ...I intend [the army] to be used, on the one hand, in such a way that it can play an independent and crucial role in relation to the whole of the war, and, on the other hand, so that it can cooperate closely with our British ally.[27]

Sikorski, however, was reluctant to deploy the Polish army on the Eastern front, as he feared that its presence would not be felt there. Therefore, he designated the Caucasus and the area bordering Iran as possible operational zones for Polish troops.

The success of the Polish effort to form an army in Russia led immediately to a dilemma. Neither Sikorski nor Anders wanted to see the Polish units put into action in just any military battle. They were an asset and a very valuable one at a time when the Poles' negotiating position was very weak indeed. But if the Poles' military contribution was to have a commensurate political influence, the army had to be seen in action.

Ultimately, it was outside forces that solved the dilemma of how and when to deploy Polish military units raised in Russia, as had often been the case in other crises of the Polish political and military leadership. On 26 September 1941 Sikorski instructed the head of the Polish Military Mission in Moscow, General Szyszko-Bohusz, to contact Churchill's military adviser, General Sir Hastings Ismay, who was accompanying Beaverbrook to the Moscow conference. It was to be suggested to Ismay that he should ask the Soviet authorities to use Polish troops in the defence of the Caucasian oil fields.[28] By contrast, on 2 October he forbade Anders to release any units for use by the Russians, who claimed that they were in need of reinforcements on the Western front. He argued in the message that the units had not completed their training and equipping and, moreover, in an underlined passage, he informed Anders that he considered him personally responsible for ensuring that the troops not be wasted by being sent prematurely to the front:[29]

> The Polish Army in the USSR is of enormous propaganda importance in the whole world but particularly the USA. If this army is to realize its propaganda role it has to be put into battle as a whole army.[30]

By October, however, the Soviet authorities appear to have decided to limit the size of the Polish army; recruitment was made more difficult and rations were cut. At the same time the British authorities sought to strengthen the Polish units in the Middle East. In March 1942 Anders was informed that from 1 April the Soviet authorities were cutting down Polish army rations to 44,000 — meaning that the Russians would only provide for an army of that size and would not allow the Poles to recruit beyond that number.[31] This decision marked the final chapter of Polish involvement in the east. Between 24 March and 3 April, 33,000 Polish servicemen and 10,000 civilians were evacuated from Krasnovodsk to Pahlevi in Iran. Between 9 August and 1 September of the same year, the remaining 40,000 servicemen were evacuated through the same route. After that, the Soviet authorities closed down all recruiting centres. The failure of the Poles to assist the Red Army in its fight against the German invasion, and the commanders' determination to go to the British military zone, spelled the conclusive end of the Polish government-in-exile's influence in the Soviet Union.[32]

Sikorski's attempts to maintain his government's standing in the east while enhancing it in the west were being thwarted not merely by the Soviet authorities but also by his own commanders. Anders, in particular, supported the view that the Polish army in Russia should be withdrawn and that Poland should associate itself unequivocally with the Western military and political effort. After Sikorski's death, Anders cautiously, but openly, concurred with calls for a war against the Soviet Union to follow the defeat of Germany.

In May 1942 Sikorski was still trying to reason with Anders, pointing out that it was not yet clear what the shortest route to Poland would be. He emphasized that the military situation remained unresolved and that this meant that the Poles could not risk concentrating their army on one front since a military defeat there could result in the destruction of the one valuable asset the exile government possessed.[33]

In the autumn of 1942, as the bulk of Polish armed forces were concentrated in the Middle East, Sikorski tried to plan possible zones of deployment for his troops. The Balkans appeared to offer both an opportunity for cooperation with the Western Allies as well as an opening to a region which could become a future Polish sphere of political influence. As early as 1941, hopes had been aroused that the Carpathian Brigade under the command of General Stanisław Kopański, which had left Syria and crossed into British controlled Palestine in June 1940, would be deployed on the Balkan front.[34] Sikorski was delighted by this possibility and telegraphed Kopański: "...the purpose is — to take part in projected battles in the Balkans, the objective is — to march to Poland through the Carpathians...".[35] These aspirations, however, never materialized as British defeats in Greece led to a decision to re-route and retrain the Carpathian Brigade for desert battle. Kopański was concerned about this change of strategy; in particular he felt that this would bring about a confrontation with Italy and abandonment of the direct route to liberating Poland. Sikorski instructed him accordingly:

> Every enemy of Britain is simultaneously our enemy. Basing oneself on this principle, the direction in which the Brigade is used is a matter of indifference to me. You have to disseminate propaganda among the soldiers that Italy, being Germany's ally, is also our enemy.[36]

The opening of a Balkan front became a possibility once more. If Polish troops were to be instrumental in the liberation of southern Europe, that is, the Balkans and Italy, their action would have to coincide with Sikorski's political initiatives aimed at creating a Central European federation. It was also hoped that Polish units, then fighting with the British in North Africa, would enter France. Sikorski stated that if the Allies opened the West European front by landing troops from North Africa in Italy and southern France, he would move his headquarters to the Middle East to supervise developments there. These plans were discouraged by the British authorities.

Polish military and political independence was a luxury which the British believed they could not afford to grant in wartime. Hence, they consistently suppressed Polish initiatives aimed at furthering the cause of their own independence, including Sikorski's efforts to create a Central European federation, his attempts to arrange periodic meetings with the heads of the other exile authorities, and the Polish approaches to the Yugoslavian monarchist Mihailovic units in 1943.[37]

Neither the Balkan front nor the second European front materialized in 1942. In April 1943, following the withdrawal of the last of the Polish troops from the Soviet Union and the discovery of the Katyn graves, the Poles broke off diplomatic relations with the Soviet Union. By then Polish standing among the Allies had changed. From being Britain's sole East European ally in 1940, Poland had been reduced to a partner of little significance and had become a thorn in Soviet-British relations. The army, which was to have been the instrument of Polish political power, could not, by itself, gain influence for the Poles. Whereas in 1939 and 1940 it was believed that the British needed the Polish army and would therefore make political concessions in return for its cooperation, in 1942 the positions were reversed and it was the Poles who sought opportunities to be needed. By that time, little hope remained of obtaining genuine commitments from the Allies.

In 1939 Sikorski's government and military planners had thought in terms of a war which would result in the liberation of Poland by the Polish army and the establishment of a democratic and pro-Western government. But the conclusion of the Tehran Conference only served to confirm what had already become apparent: the failure to open a Western front early on increased the possibility that Poland would be liberated by Soviet troops. In 1943 Polish units were preparing to go into battle in Italy, no longer thinking in terms of fighting their way back to Poland.

The Poles were the victims of military developments, but also prisoners of their own conviction that the establishment of a Polish state in its pre-1939 boundaries was essential to the stability and reconstruction of Europe. This tragedy is curiously reminiscent of Napoleon's use of the Polish Legion to suppress the slave uprising in Haiti in 1802. Similarly, it was hoped that the Legion would earn Napoleon's gratitude and therefore commitment to the revival of a Polish state. During the Second World War, as all avenues for independent action turned out to be illusory, the Poles nonetheless continued to fight on, convinced that Britain and the United States would reverse the territorial consequences of the Soviet victory over Germany.

NOTES

1. Memorandum by Lewis Namier, *The Polish Government and Its Task*, 29 Nov. 1939, Public Record Office (PRO), Foreign Office (FO) 371/23153 C19384/8526/55.
2. Record of conversation between the Prime Minister and Marshal Stalin at Tehran, 28 Nov. 1943, PRO, Prime Minister's Office (PREM) 3 136/8.
3. Record of a conversation at lunch at the Soviet Embassy, Tehran, 1 Dec. 1943, PRO, PREM 3 136/8.
4. Yves Beauvois, *Stosunki polsko-francuskie w czasie 'dziwnej wojny'* (Cracow, 1991), pp. 16–17.
5. Olgierd Terlecki, *General Sikorski* (Cracow, 1981), p. 141.
6. Yves Beauvois, *Stosunki polsko-francuskie*, pp. 26–27.
7. Maria Pestkowska, *Uchodźcze Pasje* (Paris, 1991), pp. 28–30.
8. Wacław Jędrzejewicz (ed.), *Diplomat in Paris 1936–1939. Memoirs of Juliusz Łukasiewicz, Ambassador of Poland*, (New York, 1970), pp. 338–42.
9. Sikorski's instructions to the Minister for Foreign Affairs, 30 Dec. 1939, Archiwum Akt Nowych Warsaw 3087.
10. Memorandum by the Chief of Staff, *A Note on Assistance to Finland*, 21 Feb. 1940, Polish Institute and Sikorski Museum, London (PISM) PRM 16/8.
11. Letter from Sikorski to Colonel Kędzior, 26 April 1940, PISM PRM 13/18.
12. Sikorski's personal instructions, 10 May 1940, PISM PRM 13/21.
13. Stanisław Sierpowski, *Stosunki polsko-włoskie w latach 1918–1940*, (Warsaw, 1975), pp. 611–12.
14. *Polskie Siły Zbrojne w drugiej wojnie swiatowej*, Vol. II, part 1 (London, 1959), pp. 257–60.
15. Stanisław Kopański, *Wspomnienia Wojenne 1939–1946* (London, 1972), p. 109.
16. Memorandum by Minister Stronski defining the principles of Polish foreign policy. Approved by the Council of Ministers, 30 June 1940, Archives of the Zjednoczone Stronnictwo Ludowe (ZSL), Warsaw.
17. Memorandum on Raczynski's information on the Polish government-in-exile's political talks with De Gaulle, 28 Oct. 1941, FO 371/26779.
18. *Proposal for Future Polish Foreign Policy*. Memorandum prepared by the Political Committee and approved by the Council of Ministers, June/July 1940, PISM KGA2.
19. *Polskie Siły Zbrojne*, Vol. II. part 2, p. 226.
20. Michał Sokolnicki, *Dziennik Ankarski 1939–1943*, (London, 1965), pp. 57–58.
21. Memorandum by Halifax on meeting with General Sikorski, 19 June 1940, FO 371/24482 C7880/7177/55.
22. Michał Sokolnicki, *Dziennik Ankarski*, pp. 292–99. Sokolnicki recorded these explanations given to him by Sikorski during his visit to the Middle East in autumn 1941.
23. Sikorski's message to Polish legations and to Poland, 26 June 1941, PISM PRM 59A/4.
24. Leon Mitkiewicz, *Z Generałem Sikorskin na obczyznie. (Fragmenty Wspomnien)* (Paris, 1968), pp. 68–69.
25. John Coutouvidis & Jaime Reynolds, *Poland 1939–1947* (Leicester, 1986), pp. 75–76.
26. *Polskie Siły Zbrojne*, Vol. II, part 2, p. 227.
27. Message from Sikorski to Anders, 1 Sept. 1941, PISM AXII 1/56.
28. Message from Sikorski to General Szyszko-Bohusz, Head of the Polish Military Mission in Russia, to be conveyed to General Sir Hastings Ismay, 26 Sept. 1941, PISM KGA/9a.
29. Message from Sikorski to Anders, 2 Oct. 1941, PISM KGA 18a.
30. *Ibid.*
31. Message from Anders in Moscow to Sikorski, 20 March 1942, PISM KGA 9a.
32. Piotr Zarnowski, *Kierunek wschodni w strategii wojskowo-politycznej Gen. Władysława Sikorskiego 1940–1943* (Warsaw, 1988), p. 172.
33. Message from Sikorski to Anders, 1 May 1942, PISM PRM 79/1/21.
34. Stanisław Kopański, *Wspomnienia Wojenne*, pp. 136–41.
35. *Ibid.*, p. 141.
36. *Ibid.*, pp. 147–48.
37. Message to Eden from British Ambassador to Yugoslav government in Cairo, 19 Nov. 1943, FO 371 34594 C14145/335/G55.

# 9

# The Soviet Union
# and the Grand Alliance:
# The Internal Dimension
# of Foreign Policy

## ALEKSEI FILITOV

Any examination of the Grand Alliance in the Second World War should devote equal attention to relations among the Big Three powers and the decision-making process of each. Tendencies toward cooperation or conflict reflected a very close and complex interplay within the domestic scene. The dynamics of this interaction have already been dealt with in the West.[1] However, the conceptual framework most frequently used (for example, of the State Department and the Treasury in the US, or the Foreign Office and the Chiefs of Staff in Great Britain) is inadequate. By identifying specific attitudes and approaches with certain official bodies, Western studies have overlooked the undercurrents within each institution as well as its changing influence over time.

The mechanism of Soviet decision making remains largely un-explored. There are two reasons for this. First, it is generally assumed that totalitarian rule combined with terror prevented the consideration of competing political options in foreign policy. Second, hardly any historical evidence on the subject was available. If official publications typically omitted Soviet diplomats' references to dissent in Western policy making, it goes without saying that there could be no mention of debate within the Soviet leadership.[2] The gradual opening of the archives, however, has enabled the author to unearth certain facts in the Foreign Ministry files which shed light on this "non-topic". A tentative analysis of this new evidence is presented below.

One episode which demonstrates the existence of division in the Soviet leadership was the debate between Maxim Litvinov and

Viacheslav Molotov over possible Soviet responses to the outbreak of the war in the Pacific. Litvinov, who arrived in Washington as the new Soviet Ambassador on the very day of the Japanese attack on Pearl Harbor, urged the government, in one of his first cables to Moscow, to publicly condemn Japan's aggression and declare its solidarity with the Anglo-American war effort in the Pacific. At the same time, he advised that the Russians refrain from taking any military action. His recommendations were summarily rejected by the Foreign Minister.[3]

Litvinov encountered a similar response from Molotov when he suggested that the Soviet Union respond favourably to Roosevelt's invitation to join the proposed Anglo-American Supreme War Council. Although he shared Molotov's concern that the Americans might drag the Soviet Union into the war in the Far East, Litvinov argued that Soviet participation in such a council could be reconciled if it were to be divided into a Far Eastern committee (which the USSR would not join), and a European one. Nonetheless, Molotov remained adamant in his belief that the joint council was merely a device to get the USSR involved in the Pacific war. Nor was he swayed by Litvinov's contention that Soviet participation in the council would pressure the United States into increasing supplies to Russia and hasten the opening of a second front. Molotov ultimately prevailed, concluding in his usual harsh manner that the creation of the joint Allied machinery would mean "the subordination of Soviet military planning to the whims of Washington".[4]

Between May and June 1942, Molotov visited Great Britain and the United States. The history of the difficult negotiations leading up to the signing of the Soviet-British treaty during his visit to London is well-known and need not be recounted here. A compromise solution was achieved: the Soviet side dropped its demands for recognition of Russia's western frontiers and for the conclusion of a postwar settlement in exchange for an Allied promise to open a second front. It is a lesser known fact that Molotov did not favour this deal. He was overruled by Stalin, who dismissed his reservations about the treaty and advised him to accept the British version of the text because it gave, as Stalin put it in his cable to Molotov, "a free hand to us".[5]

Likewise, Stalin disregarded Molotov's initial misgivings about a proposal made by Roosevelt to Molotov on 29 May, calling for the four Big Powers to act as "policemen" in their respective spheres of interest while joining forces to combat major global threats. The American transcript of the meeting testifies to the less than enthusiastic response by Molotov to the idea of the total disarmament of enemies and allies alike by the Big Powers. The absence of corresponding remarks by Molotov in the Soviet transcript indicates an attempt to retreat from the "incorrect" (Molotov's) line after the "correct" one (Stalin's) had been imposed.[6]

Thus, we may speak not only of clashes between Molotov and Litvinov, but even between Molotov and Stalin. These disagreements were admittedly minor and short-lived, but they are not without historical significance. They demonstrate the existence within the Soviet leadership of two differing approaches to relations with the Allies. The first may be termed the cooperative option — characterized by a trend towards narrowing the scope of unilateral actions and decisions in postwar politics. The second was the unilateral approach, expressed by the "free hand" formula. Only Litvinov consistently advocated the cooperative option. Molotov, in his dispute with Litvinov, showed a clear preference for unilateralism. With respect to the Soviet-British treaty, Stalin turned out to be even more of a unilateralist than Molotov, for whom the "free hand" did not seem to have been of overriding importance. In response to Roosevelt's "four policemen" proposal, the roles were reversed. Stalin approved of the project even though it clearly contradicted the free-hand principle by providing for a combined force of four powers.[7]

The above facts would seem to indicate that the West missed opportunities to influence Soviet policy in more positive directions by not taking a more consistently cooperative approach. One is tempted to speculate whether greater British flexibility on problems of Soviet frontiers and security in Eastern Europe and a more vigorous pursuit of Roosevelt's Grand Design might have altered the course of history.[8] It is reasonable to assume that under such circumstances the advantages of a cooperative course would have carried greater weight in the Soviet leadership's judgement and possibly won out against the trend towards unilateralism which came to dominate Soviet behaviour after the war.

Similar assessments were made at the time by British statesmen. The Ambassador to Moscow, Sir Stafford Cripps, led the criticism of Western reluctance (including that of his own government) to initiate a serious discussion in the coalition on postwar issues. The extent of the controversy was first revealed by Professor Gabriel Gorodetsky.[9] He depicts it as a confrontation between the ultra-conservative, Churchill, who was unwilling to accept the Soviet Union as a true ally and the progressive, independent and far-sighted Cripps. While harbouring no illusions about the Stalinist system, Cripps still advocated a policy of sincere collaboration with the Soviet Union, with due regard for his country's legitimate strategic and state interests. The evidence from the Soviet archives corroborates this point, as well as Gorodetsky's assertion that while Cripps' basic approach was realistic and sober, the tactics he employed to implement them undermined his case.

Between 1942 and 1943, a peculiar alliance was formed between Cripps and the Soviet Ambassadors to the USA and Great Britain, Litvinov and Ivan Maiskii. All three would send messages to Stalin (Cripps via Maiskii), aimed at convincing him of the necessity to accelerate the pace of discussion on the peace settlement and to reach a binding agreement. Their common argument was predicated on the view that America was toughening its position toward the USSR. The defeat of Roosevelt in the elections of 1944 was seen as a foregone conclusion. "Hurry, before it is too late" — was their basic message.[10] On the other hand, if Roosevelt were indeed doomed, Stalin might just as well have assumed that there was no reason to begin deliberations on postwar issues with him. Moreover, what would be the value of such a settlement, if negotiated? Would it not make more sense to wait and see and/or practise unilateralism? The unilateralist option, which Stalin ultimately adopted, did prove in the long run to be quite rewarding from his point of view.

It is not certain that a different Western tactic would have succeeded in allaying Stalin's mistrust and suspicion and led him to join the proponents of the cooperative option instead of taking the course of unilateralism, or bilateralism based on a division of spheres of influence. The Soviet dictator later miscalculated badly when he violated democratic principles agreed upon at Yalta. He did so with brazen irreverence for Western sensibilities, counting on eventual Western compliance with a *fait accompli*. The roots of this miscalculation run deep, however. In 1942 Stalin came to the possibly erroneous conclusion that the West was giving him a free hand. One may argue that a more straightforward, consistent and tactical approach from the West, especially at the earlier stage of inter-Allied relations, might perhaps have bolstered conciliatory trends in Soviet foreign relations, even though the policies were those of a totalitarian state.

NOTES

1. See, for example, P. Hammond, "Directives for the Occupation of Germany: The Washington Controversy", in H. Stein (ed.), *American Civil-Military Decisions* (Alabama, 1963); Martin Kitchen, *British Policy toward the Soviet Union during the Second World War* (London, 1986).
2. The author, while working on a paper on Soviet-Japanese relations prior to the outbreak of the Pacific war, had the opportunity to compare two sets of documents: one published in the official two volume collection *Soviet-American Relations during the Great Patriotic War* (Moscow, 1984), and the second contained in the mimeographed edition prepared by Soviet Foreign Ministry officials for "service use",

Arkhiv vneshnei politiki Rossiiskoi Federatsii (AVP RF), fond (f.) 048"z", opis' (op.) 24, delo (d.) 2–3, papka (p.) 23, 35. The latter features very interesting accounts by the Soviet Ambassador to the US, Konstantin Umanskii, on his contacts with politicians like Henry Morgenthau, who expressed views quite different from those of, say, Sumner Welles. No trace of these accounts could be found in the published version.

3. Litvinov to Molotov, 9 Dec., 1941, AVP RF, f. 048"z", op. 24, d. 2, p. 23, listy (l.) 320, 312–13.

4. Litvinov to Molotov, 23 Dec. 1941, Molotov to Litvinov, 24 Dec., 1941, Litvinov to Molotov, 25 Dec. 1941, AVP RF, f. 048"z", op. 24, d. 2, p. 23, l. 322–25. A. A. Gromyko recalls a sharp dispute that took place between Molotov and Litvinov in a car during the former's visit to the USA in 1942. Gromyko displayed a clear preference for Molotov's position: *Pamiatnoe*, Vol. 2 (Moscow, 1988), pp. 321–22.

5. The cable was not included in the official publications of the Foreign Ministry. Stalin to Molotov, 24 May 1942, AVP RF, f. 048"z", op. 1 "k", d. 10, p. 71, l. 78–79.

6. Foreign Relations of the United States, 1942, Vol. 3, p. 569; *Sovetsko-amerikanskie otnosheniia vo vremia Velikoi Otechestvennoi voiny, 1941–1945*, Vol. 1 (Moscow, 1984), p. 176.

7. *Ibid.*, p. 189.

8. Sometimes Roosevelt's Grand Design is portrayed as purely a division of spheres of influence. This seems to be a one-sided approach. Cf. J. L. Gaddis, *The Long Peace. The Inquiries into the History of the Cold War* (New York, 1987), pp. 27–28.

9. Gabriel Gorodetsky, *Stafford Cripps' Mission to Moscow, 1940–1942* (Cambridge, 1984), p. 284 and passim. The discovery of sharp dissent within the British establishment corrects the picture drawn by J. Wheeler-Bennett and A. Nicholls, *op. cit.*, p. 49. While conceding the existence of controversy in the US (Winant-Hopkins versus the "fantastic and infelicitous alignment" of Hull, Welles and Bullitt) the authors implied the existence of a monolithic British position when they spoke of a "British assault on American policy" over the non-recognition of the USSR's western frontiers.

10. Maiskii's report on his talk with Cripps on 30 Dec. 1942, AVP RF, f. 048"z", op. 1"o", d. 2, l. 2–3. Litvinov to Molotov, 19 Feb. 1943, 5 March 1943, AVP RF, f. 048"z", op. 24"l", d. 2, p. 46, l. 116–17.

# Part Three

# THE COLD WAR

# 10

## Soviet Foreign Policy and the Origins of the Cold War

### MIKHAIL NARINSKY

It was perhaps inevitable that with the defeat of the Axis powers and the loss of a common cause, the Grand Alliance would collapse. The realignment of forces resulting from profound changes in roles assumed by the Great Powers in the postwar international arena, as well as fundamental differences in socio-political structures, ideology and values, played a major part in dividing the Allies and in ushering in an era of East-West confrontation.

While one may argue that these developments were inevitable, the question remains as to whether acute military and political confrontation was the sole form the Cold War could have assumed. If one considers the mentality of the leaders of the victorious powers, the answer to this question appears to be in the affirmative. Neither the USSR nor the Western powers (in particular the United States) seems to have shown any desire to comprehend or accept postwar realities and adjust its foreign policy accordingly.

Stalin and the Soviet leadership were well aware of the con-tradictory situation which emerged on the international scene: on the one hand, the USSR had made an immense contribution to the defeat of Germany, and its prestige in the world had been greatly enhanced; on the other, the country was in dire straits at the war's end, its economy ravaged and its living standards at an unprecedented low. In this weakened state, the USSR had to take into account the increased might of "imperialism", in particular that of the United States. One response to this predicament was a broad campaign launched in the USSR against "kowtowing to the West". In foreign policy this was manifested in the stiff controls imposed on a number of countries of Central and South-Eastern Europe in the postwar Soviet sphere of influence, including the Soviet zone of occupation in Germany.

Moscow's reaction to the US draft treaty on German disarmament, proposed in September 1945, was characteristic of the campaign. After studying it, the Soviets concluded that the sole aim of the document was to achieve the earliest possible end to the military occupation of Germany. They complained that it was limited exclusively to issues of military disarmament and the demilitarization of Germany. Marshals Zhukov and Sokolovskii, together with V. Semenov, political adviser of the Soviet Military Administration in Germany, wrote in their report to the Soviet Ministry of Foreign Affairs:

> ...in its proposed form the American draft is unacceptable and...at the present time it is not in our best interests to acquiesce to any extent to possible attempts of the Americans to end the occupation of Germany any sooner, for we cannot, after such a war, allow the matter of genuine disarmament and democratization of Germany to stop half-way.[1]

The experience of World War II had instilled in the Allied leaders a common tendency: excessive reliance on military force in policy-making as a universal instrument in the resolution of socio-political, territorial and other international issues. Characteristic in this respect was Stalin's irritable remark: "The Pope...the Pope?! And how many divisions does he have?"

For its part even the US leadership gave ample evidence that it aspired to pursue its policies from a position of strength and consequently rejected the effort to seek mutually acceptable solutions through negotiations. In this context the objective correlation of forces in the initial postwar years clearly favoured the United States, for at the close of the war it was the world's leading industrial power (the US accounted for about half of the world's industrial output) and had a monopoly in nuclear weapons. The United States government was well aware of the weakness of the large Soviet army. On 21 August 1945, the French Foreign Minister Georges Bidault was informed from Washington:

> In spite of everything, Russia emerged from this war exhausted. The contacts which the American authorities had in Germany with the Soviet troops convinced them of the undeniable superiority of the United States Army. All the officials who went to Potsdam, returned with the same impression. The Russians have men, but their technology is inadequate.[2]

Despite the imbalance of forces, Stalin and his advisers believed that in time the situation was bound to change in favour of the USSR. They believed that a new economic crisis in the West, which would result in an upsurge in the development of the worker and communist movements, was inevitable. For this reason, they sought to tighten their grip on Central and South-Eastern Europe and pursued a hard-line policy, which included delaying the settlement of controversial issues such as the German question. However, the possibility of future negotiations was not ruled out. Thus, Stalin emerged optimistic from a meeting with George Marshall, the US Secretary of State, on 15 April 1947 (during the Moscow session of the Council of Foreign Ministers). He described the session as:

> ...something like combat reconnaissance. When the partners have exhausted one another, the moment for a possible compromise arrives. The result may be attained at the next session rather than at the current one, but on all important issues, such as democratization, political organizations, economic unity and reparations, compromise is within reach.[3]

The Americans decided to use their economic and military might in order to stabilize the economic and socio-political situation in Western and South-Eastern Europe. "I think," said Dean Acheson at the executive hearings of the Senate Foreign Relations Committee on 1 April 1947, "that it is a mistake to believe that you can, at any time, sit down with the Russians and solve problems," and he continued:

> I do not think that is the way that our problems are going to be worked out with the Russians. I think they will have to be worked out over a long period of time and by always indicating to the Russians that we are quite firm about them and quite prepared to take necessary actions. Then I think solutions will become possible.[4]

The Truman Doctrine was proclaimed in March 1947. The Soviet Ambassador in the US, Nikolai Novikov, reported to Moscow that the official aim of the doctrine, according to its advocates, was to check "communist expansion".[5]

On 5 June 1947, Secretary of State Marshall made his programmatic speech at Harvard University; this speech became a point of departure for the implementation of a set of economic and political measures that became widely known as the Marshall Plan. The Marshall Plan was aimed primarily at stabilizing the socio-political situation in Western Europe, incorporating West Germany into the Western bloc and reducing the level of Soviet influence in Eastern Europe.[6] At a meeting held by the US Secretary of State on 28 May, US officials decided that countries of that region could take part in the program of European rehabilitation, only if they rejected the virtually exclusive orientation of their economies toward the Soviet Union in favour of broad European integration.[7]

Marshall's speech was initially received with interest in Moscow. It was regarded as an opportunity to obtain US credits for the postwar rehabilitation of Europe. Years later, in a conversation with journalist Feliks Chuev, Molotov recalled his reaction to the invitation to discuss the Marshall Plan: "At first I agreed and, by the way, submitted a proposal to the Central Committee to include not only us, but also the Czechs and Poles in the Paris meeting."[8] Molotov gave instructions to begin to prepare in earnest for the discussion of Marshall's proposal.

The seriousness of Soviet intentions was confirmed by a cable, sent on 22 June 1947 to the Soviet ambassadors in Warsaw, Prague and Belgrade. The ambassadors were instructed to personally relay to Bierut, Gottwald and Tito the following message:

> We consider it desirable for friendly allied countries [Poland, Czechoslovakia and Yugoslavia], on their part, to take the initiative to secure their participation in working out the economic measures in question, and that they lodge their claims, keeping in mind that certain European countries (Holland, Belgium) have already done so.[9]

Moreover, the Soviet Union intended to demand that priority in granting US credits to Europe should be given to those countries which had suffered most from Nazi aggression.

It would appear, however, that the Soviets were unwilling to have Western conditions placed on the receipt of aid. They resolutely rejected any form of US control over their own economy or on the economies of Eastern Europe.

The archival material which has recently become available does not permit a complete reconstruction of the Soviet delegation's preparations for the meeting of the Foreign Ministers of France, the United Kingdom and the USSR in Paris. It does, however, reveal that erroneous notions regarding the impending collapse of capitalism hampered Moscow's ability to assess objectively the global economic and political situation.

In a memorandum to Molotov dated 24 June 1947, a leading economist, Evgenii Varga, stated:

> The economic position of the US was of decisive importance in proposing the Marshall Plan. The Marshall Plan was supposed, first and foremost, to have served as a weapon for mitigating the imminent economic crisis, whose approach was not denied by anyone even in the United States.

Varga further argued that the United States needed the Marshall Plan, above all, in order to dispose of surplus goods and take the edge off the anticipated crisis of overproduction. He concluded:

> The meaning of the Marshall Plan in this context is the following. If it is in the best interests of the US to offer, on credit, billions of dollars worth of American goods to debtors that are barely solvent, then one should try to derive the maximum political benefit from it.

The main political gain for the US would be the establishment of "a bloc of bourgeois countries under US domination..."[10]

Varga's memorandum was sent by Molotov to members of the Politburo: Stalin, Beria, Zhdanov, Mikoian, Malenkov, Voznesenskii and to Deputy Foreign Ministers Vyshinskii and Malik. That memorandum undoubtedly played a significant role in determining the Soviet stand on the Marshall Plan.

The Soviet Ambassador to the United States, Nikolai Novikov, also emphasized the "anti-Soviet" aspects of Marshall's program. In his reply to an inquiry from Moscow, Novikov informed the Soviet leadership on 24 June that, in the final analysis, "the Marshall Plan amounts to the establishment of a West European bloc as a tool of US policy". It can be assumed, he wrote, that when the Marshall plan was announced, the US did not foresee Soviet participation in the program. Hence, he viewed Marshall's assertion that any government which undertook to impede the rehabilitation of other countries could not expect to receive US assistance, as clearly directed against the USSR.[11]

The Kremlin's hard-line stance on the Marshall Plan can be explained primarily by its desire to prevent the West from holding sway over Eastern Europe, which it regarded as part of its own sphere of influence. This was evident from the directives received by the Soviet delegation at the Paris meeting of the French, British and Soviet Foreign Ministers which began on 27 June 1947:

> ...the delegation should not allow the meeting of ministers to be diverted into clarifying and examining the European countries' resources, and should reject such an approach to the question by pointing out that the meeting was intended to study the European countries' demands and explore opportunities for the US to meet them, rather than to draw up economic plans for European countries...In discussion of any specific proposals on US aid to Europe, the Soviet delegation should object to any terms of aid that might involve infringement on the European countries' sovereignty or encroachment on their economic independence.[12]

This approach, however, was totally unacceptable to the West. The Paris meeting was a complete failure due to the Soviet Union's refusal to take part in the Marshall Plan. It is the author's belief that this was a gross miscalculation of Soviet foreign policy, which only made things easier for the Marshall Plan's sponsors who did not foresee Soviet participation. This is indicated in pronouncements made by the French Foreign Minister Georges Bidault and former US Secretary of State James Byrnes during their conversation of 23 September 1947.

> Byrnes: Sometimes the communists do strange things. You know that only the Congress can take decisions in questions of money. If Molotov had stayed in Paris, he would have referred to the Potsdam accords in order to demand 50% of all available financial assets. This would have embarrassed the United States as much as yourselves. Then Molotov would have demanded aid for Yugoslavia, Poland, etc... and the total sum would have been quite different from 20 billion. It is difficult to believe that this would have been acceptable to the Congress. In deciding to act otherwise, it has greatly aided the United States.

Bidault: I admit to not being able to comprehend why he behaved that way. If he had reaped his part of the profits, or if the enterprise had failed, he could still have gained something by the fact that nobody would have gotten anything. By sticking with us, he could not lose, and he chose the only means of losing for certain.[13]

The refusal of the Soviet Union to participate in the Marshall Plan essentially dictated the negative stand taken by the pro-Soviet governments of the countries of Central and South-Eastern Europe. Moscow exerted strong pressure on them in this respect[14] and, as a result, Albania, Bulgaria, Czechoslovakia, Hungary, Poland, Romania, Yugoslavia, as well as Finland, rejected assistance under the program. Thus a major step was taken towards dividing Europe and towards creating greater international tension. The consultations of representatives of nine communist parties held in Poland in late September 1947, only increased the level of confrontation in Europe, for their resolutions emphasized the division of the world into two opposing blocs.

The events of 1947 were a turning-point in the Cold War and led to a deterioration in the international climate. The prevailing atmosphere of mutual suspicion and mistrust, exacerbated by the legacy of past relations and by new divisions, led to a situation in which military force became the predominant element in the policy of containment.

## NOTES

1. Arkhiv vneshnei politiki Rossiiskoi Federatsii (AVP RF), fond (f.) 489, opis' (op.) 24"g", delo (d.) 1, papka (p.) 19, list (l.) 51.
2. Archives Nationales, Section contemporaine, papiers privées de M. Georges Bidault, AP-80 735-1/A, pp. 2–3.
3. AVP RF, f. 489, op. 24"g", d. 1, p. 19, l. 172.
4. Quoted in D. Yergin, *The Shattered Peace. The Origins of the Cold War and the National Security State* (Harmondsworth, 1980), p. 296.
5. AVP RF, f. 489, op. 24"g", d. 1, p. 19, l. 150.
6. See M. P. Leffler, "The United States and the Strategic Dimensions of the Marshall Plan", *Diplomatic History* 12, 3 (1988), p. 283.
7. M. J. Hogan, *One World into Two: American Economic Diplomacy from Bretton Woods to the Marshall Plan* (Ohio, 1987), p. 28.
8. *Sto sorok besed s Molotovym — Iz dnevnika F. Chueva* (Moscow, 1991), p. 88.
9. AVP RF, f. 6, op. 9, p. 18, d. 214, l. 19.
10. AVP RF, f. 6, op. 9, p. 18, d. 213, l. 2–5.
11. AVP RF, f. 489, op. 24"g", p. 19, d. 1, l. 182.
12. AVP RF, f. 6, op. 9, p. 18, d. 214, l. 4–6.
13. Archives Nationales, Section contemporaine, papiers privées de M. Georges Bidault, AP-80, 735-4, p. 5–6.
14. See M. Narinsky, "Polska e plan Marshala", *Polityka* (1990) 1, XII; L. Kornilov, "A Moscow Ultimatum", *Izvestiia*, 9 Jan. 1992.

# 11

# British Policy Towards the Soviet Union 1945–1948

## MARTIN KITCHEN

British Prime Minister Clement Attlee and Foreign Secretary Ernest Bevin arrived in Potsdam on the afternoon of 28 July 1945, replacing Churchill and Eden who had left three days before for the general election, which had resulted in a resounding victory for the Labour party. The task facing Bevin was difficult in the extreme. He had virtually no experience in foreign affairs and the laconic Prime Minister left him to do most of the talking. But Bevin, who knew that he had a very weak hand to play, was in a fighting mood, telling General Sir Hastings Ismay, who met the new team at the airport, "I'm not going to have Britain barged about."[1] British power and influence had diminished dramatically during the war and the economy was in ruins. The Labour party had no coherent policy to guide the Foreign Secretary and there was nothing specifically socialist about his views in this area. He was a pragmatist and a fierce patriot, determined to defend what he considered to be Britain's vital interests.

Both Truman and Stalin were somewhat taken aback by Bevin's truculent opening shots at the conference. Bevin expressed the strongest disapproval of Molotov's demand that the western Neisse should form Germany's eastern boundary, and it seemed as if a speedy conclusion of the conference would be prevented by the intransigence of this expert and tough negotiator. Secretary of State James F. Byrnes decided to frustrate the troublemaker by agreeing to Molotov's claim concerning the western Neisse, and he also offered the Russians additional reparations from the western zones of occupation. This infuriated Bevin, the more so since these increased reparations would come largely from the British zone which included the Ruhr. The Soviets, certain of American support, decided to go on the offensive against Bevin and suggested that the Ruhr should be internationalized. Bevin fought off this attack, but he had to give way over the frontier and reparations, the result of a deal which had been made behind his back.

Bevin returned to London resentful that Byrnes had refused to accept the British as equal partners and fearful that the Soviets would exploit the differences between the British and Americans to win further concessions. His views were fully endorsed by the staff of the Foreign Office, who were becoming extremely enthusiastic about their new boss. But it was very difficult to know how best to serve Britain's interests. Britain was in no position to stand alone against the Soviets and it was feared that a Western European bloc, which might include western Germany, would only serve further to irritate the Russians.[2] In August 1945 Attlee wrote to South African Prime Minister Jan Smuts:

> The growth of Anglo-Russian antagonism on the Continent and the creation of spheres of influence, would be disastrous to Europe and would stultify all the ideals for which we have fought. But I think we must at all costs avoid trying to seek a cure by building up Germany or by forming blocs aimed at Russia.[3]

This view was strongly endorsed by Bevin.

In August the Americans delivered a devastating blow to Britain when President Truman announced that Lend Lease would cease immediately. Britain could only survive what economist John Maynard Keynes described as a "financial Dunkirk" by going cap in hand to the Americans for a loan. The State Department regarded the British as "cry babies" and had no desire to subsidize a government which seemed to be socialist at home and imperialist abroad and thus doubly evil. They demanded that the British ratify the Bretton Woods Agreement on free trade, lift restrictions on American imports and agree to the convertibility of sterling. The British government had no alternative but to accept. They got the loan, but it seemed that the much vaunted "special relationship" was now in ruins.

The British were thus in an unenviable position when the Council of Foreign Ministers met at Lancaster House in London on 11 September. Both the Chiefs of Staff and the Foreign Office were very concerned that the Soviets would exploit British weakness to extend their influence in the Mediterranean. It was agreed that the British had to resist any Soviet attempts to secure Cyrenaica as a military base and that they should claim it for themselves as essential for the defence of Britain's vital interests in the Middle East.[4] In return the Soviets should be granted a revision of the 1936 Straits Convention, which limited the passage of Russian warships from the Black Sea to the Mediterranean.[5] Otherwise it was feared that the Soviets would start meddling in the internal affairs of Turkey and Greece. Bevin believed that the preservation of Britain's position in the Middle East was a top strategic priority and he was fully aware that this was an area which was extremely vulnerable to Soviet pressure. The question was whether Britain had the power, the resources and the tenacity to hang on to the Middle East. Attlee believed that the country could not afford such a policy; the left criticized it as blatantly imperialistic; the right praised it for the same reason; and Bevin's pro-Arab policy exacerbated the Palestine question, thus endangering the whole enterprise.

Many British officials were still uncertain about the desirability of forming a Western European bloc. Some, like Frank Roberts at the Moscow embassy, favoured a series of bilateral agreements beginning with an Anglo-French alliance which, because it was ostensibly aimed against Germany, would be unlikely to arouse Soviet suspicions. This proposal met with a cold reception as the French were proving most uncooperative over Germany and the Levant. Others could not see what all the fuss was about. In July, Deputy Under-Secretary of State Bruce Lockhart wrote in all seriousness that "Anglo-American military strength is at its peak; Russia's has long since passed." Gladwyn Jebb, head of the Reconstruction Department of the Foreign Office, argued that the Russians were "very apprehensive of the Anglo-American lead in technique and modern methods of warfare".[6] Britain was in the enviable position of being strong enough to stand up to the Soviet Union "even to the point of risking a showdown". Permanent Under-Secretary of State Sir Orme Sargent felt that all this talk about blocs was a "council of despair" and suggested that Britain still had enormous influence since, unlike the Soviet Union or the United States, "we are not regarded either as gangsters or go-getters".[7]

At Lancaster House it was clear from the outset that Molotov was singularly unimpressed by Britain's military might and diplomatic prestige. Far from being apprehensive, he once again exploited the obvious differences between the British and Americans and came up with the shocking proposal that the Soviets should take Tripolitania into trusteeship for at least ten years. No resolution to this problem was found, somewhat to the relief of the British who had troops stationed in Tripolitania and thus preferred to leave things as they were, rather than have as Bevin phrased it, the Soviet Union "across the throat of the British Commonwealth".[8]

Molotov's attitude was so aggressive that it served to bring the Americans and British closer together and they counter-attacked by refusing to recognize the governments of Bulgaria and Romania until they were satisfied that they were genuinely representative. Molotov complained of the undemocratic nature of the regime in Greece and denounced the Western powers' support of fascist regimes in Spain and Argentina. For the British this was merely bluff. They had long since accepted that Eastern Europe was firmly in the Soviet Union's grasp and had simply complained about the undemocratic nature of its client states in order to ward off the Soviet claim to Tripolitania. Bevin, with his obsession over the Middle East, seriously misjudged Molotov's intentions. The latter had come to London to secure recognition of Soviet domination of Eastern Europe, not to establish a colony in North Africa. In a private meeting with Bevin at the Soviet Embassy on 1 October, he made this perfectly clear.[9]

The conference dragged on for three more days. Bevin, in exasperation, accused Molotov of acting like a Nazi and later apologized in a vain attempt to save the conference. Molotov, who had shown no inclination to reach a settlement, left London having refused to sign the protocol.

The conference was doubly frustrating for the British: the Soviets had refused to compromise and the Americans had proved very reluctant to consult their ally.[10] They felt that Byrnes had been feeble in the face of Soviet attacks and "slippery" in his dealings with them; but they greatly admired his adviser John Foster Dulles who had stood up valiantly to Molotov's assaults. They simply could not fathom why Molotov had been so needlessly intransigent, although Bevin was still convinced that it had something to do with the Soviet determination to secure a base in the Mediterranean.[11] He was careful, however, to keep this to himself for fear that the Soviets might take this concern as a sign of weakness, and he did not even mention it in his report to the cabinet. But he warned that the government should not over-react to the failure of the conference:

> We should keep our eye on the ball and not be distracted into making special treaty arrangements with small states which might produce dissension in the ranks of the big five.[12]

Dulles echoed these sentiments in a widely publicized radio speech in which he said "there will be no bloc of Western Powers if the US can avoid it".[13] The failure of the Lancaster House conference was thus in no sense a turning point in the history of the Cold War.

The Foreign Office now braced itself for a Soviet ideological offensive. In an influential memorandum, written at the end of October 1945, Thomas Brimelow suggested:

> The Russians are being slow and cautious in all questions of international collaboration, but they have not decided to be uniformly obstructive. They show no signs of departing from old animosities or their established habits, and they place their short term selfish interests above the less certain long term advantages of collaboration. But they are quite willing to collaborate when it pays.[14]

On the other hand, Frank Roberts in Moscow speculated that the

Soviets would withdraw "the Red Army occupation troops as soon as their presence is no longer required to consolidate Soviet political influence".[15] The British hosted a highly successful party for their NKVD contacts in Moscow, showing that some of the wartime camaraderie still remained.[16] E. H. Carr continued to write pro-Soviet leaders in *The Times*, much to the fury of the Foreign Office and of the Prime Minister who complained to the editor Barrington-Ward.[17]

The British realized that there was precious little they could do to stop the Soviet Union from dominating Eastern Europe and that the most they could hope for was the wringing of a few concessions from the Soviets. Brimelow summarized the frustrations of the Foreign Office:

> There seems to be no way out; so long as the outside world is stronger than the Russians they will be full of suspicion and fear; and if the outside world is weaker than they are, it is bound to live in fear and suspicion of the Russians, for they are now showing a determination to live up to the limits of their power.[18]

Clearly the British were in no position to stand up to the Soviets alone; they needed a close alliance with the United States and relations between the two countries were highly strained. This was a matter of the greatest concern to Bevin who told his private secretary, Pierson Dixon, "if we are not careful our victory in the war may lead to us being plucked by our allies".[19] It was therefore decided to try to scare the Americans into a more cooperative mood. The Foreign Office prepared a memorandum for the Secretary of State, which was forwarded to the Ambassador in Washington, Lord Halifax. It stated:

> ... my guess is that [the Soviets] have no intention of confining themselves to Europe, and that they intend to embark on a general campaign to establish Russian influence in every quarter of the globe.[20]

The British government announced that it was prepared to give the Americans a number of bases in the Atlantic and the Pacific to meet this threat. In addition, the British followed the Americans in refusing to recognize the governments of Romania and Bulgaria, even though they had at first been prepared to do so for reasons of expediency. They knew that the elections had been rigged, but felt that nothing could be done about it. Also in line with the Americans, they did recognize the Hungarian government, even though they believed that the majority of the ruling Smallholders party were communist stooges. They accepted the Soviet sponsored governments in Austria and Czechoslovakia, although they were increasingly impatient with Beneš and Masaryk for continuing to make concessions to the communists. In Poland Bevin was prepared to accept Mikolajczyk's glowing reassurances and said of his government: "I like to see the plant growing, and I am not going to pull it up every moment to make sure it is growing."[21]

The Americans did not respond to these advances and continued to ignore the British. Secretary of State Byrnes proposed to Molotov that there should be another meeting of foreign ministers in Moscow as soon as possible. He did this without consulting the British and Bevin was understandably incensed. He felt it was absurd to go running after the Russians in light of their outrageous behaviour at Lancaster House and Byrnes had allowed no time for discussions with the British before the planned meeting.[22] His inclination was to refuse to attend, but he was persuaded otherwise by Ambassadors Clark Kerr in Moscow and Halifax in Washington, both of whom agreed that Byrnes' diplomacy was singularly inept but who warned that if Bevin did not go to Moscow the Soviets would do everything possible to split the already badly strained "atomic bloc".[23] Bevin eventually gave way, heeding Clark Kerr's advice to bring plenty of cigarettes and whiskey for their mutual enjoyment and plenty of "bumf" and plum puddings in case the conference lasted until Christmas.

Bevin's worst fears were confirmed in Moscow. Byrnes treated him so badly, constantly harping on the British mania for spheres of influence, that US State Department adviser Charles Bohlen and US Ambassador to Moscow, Averill Harriman, felt obliged to apologize for his behaviour to the Foreign Office's Assistant Legal Adviser, Patrick Dean.[24] Molotov was delighted to see the feathers flying in the rival camp and exploited the situation for all it was worth. He negotiated directly with the Americans, offering a few minor concessions, while he continually attacked Bevin. The British were unable to initiate a discussion of the problems of Iran and Turkey, matters of the utmost importance to them, and they got no support at all from Byrnes. They felt patronized by the Americans and insulted by the Russians. Nonetheless, Bevin was somewhat encouraged by two talks that he had with Stalin, which he found helpful; and at least, unlike the previous conference, this one did not end in a total fiasco, in spite of Molotov's heavy-handed attempt to alter the text of the final communiqué. Bevin also got a certain satisfaction from the report that President Truman had accused Byrnes of appeasing the Soviets during the conference and it seemed that the days of this unfortunate diplomatist were numbered.[25]

Many British officials, among them the increasingly influential Frank Roberts and Clark Kerr, felt that the Soviet Union was concerned principally with its own security and the possibility of a revival of German power, but Bevin disagreed.[26] At an unofficial meeting with diplomatic correspondents on New Year's Day, he condemned the

Soviet Union as an imperialist power and argued that its repeated insistence on the need for security was not to be taken seriously. When asked by the correspondent from the *Daily Telegraph* whether Britain was prepared to go to war with the Soviet Union he was horrified and hastily replied, "Good God, no". In the course of further discussions he let it be known that he blamed the Americans for not giving him the support he needed to counter the Russians by diplomatic pressure. It was clear that he was as much concerned by the Americans as he was by the Russians, for he felt that unless the Americans toughened their stance, the Soviets would probably extend their influence to Turkey and the Balkans, as well as to China and much of the Far East.

The next round of Big Power diplomacy was at the first meeting of the United Nations General Assembly held in London in January 1946. Deputy Foreign Minister Andrei Vyshinskii, who led the Soviet delegation, launched a massive attack on British policy in Greece, in order to counter Bevin's suggestion that a commission of inquiry be established to investigate Iranian complaints of Soviet meddling in its internal affairs. Bevin parried Vyshinskii's endless jibes and, in the opinion of many observers, won most of the debating points. Public opinion, which was still largely pro-Russian, began to shift as a result of the coverage given in the press to Vyshinskii's outbursts. Even the left-wing press became much less critical of the Foreign Secretary. Bevin was convinced that he was right to stand up to the Russians for in private talks Vyshinskii was remarkably reasonable and moderate.[27]

Both the Soviet Union and the United States agreed that Greece lay within Britain's sphere of influence and Bevin was determined that Britain's position in the area should be strengthened. For supporters of the left this was an unpopular policy. They argued that Britain was propping up a corrupt and incompetent populist government while the pro-communist National Liberation Front (EAM) enjoyed widespread support in the country. In a fresh round of fighting the Greek army proved useless and was only saved from defeat by the intervention of British troops. Bevin believed that in a free election Greece would go the same way as Yugoslavia, a brutally repressive dictatorship at that time, solidly in the Stalinist camp. Attlee strongly disagreed with his Foreign Secretary. He felt that they were "backing a lame horse" in Greece and that Britain simply could not afford to maintain a military force there in order to prop up an unpopular and inept government.[28] He believed that the Soviet Union was too shrewd to become involved in the appallingly tangled internal affairs of Greece and that a neutral Greece would have a fair chance of survival. The cabinet agreed with the Prime Minister and it was thus decided to withdraw from Greece, leaving the entire problem to the Americans who alone were able to offer the economic assistance the country so badly needed. The Americans eagerly accepted the challenge and support for Greece became a key element of the Truman Doctrine.

The Soviets constantly attacked British policy towards Greece, the Middle East and Iran, and denounced the idea of a Western bloc as a hostile move; but the Foreign Office did not take these outbursts too seriously. This sober view of Soviet intentions was due in large part to the balanced reports for the Foreign Office written by Frank Roberts in Moscow. He argued that comparisons between Nazi Germany and Stalinist Russia were wide of the mark. The Soviets had no need for living space, the leadership was more flexible and pragmatic than the Nazis, they did not subscribe to any fanciful notions of racial superiority, their economy was hopelessly weak and the Red Army ace had been trumped by the atomic bomb. The Soviet Union was worried by the sheer strength of the Anglo-American alliance which it had hoped to weaken by attacking the junior partner. Roberts cautioned against any hint of panic or extremism and counseled a policy of "distant realism".[29]

The Joint Intelligence Committee did not share the Foreign Office's relatively optimistic assessment of Soviet policy. In March 1946 the Committee reported:

> It is agreed that the long term aim of the Russian leaders is to consolidate around her boundaries a belt of states subservient to Russia so that she may build up strength without fear of attack. It is considered, however, that such an aim implies the gradual but continual broadening of the belt.[30]

In a further report written a few days later, the Committee suggested that the Soviet Union was determined to challenge Britain's position in the Middle East.[31] The Committee argued that the Soviets would not be ready for a major war for at least another five years but that they were in an excellent position to extend their influence in the Middle East. Within the Foreign Office, Thomas Brimelow, an enthusiastic social democrat, argued that the Soviets could exploit the backwardness, corruption and mistreatment of minorities in the Middle East while the British continued to support unpopular, venal and incompetent élites. He felt that social democracy was an attractive philosophy that could be used to strengthen Britain's standing in the world, but he realized that the United States would never support such an ideological crusade even though it was designed to counter the attractions of communism.[32]

The British government was thus uncertain as to whether there really was a Soviet threat, and if there was one, what could be done about it. The economy was in such a parlous state that it was agreed there had to be drastic cuts in defence spending.[33] The Chiefs of Staff argued that the Middle East was not vital to the strategic defence of Britain. Attlee believed that the region should be abandoned. Bevin was vehemently opposed to these views and insisted that the Middle East was politically, economically and strategically vital to Britain. He did not share Frank Roberts' cautiously optimistic assessment of Soviet policy. In April 1946 he wrote to the Prime Minister of his concerns about the Soviet Union's "aggressive policy based upon militant communism and Russian chauvinism" and later told Attlee of his fears that the internal dynamics of Soviet society were such that war might well result and that even Stalin would be unable to control this aggressive and expansionist system.[34]

Bevin's panic-stricken outburst has to be seen against the background of the Iranian crisis of March 1946. British and American forces had been withdrawn from Iran by the 2 March deadline but Soviet troops not only remained, but were reinforced. On 9 February Stalin had delivered a speech in which he insisted on the inevitability of conflict between capitalism and communism. Shortly afterwards it was reported in the *New York Herald Tribune* that a Soviet spy ring had been uncovered in North America: Igor Gouzenko, a cipher clerk in the Soviet Embassy in Ottawa had defected with evidence that Soviet agents had penetrated the Manhattan Project and had passed on atomic secrets. This made public an affair which had been kept secret since Gouzenko's defection on 5 September 1945. The Canadian government had not wished to strain relations with the Soviet Union and had wanted to conduct a full investigation of Gouzenko's allegations without the distractions of a public outcry, such as that which followed the publication of this spectacular news. Then, at the end of February, the US Chargé d'Affaires, George Kennan, sent his enormously influential "long telegram" from Moscow arguing the case for containment.

On 5 March, at the height of the Iranian crisis, Churchill, with consummate timing, delivered his famous address at Fulton, Missouri. He issued a dire warning against Soviet aggressive ambitions, and the dangers of appeasement, and called for the closest cooperation between Britain and the United States. The term "Iron Curtain" now became part of the standard vocabulary of international affairs. Churchill had shown the text of his speech to Halifax in Washington who treated it as a purely private matter. It was also given to the Ministry of Information, which did not see fit to pass it on to the cabinet.[35] Attlee did not mind that he had not been consulted, but he was very concerned about the effect the speech might have on

American public opinion. His fears were unfounded. Both Truman and Byrnes had seen the text prior to the speech and found it excellent. The American public also reacted favourably, and only the left-wing press complained of its strident tone.[36] Attlee told Churchill that he was sure that the speech would "do good".[37] This was glowing praise from a man of so few words. Bevin, who shared most of Churchill's sentiments, did nothing to distance himself from the speech when the Soviets began an endless litany of complaints. He preferred to remain silent when Stalin compared Churchill to Hitler in an interview published in *Pravda*. There was also some criticism from the left of the Labour party about the unfortunate consequences of an Anglo-American alliance and the usual ritual denunciations of Bevin's policy in Greece. At a meeting of three hundred Labour MPs, Bevin demanded a vote of confidence for his foreign policy. Only six members voted against him and thirty abstained.[38]

The lesson of the Iranian crisis, Attlee believed, was that in the event of war it would be impossible to keep the Mediterranean open or stop a determined Soviet thrust into Iran, Iraq or Turkey, and that therefore all British forces should be withdrawn from the Middle East, Egypt and Greece. With India soon to become independent, the Suez Canal would lose its significance for Britain, and the Cape of Good Hope route would become the vital link to Australia and New Zealand. Bevin continued to stress the crucial importance of the Middle East and insisted that without a strong British presence in the Mediterranean, Turkey, Greece, Italy and France were likely to fall prey to totalitarian communism. He was given powerful support by the Chiefs of Staff who argued that if the Soviet Union was considered to be Britain's most serious potential enemy, the best way to defend Britain was for it to maintain a strong presence in the east. No decisions were made on these important issues in the spring and summer of 1946 and the government remained uncertain of how to assess the Soviet threat or how best to meet it.

The hardening of attitudes towards the Soviet Union in early 1946 was also noticeable in the Foreign Office. Christopher Warner, the head of the Northern Department, wrote a lengthy assessment of Soviet policy in April, in which he argued that the country had returned to the pure gospel of Marxism-Leninism-Stalinism and was strengthening its industrial and military power in order to pursue an aggressive policy.[39] The Soviets refused to cooperate in international efforts at reconstruction and rehabilitation and were despoiling those countries unfortunate enough to be within their sphere of influence. Warner discounted the belief, previously held by many in the Foreign Office, that Soviet policy was dictated by security interests, and complained that the Soviet Union "is practicing the most vicious power politics, in the political, economic, and propaganda spheres and seems determined to stick at nothing, short of war, to obtain her objectives". He concluded, therefore, that Britain should avoid appeasement and make no concessions, and be prepared resolutely to defend its interests.

Although accepting the service chiefs' assessment that the Soviet Union would not be ready for war for at least five years, Warner suggested that the Soviets might stumble into war by miscalculation as Hitler had done over Poland. Britain had therefore to be constantly vigilant, making certain that no countries where its vital national interests were involved became communist. A massive anti-communist campaign should be mounted, and full support given to progressive anti-communist forces abroad. One result of this campaign was the commissioning of Carew-Hunt's widely disseminated and influential study of communism.[40]

Warner insisted that the Soviet Union had a master plan to subvert and undermine the capitalist states and that it intended to conduct a full scale ideological, economic, political and ultimately military campaign against the capitalist-imperialist world. It was thus far more gloomy and outspoken than Kennan's memorandum and clearly foreshadowed the Truman Doctrine.

The next meeting of the Council of Foreign Ministers was scheduled to begin on 25 April 1946. The British were in a reasonably confident mood after the Soviets had been forced to back down in Iran and they observed that the Russians were now concentrating their fire on the Americans, possibly because they were impressed by Bevin's firmness at the negotiating table and by Churchill's Fulton speech which they felt had been sanctioned by the British government. They were also delighted to find Byrnes in a tougher mood after the success in Iran. He was now no longer prepared to allow the conference to drag on, and after nearly three weeks of absurd wrangling with Molotov, he called for a one-month recess.

Germany, predictably, was by far the greatest problem. The French wanted to separate the Rhineland and Ruhr from the rest of Germany; the British argued that this would cripple the German economy and that they could not afford to continue propping it up. The British Chiefs of Staff wanted western Germany to become part of a Western defensive bloc, although they knew the French would protest vigorously. The Foreign Office objected to the western Neisse as the final frontier with Poland but realized that precious little could be done about it. British officials agreed that a divided Germany was desirable. Only a divided Germany would make it possible for the three western zones to be integrated fully into a Western bloc. In addition, demo-cratic, hopefully social democratic, institutions were to be encouraged so that communism would hold no attraction for the Germans. It was feared that a united Germany would be likely to play the East off against the West and might even be tempted to make a common cause with the Soviet Union. The major problem for Bevin was to ensure that the Russians appeared to the world to be solely responsible for the division of Germany, and that the British seemed to be in full support of the unity of the country.

The British were unsure whether this policy would prove success-ful. It was doubtful whether the Americans and the French would go along with the proposal to form an anti-Soviet bloc which would include western Germany. The British did not relish the idea of having the Germans as their allies against the Soviet Union — a curious outcome after six years of war. Bevin, especially, shuddered at the thought. As he said to General Robertson, the British Military Governor in Germany, "I tries 'ard Brian but I 'ates 'em."[41] There were also considerable risks involved. The division of Germany would make it virtually impossible to come to an understanding with the Soviets. For the rest of the year the pros and cons of this policy were debated, but a final decision was not taken until the following year.

As the Soviets argued endlessly about the problems of inter-zonal inspection and complained of violations of previous agreements on occupation policy, General Clay's proposal that the British and American zones be united was given a sympathetic hearing by both American and British officials.[42] Clay's suggestion, which amounted to a rejection of the Potsdam agreement, was all the more remarkable in that only a few days previously he had informed the State Department that the Soviets were adhering scrupulously to the Potsdam agreement in the Allied Control Commission and that they were genuinely trying to be friendly to the United States. Clay had emphatically distanced himself from the Kennan doctrine and was convinced that the Soviets harboured no aggressive intentions.[43] These views were shared by Clay's political adviser Robert Murphy.

Bevin was concerned about Clay's proposal because he wanted to make sure that the blame for the division of Germany was placed on the Soviets. The Americans were also hesitant. There was considerable opposition in Congress to the loan to Britain; there was widespread reluctance to become locked into a Western bloc; American Jews were strongly critical of British policy towards Palestine, making un-favourable comparisons between Ernest Bevin and Adolf Hitler; and there were lingering hopes that an agreement might still be reached with the Soviet Union. It was therefore decided to postpone the whole issue until the second round of the Paris talks. When the conference resumed, discussions concentrated on the main issue of the peace treaties. Agreement was soon reached on the drafting of treaties with Italy and the four satellites (Romania, Bulgaria, Hungary and Finland), but there was no agreement over Austria or Germany.

In May 1946 the new British Ambassador, Sir Maurice Peterson, arrived in the Soviet Union. His appointment was seen by some as a calculated insult to the Soviets as he was not particularly highly regarded and had been Ambassador to Franco's Spain. In his first interview with Stalin he launched into a massive attack on Soviet policy, on the hostility of the Soviet press towards Britain, on Molotov's refusal to consider free trade throughout the Danubian basin, and on the behaviour of the Soviet delegation at the Paris conference. On the Middle East, an area which he defined in exceedingly generous terms, he asked:

> Could not the Russians realize that this was our area, that we had done and were doing great works in it and that frankly, as regards the Arab countries, we know a great deal about them while the Russians know nothing at all?

Stalin was hardly the man to sit silently through such an outburst. He accused the British of having destroyed the wartime alliance — by refusing to allow the Soviets bases in the Mediterranean, by objecting to a revision of the Montreux Convention and thus attempting to deny the Soviet fleet access to the Mediterranean, and by the government's refusal to distance itself from Churchill's Fulton speech. Having thus let off steam, Stalin thanked the Ambassador for a most helpful chat.[44]

Bevin had finally agreed to accept General Clay's proposal to unite the American and British zones of occupation in Germany. On 25 July 1946 the cabinet agreed to push ahead, although Bevin still had some misgivings. He hoped that the Soviets would also be willing to drop their zonal barriers in return for access to the Ruhr, but he realized that this was an outside chance. His main motive for accepting the proposal was that without firm American support, conditions in the British zone would deteriorate rapidly. Meanwhile the British and American service chiefs began to discuss means of defending Greece and Turkey and the British were delighted to hear that the Joint Chiefs were convinced that the defence of Middle Eastern oil supplies was a strategic necessity.

As the Paris conference dragged on towards its unsatisfactory conclusion, the British became increasingly pessimistic about relations with the Soviet Union. Bevin told Attlee that the British and Americans could make no further concessions and that they now faced "a war of nerves all over the world". Stalin gave a conciliatory interview to

Alexander Werth of the *Sunday Times* and Molotov attempted, unsuccessfully, to make a few jokes at the Paris conference, but none of this did anything to relieve the gloom.

In September Thomas Brimelow wrote another lengthy assessment of Soviet policy.[45] He did not concur with Frank Roberts that it might still be possible to reach limited agreements with the Soviets. The Soviets were building up their armed forces and strengthening their hold over bordering states. Any attempt by the Western powers to resist this would confirm the Soviet belief in the inevitability of conflict between the capitalist and the communist worlds and would thus strengthen their determination to build up their armed forces and avoid any concessions. On the other hand, if the West made concessions this would convince them that their confrontational policy was paying off. Brimelow was thus convinced that nothing would come of "diplomatic courtesies or tactical manoeuvres" and that all Britain could do was to strengthen those countries which seemed to be susceptible to communism. This could best be done by an ideological offensive stressing anti-communism and the virtues of social democracy. Britain would set the example by establishing a national health service, ensuring full employment and equal educational opportunities, promoting technological progress, and determinedly opposing any signs of oppression or violence. Although some officials thought this paper was unduly pessimistic, it was given a warm reception at the Foreign Office.

The Prime Minister did not share these views and found them unduly alarmist. He continued to insist that Turkey, Greece, Iraq and Iran could never be strengthened sufficiently to meet a determined Soviet attack. He suggested that possible Soviet fears of Britain and America could be assuaged by establishing a ring of neutral states around the Soviet Union. Bevin, who was attending yet another unsatisfactory round of the Council of Foreign Ministers in New York, was highly alarmed at this suggestion, which came at a time when the Americans seemed at last to have understood the strategic importance of the Mediterranean and were taking a tougher line with the Soviets. Attlee believed that Bevin's foreign policy aims would place far too great a strain on Britain's economic resources; he was fully supported in this view by the Chancellor of the Exchequer. The Prime Minister had told the Chiefs of Staff that he had serious misgivings about their Middle Eastern strategy, which he thought far too costly and unnecessarily provocative towards the Soviet Union. He believed that only if there was incontrovertible evidence that the Soviets were prepared to run any risks to achieve world domination should such a policy be pursued.

Bevin replied that were the British to withdraw from the Middle East the Soviets would simply move in and such an obvious sign of weakness would encourage them to continue with their policy of bluffing and bullying. The Americans, who had gradually come round to the British point of view, would write off the British government. Bevin urged Attlee not to despair, to wait until the economy recovered and to remember that the British would soon have their own atomic bomb, of which he had said: "We've got to have the bloody Union Jack flying on top of it!"[46] Attlee reluctantly accepted these arguments and was prepared to wait before taking any drastic measures.

In October, much to the alarm of the Foreign Office, Field Marshal Montgomery, now Chief of the Imperial General Staff (CIGS), accepted an invitation, first made at Potsdam, to visit Moscow.[47] Montgomery announced that he was on the best possible terms with Stalin, Molotov and Vyshinskii and could not see why the diplomats should have any objection to his visit. The Foreign Office decided that the best they could do was to give Montgomery a detailed brief which hopefully would stop him from making one of his horrendous *faux pas*. Montgomery was asked to deny that there was any attempt to create a "Black Reichswehr" in the British zone of Germany and was told to invite the Russians to send an inspection team, provided that the British were granted similar rights to visit the Soviet zone. He was further told to explain to the Russians that the so-called area of Bizonia had been created out of the British and American zones because the Soviet Union had refused to treat Germany as a whole and had been shipping goods and equipment from its zone back home instead of distributing them as agreed upon at Potsdam. Montgomery was asked to stress the vital importance of the Middle East to Britain both economically and strategically, should the question arise, and to insist that this posed no threat whatsoever to the Soviet Union. He was asked to head off suggestions that the Russians should have any strategic bases abroad, particularly in the Mediterranean.

Montgomery left for Moscow on 4 January and put on a characteristically abrasive performance. He deeply offended his official host Marshal Vasil'evskii. The British Ambassador politely remarked of Montgomery: "I should not judge him to be among the most tactful of men."[48] US Ambassador Gen. Walter Bedell Smith noted, with complete understanding, that even Gen. Omar Bradley, a remarkably tolerant man, hated Monty's guts. The Imperial Chief of Staff refused to attend the festivities in his honour and went to bed demonstratively early. He had one meeting with Stalin on 10 January at the unusually early hour of five o'clock in the afternoon.[49] He presented Stalin with copies of his two books and a case of whiskey and further attempted to flatter him by talking of "we fighting men". Stalin rejected Montgomery's proposal for an exchange of officers and mutual visits to military schools. Then Montgomery made the absurd proposal that there should be a military alliance between their two countries. Stalin replied: "That is what I would like, and I think it is essential."

Montgomery returned to Britain convinced that there was nothing to fear from the Soviets for years to come and that they would not even be able to "thump the table" for the next fifteen to twenty years. He felt that the army officers were uneducated and lacked professionalism. He described Molotov as "not a very nice character" and reported, much to the surprise of those who had seen the Soviet dictator in action, that Stalin drank very little. His conclusion was that Britain should take some initiative to break down the suspicions which existed between the two countries.[50] The Foreign Office did not know quite what to make of all this. One official, Robin Hankey, reflected the feelings of many when he minuted that he found Montgomery's proposal for a military alliance "embarrassing"; but at least CIGS had not caused quite the havoc in Moscow many had feared.[51]

Bevin was convinced that Stalin's acceptance of the proposal for a military alliance was part of an effort to divide the British and the Americans at a time when they were reaching a joint solution to the German problem and when an agreement was near on the standardization of military equipment and the exchange of military information. On the other hand, the Council of Foreign Ministers was due to meet in March and the British could not afford to risk being condemned for refusing Stalin's offer of friendship. Bevin tried to wriggle out of this difficulty by assuring Stalin that as far as the British government was concerned the 1942 treaty between the two countries was still in effect. He also urged that the Soviets be kept fully informed of the Anglo-American military talks, otherwise they would become even more suspicious.

None of this implied that Bevin was more favourably disposed towards the Russians. In January he addressed a number of heads of missions in terms which showed that he had studied the Brimelow memorandum carefully. He said:

> Our general objective should be to hold the position against the spread of communism in order that Western concepts of social democracy may if possible in the course of time be adopted in as many Eastern European countries as possible.[52]

The aim, therefore, was not so much to attack the Soviets as to extol the virtues of British social democracy by means of the BBC, the British Council, the Inter-Parliamentary Union, and by encouraging cultural exchanges. Given the parlous economic conditions in the

Eastern European states and the fact that only the Yugoslavian government enjoyed a reasonable degree of popular support, Bevin believed this program had a reasonable chance of success. A few days later, on 18 January 1947, Bevin submitted a paper to the cabinet suggesting a Western European customs union which would include the western zones of Germany. This proposal was enthusiastically endorsed by Duff Cooper, then British Ambassador in Paris, and the cabinet suggested further serious study of its implications.[53] Bevin's containment policy now had its military, ideological and economic components.

The Council of Foreign Ministers met again on 10 March in Moscow and the talks soon got bogged down in endless wrangles about Germany. The British, probably knowing full well that the Russians would never agree, demanded unification and freedom of movement; the Soviets called for four-power control over the Ruhr and the dismantling of Bizonia. They further demanded massive reparations from western Germany, but the British and Americans argued that this would result in Germany continuing to be an economic liability for the Allies.

The conference had only just begun when the American President proclaimed the "Truman Doctrine" in a speech to Congress. It was such an ambiguous statement that the Foreign Office was at a loss to know what to make of it.[54] The Soviet press virtually ignored the speech and the comment in *Izvestiia* was moderate by Soviet standards. The talks dragged on with no agreement reached on either Germany or Austria. After a total of forty-three meetings the delegates reached one decision — to meet again in London in November.

Bevin fended off an attack from the Labour party left wing accusing him of reducing the country to a dependency of the United States, but this only served to remind him of the severe financial crisis facing the country. The news of Marshall's speech, given at Harvard on 5 June, came to Bevin, as he later said, "like a life-line to a sinking man".[55] He reacted speedily and vigorously to Marshall's proposal for a European recovery scheme. While he was anxious to make it appear that he wished to include the Soviet Union in the scheme, he hoped that the Soviets would refuse to have anything to do with it. He knew from his Minister of State, Hector MacNeil, that the Americans did not want to have the Soviets involved, or even socialist economists such as Gunnar Myrdal.

The British assumed that the Soviets had no interest in seeing the economic recovery of Europe, since they stood to profit politically from Europe's economic miseries. Nor would the Soviets look favourably on an American-sponsored scheme for European recovery. It came therefore as no surprise when the Soviets raised an endless series of objections at the Paris talks which began on 27 June. The British and French agreed that the European states should work out a common program, which they would then forward to the Americans for approval. The Soviets insisted that each state should send its own shopping list, and complained that the Anglo-French proposals were a violation of national sovereignty. Supported by the French and certain of his Prime Minister's backing, Bevin announced that the Western European states would go ahead with their program even if the Soviets continued with their obstructionist tactics.[56]

The Conference on European Reconstruction was scheduled to begin on 12 July in Paris. Eight of the twenty-two nations invited were in the Soviet orbit and therefore refused to attend. The conference established the Organization for European Economic Cooperation (OEEC) which, in 1960, was renamed the Organization for Economic Cooperation and Development (OECD). This marked a significant step towards the division of Europe. The Soviets responded by creating the Cominform at a conference held in Wiliza Gora in Poland at which it was proclaimed that the world was now divided into two hostile blocs. It was solemnly announced that Attlee and Bevin "are facilitating by their grovelling and servility the task of American capital, provoking it to extortion and pushing their own countries on the road of vassal dependence on the United States".[57]

Frank Roberts, the Foreign Office's most respected commentator on Soviet affairs, was not particularly perturbed by these outbursts from the Soviets which he interpreted as responses to the Truman Doctrine and the Marshall Plan. In his view the Soviets accepted the fact that the world was divided and were acting accordingly.[58] Even less sanguine diplomats agreed that there was no likelihood of war. The French were not so confident and, on their initiative, strongly supported by Duff Cooper, Anglo-French talks began in October 1947 on a possible military alliance with the United States to protect a European frontier running through the middle of Germany. The talks were held secretly in order to avoid alarming public opinion and Bevin, who enthusiastically encouraged the talks, minuted: "What we have to get into the heads of our people is western security regionally and less anti-attitude."[59]

The main impetus behind the military talks was the breakdown of the deliberations of the Council of Foreign Ministers which met in London on 25 November 1947. The French were concerned that should the talks break down the Soviets would establish a puppet government in East Germany.[60] The Western powers would then have to sponsor a government in West Germany. The French, however, were anxious not to fuse their occupation zone with Bizonia before they had military guarantees against the Soviet Union from Britain and the United States. The Americans were hesitant to go so far, proposing currency reform in Bizonia and political reform short of actually forming a separate West German state. The British supported the American proposals, hoping that such economic and political restructuring of the western zones would serve to expose the shortcomings of the Soviet zone.

The conference had opened with Bevin delivering a lecture to Molotov in which he pointed out that negotiations implied concessions, not unanimous approval of Soviet proposals. Molotov replied by calling for a united Germany, but the Western powers pointed out that without four-power agreement this was nothing but a propaganda sham. Molotov replied that the Western powers were deliberately trying to divide Germany. Bevin and Bidault agreed that Molotov was simply keeping the talks going in order to have a forum for his propagandistic outbursts. Marshall felt that since the Russians had no intention of relinquishing control over their satellite states, including their occupation zone in Germany, they had no interest in the talks succeeding. After several more days of fruitless talk the Western powers decided to end the conference. On 15 December the Council broke up and no date was fixed for a further meeting.

The talks having failed, Marshall and Bevin agreed that Trizonia would have to be formed as soon as possible.[61] The French were still hesitant and Bevin's unfortunate remark that the Soviet Union was less of a danger than a resurgent Germany, encouraged the French to demand that the Ruhr be separated from Germany.[62] The British and Americans were now determined to go ahead regardless of French objections and Soviet denunciations. Yet even at this point the break between East and West was far from final. While Molotov denounced the British imperialists in London, the final touches were put on an Anglo-Soviet trade agreement in Moscow. The negotiations, which had been conducted with considerable skill by the young Harold Wilson (at that time Overseas Trade Secretary), resulted in a substantial exchange of goods, machinery and grain, and was denounced by the Americans as far too favourable to the Soviets.[63] The British felt that they had to continue to attempt to reach limited agreements with the Soviets since they were uncertain as to how Congress would react to the Marshall Plan.

In early January Bevin prepared a number of papers on Soviet policy which were presented to the cabinet on 8 January 1948. He warned of the Soviet hopes that the Marshall Plan would fail and that the Western allies would fall out. He predicted a communist coup in Czechoslovakia which actually took place the following month. He did not agree with the Americans that reparations payments from the western zones to the Soviet Union should stop, arguing that this would only make the Soviets even less cooperative in other areas.[64] At the same time he strongly supported the idea of currency reform and the creation of a political authority in the western zones which would stop just short of a provisional government. Plans for a Western European union should also go ahead, but it should not appear to be too overtly anti-Soviet nor too right wing in order not to alienate socialist opinion. On 22 January Bevin made a major speech on foreign policy in the House of Commons in which he repeated these ideas. He denounced the dictatorial Soviet methods in Eastern Europe and called for a Western union to contain Soviet expansionism. The speech was well received by all but the extreme left, and Churchill impishly remarked that it "signalled the final conversion of the Labour Government to the principles of the Fulton speech".[65]

British strategic thinking reflected this conviction that balance of power politics had to replace the futile attempt to reach an under-standing with the Soviets. At the end of January 1948 Montgomery produced a remarkable paper entitled "The Problem of Future War",[66] in which he argued that the Soviet Union was seeking to capture the German "soul" as a first step towards world domination. The West had therefore to ensure that a united Germany was firmly in its camp. Montgomery argued that the Germans would never accept the division of their country and that the Eastern satellite states would revolt against the Soviet Union for having refused to accept the Marshall Plan. He suggested that the Soviets might go to war so that they could offer their client states the fruits of victory, but he believed this would not happen before 1957 and possibly not until 1960.

Montgomery insisted that, in the long run, the British Empire would be unable to fight this war alone and would have to have the full sup-port of the United States. Nonetheless, in the initial stages of the war Britain would have to secure, unaided, strategically vital areas, such as the United Kingdom, the Middle East and the lines of communication to the United States. An air offensive would be mounted against the Soviet Union from bases in Britain, the Middle East and northwest India using atomic bombs against selected strategic targets. The Soviets would have to be held as far east as possible, the Rhine providing the most suitable defence. Montgomery pointed out that were Western Europe to fall, the defence of the United Kingdom would be exceed-ingly difficult, and that it might also prove impossible to hold on to the Middle East and the Mediterranean. He proposed that a major base should therefore be built in East Africa to secure communications across the African continent.

The Chairman of the Chiefs of Staff, Lord Tedder, objected vigorously to Montgomery's proposal to commit a large British force to a continental war from the outset, and argued that it was foolish to work out a detailed strategy until the Americans had been fully consulted, and until the results of a study of the effects of an atomic war were known. Sir John Cunningham of the Royal Navy supported Tedder, saying that such a commitment was beyond the financial resources of the country and that it would probably end in another Mons or Dunkirk. He was also appalled at the prospect of a rearmed Germany which he felt might be tempted to pursue its own selfish aims. Furthermore, he did not share Montgomery's belief that the Soviets were seeking world domination, suggesting that they had more limited objectives. Montgomery's only support came from Sir Henry Tizard, the government's scientific adviser, who felt that it was essential to hold the Rhine frontier and suggested that a pre-emptive atomic strike against the Soviet Union should be seriously considered as soon as it was known that the Russians had the bomb. He insisted that war with the Soviet Union was inevitable within the next fifteen years unless there was a radical change in Soviet policy.[67]

It was agreed that Montgomery's controversial paper should be discussed at a conference attended by the Chiefs of Staff, the Prime Minister, the Foreign Secretary and the Minister of Defence. Attlee supported Tedder's view and had serious reservations about bringing the Germans into the Western union. Bevin also had misgivings about the Germans and feared another Dunkirk, but insisted that the Rhine had to be held, proposing that the armed forces of the Western union be integrated. He wrote:

> The past actions of the Soviet government, culminating in the recent events in Czechoslovakia and Finland, showed beyond any doubt that there was no hope of reaching a satisfactory settlement either by agreement among the four Great Powers or through the United Nations Organization, and that resolute action must be taken to counter the Soviet threat to Western civilization.

He suggested a five-power treaty for the defence of the non-Soviet world which would act, in the words of his new Private Secretary Frank Roberts, as "a UNO as it would have been had the Soviets cooperated".[68]

The Soviet-backed coup in Czechoslovakia made it imperative to press on with the formation of the Western union. Bevin wrote to Pierson Dixon, whom he had sent to Prague as Ambassador, in a fit of anger and frustration:

> Living through a Communist revolution as you have done, is unequalled as an education in the utter ruthlessness and perfidy of Communism,

which is difficult, if not impossible, to grasp fully until one has seen it at work.[69]

On 17 March, Britain, France and Benelux signed the Brussels Pact in which the signatories agreed to mutual military assistance in the event of an attack and to the highest possible degree of economic cooperation. At the beginning of April the President signed the Marshall Plan legislation. On 28 June the Soviets imposed the Berlin blockade. At the Labour party conference Bevin said:

> We cannot change the communism of Russia, and I am not going to try. We cannot pursue, and we have no intention of pursuing, a policy in Eastern Europe of trying to change by force many of the things done in those states with which we do not agree. Those things will have to be worked out in the process of time. But equally we are not prepared to sit idly by and see a similar process of communization carried on over a weakened, distracted and disunited Europe.[70]

This is an admirably concise statement of British policy towards the Soviet Union which was to remain essentially unchanged until the collapse of the Soviet empire proved the wisdom of Bevin's words.

NOTES

1. Alan Bullock, *Ernest Bevin: Foreign Secretary 1945–1951* (London, 1983), p. 25. For the British papers on the Potsdam Conference see Public Record Office, Cabinet Papers (CAB) 99/38, CAB 99/39 and 99/40 and the relevant Foreign Office files in FO 371.
2. See FO 371/50826 for extensive discussion of the pros and cons of a Western bloc.
3. Bullock, *Bevin*, p.117.
4. The Soviet ambitions for a base in Cyrenaica had been discussed at a meeting of the Chiefs of Staff, 23 Aug. 1945: CAB 79/38.
5. See CAB 80/97 for Foreign Office memorandum on the Montreux Convention in which it was argued that it would be better to amend the Convention than to run the risk of direct Soviet intervention in Turkey and Greece.
6. Gladwyn Jebb, 20 July 1945, FO 371/50912.
7. Sir Orme Sargent, 11 July 1945, FO 371/50912.
8. Bevin to Molotov, 1 Oct. 1945, FO 371/50919.
9. FO 371/47857.
10. Bevin reported to cabinet on the failure of the CFM conference on 25 Sept. 1945: CAB 128 CM (45) 35th Conclusions Minute 1.
11. FO 371/50917 contains a number of minutes asking why the Soviets were being so difficult. Halifax reported from Washington on 25 Sept. 1945 that President Truman was also at a loss to know what the Soviets were up to.
12. Bevin minute, 6 Oct. 1945, FO 371/50826.
13. FO 371/50826. Dulles' speech was broadcast on 6 Oct. 1945.
14. Brimelow memorandum, 29 Oct. 1945, FO 371/47857.
15. Roberts to Foreign Office, 22 Oct. 1945, FO 800/501.
16. FO 371/47857.
17. The Foreign Office felt that Carr's support in his *Times* leader of 3 Oct. 1945 for Molotov's view that three powers were better than five was "sabotage": FO 371/50921. Bevin complained that the *Times* had a "jellyfish" attitude on foreign affairs and by always demanding "useless compromise" could hardly be considered a national newspaper: FO 800/498.

18. Brimelow memorandum, 12 Oct. 1945, FO 371/47856.
19. Bevin to Pierson Dixon, 16 Oct. 1945, FO 371/50921.
20. FO 371/50921.
21. In a statement to the House of Commons, 23 Nov. 1945. Bullock, *Bevin*, p. 141.
22. In a letter to Byrnes, Bevin said he disliked three-power diplomacy and wanted the UN, or at least the French, involved in any further talks: FO 800/446.
23. Clark Kerr to Bevin, 29 Nov. 1945 and 3 Dec. 1945, FO 800/47.
24. *Ibid.*
25. For an assessment of the conference, see FO 800/447. Bevin was angry with the Americans for adopting a piecemeal rather than a comprehensive approach to the German question and felt that Truman's statement on Greece and Turkey made the situation even more difficult. However he noted: "My impression from the Moscow meeting is that Mr. Molotov was beginning to come to a better understanding of the attitude of His Majesty's Government and thus to show some sympathy for it."
26. Roberts to Bevin, 16 Jan. 1946, FO 371/52327. Geoffrey Warner was less optimistic, minuting, "I wish I could believe this was the whole story."
27. For record of Vyshinskii-Bevin talks on 26 Jan. 1946, see FO 371/56780.
28. Attlee to Bevin, 1 Dec. 1946, FO 800/475.
29. Roberts to Bevin, 28 March 1946, FO 371/56763.
30. Joint Intelligence Committee (JIC) report, 23 March 1946, FO 371/56831.
31. JIC report, 29 March 1946, FO 371/56831.
32. Brimelow memorandum, 24 March 1946, FO 371/56831. Brimelow agreed with Roberts that strong ties with the United States were needed to stop the "artichoke effect" of Soviet policy in their sphere of influence. Much of this confusion over British policy towards the Middle East is reflected in the briefing of Sir Maurice Peterson given on 18 March 1946, prior to his departure to Moscow.
33. Cabinet meeting, 18 Feb. 1946, CAB 128/16 (46), where the need for economy was stressed.
34. FO 800/501/SU/46/15.
35. CAB 23 (46) 11 March 1946; also Bevin to Attlee, 7 March 1946, FO 800/498.
36. For the Foreign Office's comments on the favourable reception given to the speech in the United States, see FO/51624.
37. Attlee to Churchill (who was still in the United States), 25 Feb. 1946, Prime Minister's Office (PREM) 8/197.
38. FO 800/492.
39. Warner memorandum, 2 April 1946, FO 371/55581.
40. R. N. Carew Hunt, *The Theory and Practice of Communism* (New York, 1962).
41. Bullock, *Bevin*, p. 90.
42. Lucius D. Clay, *Decision in Germany* (London, 1950), p. 165.
43. Wilfried Loth, *Die Teilung der Welt 1941–1955* (Munich, 1989), p. 147. Jean Edward Smith, "The View from UFSET: General Clay's and Washington's Interpretation of Soviet Intentions in Germany, 1945–1948", in Hans A. Schmitt (ed.), *US Occupation in Europe after World War II* (Lawrence, 1978), pp. 64–85.
44. Peterson met Stalin on 27 May 1946: PREM 8/349.
45. Brimelow memorandum, 9 Sept. 1946, FO 371/56835.
46. Bullock, *Bevin*, p. 352.
47. Roberts was not at all keen on the idea of allowing Montgomery to go to Moscow. He pointed out that the Soviets refused to be represented at the British victory parade. He did not want it to seem as if they were running after the Russians. The formal invitation, however, made it difficult for the Foreign Office to find an adequate excuse not to accept: FO 371/56904.
48. FO 371/66279.
49. See FO 800/502 for a full record of this astonishing conversation. The Foreign Office reacted to the proposal for a military alliance by suggesting that the Anglo-Soviet treaty could be brought up to date. In a letter to Bevin of 8 Nov. 1947, Montgomery had blamed the whole mess in Europe on Eisenhower's refusal to accept his strategy after the break-out from Normandy: FO 800/451.
50. See FO 371/66279 for Montgomery's report on his visit to Moscow.
51. Hankey minute, 17 Jan. 1947, FO 371/66279.
52. The meeting was held on 14 Jan. 1947: FO 953/4E.

53. The memorandum from Duff Cooper is dated 10 Jan. 1947: FO 371/62398.
54. See FO 371/67582A for comments by Gladwyn Jebb, Wilson Young and Sir John Balfour from Washington.
55. Bullock, *Bevin*, p. 405. At the time no one had any idea what the "Marshall Plan" involved. As one American official wrote, it was like a flying saucer: "nobody knows what it looks like, how big it is, in what direction it is moving, or whether it really exists". The important thing was that Bevin took up Marshall's phrase, "the initiative, I think, must come from Europe", and did everything he could to make sure that the opportunity was taken. Bullock is surely right in claiming that this was Bevin's greatest achievement as Foreign Secretary.
56. For the debate on European reconstruction, see Bullock, *Bevin*, pp. 405–27; M. J. Hogan, *The Marshall Plan* (London, 1987); A. S. Milward, *The Reconstruction of Western Europe 1945–51* (London, 1984).
57. FO 371/66475.
58. Roberts to Bevin, 7 Oct. 1947, FO 371/66475. Roberts urged Bevin not to take the foundation of the Cominform too seriously, saying that the Comintern had never been properly dissolved and that "The Kremlin thus seem to have taken up the original American challenge inherent in the Truman Doctrine, and have accepted the division of the world into two camps."
59. General Revers, the French Chief of Staff, favoured an "anti-Soviet bloc", a phrase which Bevin found "most unfortunate": FO 371/67674.
60. FO 371/64633.
61. Bevin's conversation with Marshall, 17 Dec. 1947, FO 371/64250. Bevin favoured an informal understanding among the Western powers and added: "If such a powerful consolidation of the West could be achieved it would then be clear to the Soviet Union that having gone so far they could not advance any further." Several proddings from Duff Cooper can also be found in this file.
62. Bullock, *Bevin*, p. 265.
63. Roberts to Foreign Office, 17 Dec. 1947, FO 371/64250, reporting that the American Ambassador in Moscow, Bedell Smith, had complained about the trade agreement and urged the British to take a tougher line with the Soviets over reparations from Germany. Details of the trade negotiations, in which Wilson's formidable opponent was Mikoian can be found in FO 371/66323 to 66339. Wilson's delegation was accused by the Soviet authorities of "rowdy behaviour". It appears that they played cricket and gave sandwiches to a group of children: FO 371/66332.
64. CAB 128/2(48).
65. The Soviets were deeply suspicious about the Western union. Lord Duncannon was treated to lunch by Starikov at the Soviet Embassy, plied with claret (Mouton Rothschild 1922), cognac (Clos des Ducs) and quizzed about the proposal. He detected Bogomolov of the NKVD listening in at the door; when discovered, Bogomolov "looked sheepish": FO 371/66332.
66. FO 800/452.
67. *Ibid.*
68. FO 800/460. Bevin's ideas are contained in the Cabinet Papers (48)71 of 3 March 1948 and CP(48)72. They were discussed in cabinet on 5 March 1948: CAB 128/19(48).
69. Bevin to Pierson Dixon (Prague), 22 April 1948, FO 800/450. Although British officials were appalled by the Prague coup there was a certain feeling that it served the Czechs right. Pierson Dixon wrote of Masaryk on 10 March 1948: "Lacking moral and physical courage, he joined the communists and then found it intolerable to sing for his supper." Robin Hankey wrote on 16 March 1948: "The Czechs are professional serfs": FO 371/71286.
70. Bullock, *Bevin*, p. 555.

# 12

# The Origins of the Cold War in the Near East

## BRUCE R. KUNIHOLM

Recent developments in the Commonwealth of Independent States (CIS) will have a profound impact in general on the history of our time, and in particular on interpretations of the origins of the Cold War. John Gaddis, perhaps the pre-eminent American diplomatic historian of the Cold War, has observed that the difficulty of assessing differing interpretations of the Cold War has been due to the impossibility of verifying one or another argument without access to Soviet sources. As he has put it: "one cannot credibly assess responsibility when one can confirm the motives of only one side".[1] In short, without evidence, historical arguments remain just that.

We now have good reason to anticipate a change in this situation because of the new climate in the CIS. In August 1990 the Soviet Foreign Ministry allowed access to documents over 30 years old, except for those containing especially important state secrets — a category that will no doubt deserve careful scrutiny. The Communist party's archives were opened to scholars after the attempted coup in August 1991. By October 1992 a number of documents had been released — most notably on the Katyn Forest massacres and the shooting down of the Korean airliner, KAL-007 — engendering lively discussion. As Russia struggles toward democracy, it is grappling with the same problem that all democracies confront: public accountability. A touchstone of democracy, public accountability is an ongoing and never-ending process that has been especially difficult in the era of secret and covert operations from which we are emerging.[2]

While contending with the evidenciary obstacles to reconstructing the past — and it is explaining the past that is the task of historians — US diplomatic historians have disagreed over methodological approaches. What frequently separates them are conflicting opinions not only about what constitutes sufficient evidence, but also about what needs to be explained. And even if they can agree on that, and can identify a set of causes that contribute to an explanation, they may differ over which causes deserve priority.

American diplomatic historians writing about the origins of the Cold War reflect these differences in the many debates among the Cold War traditionalists, revisionists, post-revisionists, neo-revisionists and corporatists.[3] Suffice it to observe that whatever the cause of such divisions, they also reflect different methodological assumptions about the need for and value of systemic explanations (as advocated by what one might loosely call the *open door* and the *corporatist* schools).

Those advocating systemic interpretations, criticize traditional, diplomatic historical interpretations as begging fundamental questions that are answered only by what they see as their own rigorous systemic analyses. Such interpretations have the potential for systematizing not only economic assumptions, but ideological, political, cultural, social, strategic, perceptual and other often inextricably intertwined ones as well. At best they can sweep away familiar frames of reference which, because they are taken for granted, present us with credible though distorted images, whose deviance from the true picture would otherwise go unperceived. They address the fact that how things happen is not synonymous with why they happen, and in attempting to infer the real reasons behind the actions they seek to explain, they are doing what historians must always do.

Systemic interpretations have made important contributions to explaining the origins of the Cold War. In the eyes of critics such as A.J.P. Taylor, however, general explanations such as those provided by systemic points of view often explain everything and nothing.[4] This is because they allow almost anything to be rationalized on their behalf and, on occasion, in the words of one historian, "reduce diplomatic history to a branch of sociology".[5] Many critics of systemic interpretations believe that multi-causal interpretations, however untidy, better reflect the manner in which human history unfolds, and that to impose a comprehensive order on political behaviour often does violence to those individual actions of which it is comprised. Their judgment, ultimately, is that more elaborate explanatory frameworks, while useful from an heuristic point of view, do not necessarily result in better or more accurate explanations of the past. From their point of view, one should rein in a desire to make exorbitant claims about the explanatory power of systemic frameworks and new techniques, and apply them carefully to problems posed by international history in order not to diminish their nonetheless important contributions to the illumination of human behaviour. The cautionary lesson in the American experience is that Soviet historians, in "preparing tools of analysis" for the "new thinking" that they see as necessary,[6] should be clear about these differences among us, should stick as closely as they can — at least initially — to the evidence that they begin to uncover, and should think carefully as they sally forth with their own revisionism.

The most fundamental questions that arise in debates among American historians on the origins of the Cold War are neither evidenciary nor methodological; rather, they involve the norms that one should apply to the difficult judgments that historians must make.[7] While judgments are involved in every step of the process of acquiring evidence, sifting through it and developing an interpretation of the past, the key questions are often raised at a level of abstraction where even historians who can agree on much of the evidence and a common methodology, nonetheless have serious differences. For example, in assessing great power differences during the Cold War, how do we define "legitimate" security concerns and to what extent can dominant perceptions and policies (whether in the United States, Britain or the Soviet Union) be seen as "legitimate" in the context of the 1940s? Given "legitimate" security concerns, the question then becomes the extent to which the policies pursued by particular leaders were appropriate to their countries' legitimate security concerns? How, in short, do we get beyond the chauvinistic assumptions implicit in various nationalistic perspectives and assess the methods used by various leaders to achieve their ends, given their different political systems and the strengths and weaknesses of their respective countries? Where, to ask the question in a different way, does justifiably defensive behaviour stop and unjustifiably aggressive behaviour begin?

There is an insurmountable difficulty in differentiating between aggressive and defensive actions, just as there is in distinguishing between nationalistic and ideological elements of a nation's policies, or between ideals and self-interest in the foreign policy of one or another country. This was particularly true when perceptions of the world held by American and Soviet policy makers were grounded in a fundamental belief that their interests were compatible with those of other nations, and an even more profound conviction that the system of government they represented could best serve mankind. The question of the relative merit of each system is essentially a moral one, which continues the debate between Wilsonianism and Leninism dating back to the First World War.

The problem of assessing the relative merits of different systems of government raises an important question: Which principles should we invoke as a basis for judging the arrangements that leaders believe will best serve national interests as well as international security? Given the profound differences such as those that separated Soviets and

Americans, and the fact that their leaders preferred an international security system that was compatible with their political systems and ideologies, such a task begs the question of a common standard and risks dissolving into moral relativism. If we exclude the two main principals in this debate, judgements about the relative merits of international security arrangements are subject to a host of considerations, including a country's historical experience, and, occasionally, the dictates of propinquity. The closer a country is to a great power, we might generalize, the more it is vulnerable to and tends to resent the great power's imperial sway; the further away a country is, the less vulnerable it is, the less it has to fear, and the more it can call on that power to assist it.

When it comes to the early years of the Cold War, for example, the vast majority of people in countries that bordered the Soviet Union, such as Poland, Turkey and Iran, resisted a close alignment with the Soviets and, needless to say, preferred the US emphasis on self-determination to the Soviet desire for a sphere of influence over them. Clearly, in the eyes of those whose territorial integrity was in question, the United States was seen as a counterweight to the Soviet Union, whose influence was resented and feared and whose territorial aspirations were seen as illegitimate. Only principles such as those espoused by the United States could provide for the future independence of small countries which otherwise feared absorption into a Soviet sphere of influence.

Although geography can have a profound influence on the orientation of a country's national security policies, so too can history. However American historians might question the primacy of security as a motive for Soviet control of Eastern Europe in the early years of the Cold War, the fact that the Soviet Union suffered more than 60 times as many casualties as the United States in World War II obviously had a profound effect on Soviet priorities. One does not have to deny Stalin's cynicism, excuse his ruthlessness or make the case that his motives were based solely on security concerns, to see how the notion of a Soviet sphere of influence in Eastern Europe followed logically from the Soviets' view of their own history.

The point here is that critical historical questions depend to a great extent on the norms that one applies as a standard of judgement, and that norms are not so easy to agree upon. The complicating factor is that they may well dictate the questions that one asks, the evidence through which one sifts, the methodologies one uses and the explanations one arrives at. Who we are and what we believe has a lot to do with the results we come up with. It is important to keep this in mind and to try to be as honest as we can as we look at the past, because what we write will shape our understanding of the past and inform our relationships in the future.

The origins of the Cold War in the Near East have been dealt with extensively by this author.[8] Some of the contentious issues that Western historians have debated among themselves will be outlined below. Hopefully, Russian historians examining Soviet archives, will take some of our differences as a point of departure and help shed light on these debates.

US-Soviet rivalry in the Near East during the Cold War appears to have evolved from, and eventually superseded, earlier Anglo-Soviet rivalry there. This can be seen as a response to the vacuum created by the declining influence of the British Empire in the region after World War II. American and British sources point to the fact that in the period 1944–46 Stalin was willing to risk diplomatic conflict in order to expand his sphere of influence in the Near East, but was prepared to stop short when there was a risk of war. They also show that he counted on wearing down the resistance of the more democratic and less easily-managed governments of his former allies.

In Iran, the Soviet government violated Allied understandings and exploited the opportunities that occupation afforded in an apparent effort to control the government in Tehran. Oil concessions, which the Soviets demanded, and Kurdish and Azerbaijani separatist movements, which the Soviets supported in occupied northwest Iran, were means to the same end. So were over 200 tanks that the Soviets moved into Tabriz in March 1946. The Soviets also sought, through a war of nerves and constant diplomatic pressure, to annex Kars and Ardahan in eastern Turkey and gain control of the Turkish Straits. A number of Soviet moves, including media attacks against "hostile" governments, attempts to effect the ouster of various government leaders, and irredentist Armenian and Georgian claims coupled with troop movements, suggested the need for a more forceful policy by the United States if it were to oppose Soviet ambitions in the Near East.

If the United States had not stood firm in Iran and had not confronted Soviet pressures on Turkey in 1946, it is likely that Stalin would have been tempted to expand the Soviet sphere of influence in the Near East as he did in Eastern Europe and the Far East at the end of World War II. That is why, despite its shortcomings, a British stand similar to the Truman Doctrine may have been necessary when they started withdrawing from the region. Subsequent to the Truman Doctrine and the articulation of the policy of containment, the Cold War was well underway, positions had begun to rigidify and the actions and reactions of the United States and the Soviet Union toward each other became much more difficult to disentangle. Events leading up to the enunciation of the Truman Doctrine have been the subject of considerable debate. This stems from the fact that the Truman Doctrine was a benchmark in the evolution of the Cold War. Moreover, the commitment to maintaining the balance of power in the New East served as a precedent for the Administration's policy in Europe.

Where do American scholars disagree? Melvyn Leffler has argued that the American conception of national security during the Cold War was a consequence not so much of Soviet actions as of America's perceived vulnerabilities and of the resulting strategic and economic imperatives. Central to his argument is the belief that implementation of this conception was unnecessarily provocative and, hence, primarily responsible for many of the Cold War's most enduring characteristics. To support this systemic argument, Leffler plays down the significance of serious Soviet pressures on Iran and Turkey, placing such actions, whose importance is central to the debate on the origins (as opposed to the evolution) of the Cold War, in the context of contradictory evidence of Soviet intentions. Leffler has argued that Soviet initiatives in Iran and Turkey were for the most part "tentative and circumspect", that Soviet behaviour, "while worrisome, did not constitute relentless pressure or systematic intimidation", and that in Iran, Stalin may have been concerned about the vulnerability of Russian oil fields and petroleum refineries, prompted by strategic and defensive calculations rather than by offensive. While Leffler concedes in his most recent publication that Soviet intervention in Iran was neither legal nor moral and that the Soviets were probing in Iran, he equates Soviet actions with those of the Americans, arguing that both governments were acting defensively, triggering a spiraling crisis of misperception and trust.[9] He dismisses as contrived the allusions to Soviet threats of force against Turkey in President Truman's decision of August 1946 to take a tough line against the Soviet Union, arguing that the Soviets had "done little more than send a diplomatic note", that Turkey only "supposedly" was subject to pressure from the Soviet Union, and that "it is questionable whether there was a crisis in Turkey except in the minds of American officials". In his recent book he suggests that the real problem was a vacuum of power in the region as well as other problems associated with the aftermath of World War II.[10]

Leffler also asserts that there is "reason to assign as much of the responsibility for the origins of the Cold War to the United States as to the Soviet Union".[11] But if he is more persuasive in characterizing Soviet actions in the period following the Truman Doctrine as reactions to Western initiatives, he is less so in arguing that, in the period prior to the Truman Doctrine, Soviet actions were either as reactive or as benign as he would have us believe, or that United

States' interpretations of and responses to those actions were not reasonable under the circumstances. Nor is he any more convincing than he was in his earlier writings[12] in his assertion that the United States had a conception of its security interests in the region that caused it to interpret Soviet behaviour in an alarmist way, or that the United States deserves as much of the responsibility for the origins of the Cold War.

This is not to say that the United States does not deserve harsh criticism for many of its polices during the Cold War, or that it does not share substantial responsibility for the manner in which the Cold War evolved. The overthrow of Mossadeq in Iran would be a prime example.[13] But that is not the question we are addressing here. The question concerns the origins of the Cold War in the Near East. In a debate on the relative legitimacy of Soviet and American security concerns in the Near East in the early Cold War period (1944–1947), it could be argued that even if the Soviets had legitimate security interests in Eurasia, their policies toward the countries on their southern flank (the northern tier of the Middle East), were unacceptable to the majority of the international community, especially in light of Soviet expansion into Eastern Europe and the Far East.

In the case of the Near East, the problem for US officials was hardly ever (as it was in Iran) whether or not a Soviet attack was imminent, but whether Soviet intimidation, unopposed by the United States, would force the countries on its southern flank to accommodate Soviet interests; the extent to which those countries might have to do so; and whether the United States, the only country that could oppose Soviet pressures, should reject requests for assistance by the governments in question and acquiesce in such developments. As Molotov's memoirs suggest, this is exactly what Stalin would have liked.[14] From the point of view of US officials the issue, ultimately, was how to respond to repeated Soviet pressures — before rather than after they became a problem. Policy had to be formulated on the basis of rational analysis of Soviet activity. It had to deter Soviet initiatives and at the same time appeal to a public confused by wartime rhetoric. Recent history indicated to US and other foreign officials that the Soviet government would not act in a manner appropriate to reasonable standards of international behaviour and that something had to be done about it. The driving fact in the region was inauspicious Soviet conduct that provided a context within which developing (but not yet formally accepted) strategic conceptions gained currency. Not to have anticipated such Soviet behaviour, particularly after the long and drawn-out crisis in Iran in 1945–46, and in view of previous pressures on Turkey, would have constituted a dereliction of responsibility.

The resulting US commitment to maintain the balance of power in the Near East and Europe appears to have made good sense, even if the rhetoric associated with that commitment was misleading. Vojtech Mastny has argued convincingly that the primary source of conflict between East and West — at least in the initial years of the Cold War — was the Soviet Union's striving for power and influence far in excess of its reasonable security requirements. Mastny suggested that Stalin, premising success on his ability to rule his empire without arousing alarm about his intentions, could have taken a more enlightened and less exaggerated view of what security meant only if he had not been Stalin.[15]

Clearly, in order to debate the question in any real depth, one would have to get into great detail, checking footnotes, looking at the manner in which conclusions have been drawn, judging whether or not one's selection of evidence has been reasonable and representative. In the final analysis, whatever the differences, Western inferences about Soviet motives are precisely that. There is little consensus now about Soviet motives, and there was little consensus at the time the Cold War was beginning in either the United States or Britain.[16] It is the absence of any documentary evidence about Soviet motives and internal debates that makes normative judgments so difficult. Historians who are able to gain access to the Soviet archives may be able to tell us about Soviet strategic and defensive concerns (and whether, in their judgment, defensive concerns became aggressive), the vulnerability Stalin actually felt about Soviet oil fields in Baku, and the extent to which Soviet policies in the region were formed by perceived threats from the United States or were a response to US initiatives. It would also be interesting to know how far Stalin was prepared to go as he probed in the region — Molotov's memoirs suggest that he knew when to stop — and what his fundamental attitudes were toward Turkey and Iran. We do know, for example, that he negotiated the Soviet Union's borders with Turkey and Iran in 1921, that in opposition to Lenin's wishes he reinforced Soviet troops in the Soviet Republic of Gilan in 1921, and that he installed the Minister of the Interior of that republic in the puppet government that was set up in Iranian Azerbaijan in 1945–46.

Most historians would probably accept the notion of a power vacuum and other problems associated with the aftermath of World War II as causes of the Cold War. It could be asked whether such an explanation clarifies everything or nothing. Is it sufficient to explain the origins of the Cold War as one would a road accident, in terms of general causes,[17] or is there some utility in more particular explanations? The difficulty, however, with this line of analysis is that in elaborating on general explanations, it divests national leaders of their responsibilities as leaders of nations and therefore their accountability to their people as well. Was the Cold War just another road accident, to be explained by general causes and covered by no-fault insurance? If that is the case, the Russian people and those who were absorbed by the Soviet empire had to pay a disproportionately high premium.

In this era, Mikhail Gorbachev is highly esteemed in the United States because it was he who had the courage to take the initiatives that brought an end to the Cold War. When his leadership was challenged, he was not willing to risk the lives and well-being of his countrymen to maintain his position in power. Rather, he facilitated (with some prodding from Boris Yeltsin and others) the transition through which his country was moving. For these and other reasons, he deserves credit. Stalin, on the other hand, who could have done the same, pursued policies which risked the lives of his countrymen not for the purpose of bettering their lot, but to maintain his position in power. Millions of people died for the sake of this goal before World War II, and millions suffered during the Cold War under his oppressive rule for the same reason. If the Cold War played into his hands by providing him with a rationale to clamp down on the territories he controlled, as Leffler asserts that Soviet scholars have argued,[18] is it not fair to ask what role he (and the system he created) played in initiating the conflict? Should the West have acquiesced to him and allowed him to oppress people in other countries (such as Iran and Turkey) as well? To absolve him of responsibility for his actions by merely addressing the question "what happened", to circumvent the moral issues that are at stake, and to characterize his actions as little more than part of an action-reaction syndrome, is to do a disservice to leaders such as Mikhail Gorbachev who have been less self-serving, more willing to be accountable for what they do and ready to confront their responsibilities as national leaders. It has already been mentioned at the beginning of this paper that one of the touchstones of democracy is public accountability. In Stalin's time there was no accountability. It can only be hoped that findings in the Soviet archives will make it possible for Russian scholars to gain new insights into the history of the origins of the Cold War, and thus provide an instructive example to future leaders of Russia and the CIS that they are answerable — to their own people and to history.

NOTES

1. John Gaddis, *The Long Peace: Inquiries into the History of the Cold War* (New York, 1987), p. 44.
2. For an illustration of this difficulty in the United States, see Bruce R. Kuniholm "Foreign Relations, Public Relations, Accountability, and Understanding", *Perspectives* 28, 5 (May/June 1990), pp. 1–12.
3. See John Gaddis, "The Emerging Post-Revisionist Synthesis on the Origins of the Cold War", *Diplomatic History* 7, 3 (Summer 1983), pp. 171–90, as well as the subsequent responses by Lloyd Gardner, Lawrence Kaplan, Warren Kimball and Bruce Kuniholm; Bruce Kuniholm, "The Origins of the First Cold War", in Richard Crockatt and Steve Smith (eds.), *The Cold War Past and Present* (London, 1987), pp. 37–57 and Geir Lundestad, *The American "Empire" and Other Studies of US Foreign Policy in a Comparative Perspective* (Oslo, 1990), and the sources cited therein.
4. See A. J. P. Taylor, *The Origins of the Second World War* (Greenwich, Conn., 1969), pp. 102–3, who points out that wars are like road accidents in that they have general and particular causes. "Every road accident is caused, in the last resort, by the invention of the combustion engine and by men's desire to get from one place to another." The police and the courts do not weigh general causes because general explanations explain everything and nothing. The "cure" for the problem — forbidding cars — is of little help and leads the court to address specific causes.
5. See Kuniholm, "The Origins of the First Cold War"; and Frank Ninkovich, "The End of Diplomatic History?" *Diplomatic History* 15, 3 (Summer 1991), pp. 439–48.
6. See Samuel Lewis' discussion in Kenneth J. Jensen (ed.), *Origins of the Cold War: The Novikov, Kennan, and Roberts 'Long Telegrams' of 1946* (Washington, DC, 1991), p. xiv.
7. Some of the material discussed here is elaborated in much greater detail in Kuniholm, *The Origins of the Cold War in the Near East: Great Power Conflict and Diplomacy in Iran, Turkey and Greece* (Princeton, 1980); Bruce Kuniholm, "Comments", *American Historical Review* 89, 2, pp. 385–90; and Kuniholm "The Origins of the First Cold War".
8. See Kuniholm, *The Origins of the Cold War in the Near East*; Bruce Kuniholm, "Loy Henderson, Dean Acheson, and the Origins of the Truman Doctrine", in Douglas Brinkley (ed.), *Dean Acheson and the Making of US Foreign Policy* (London, 1992); Bruce Kuniholm "US Policy in the Near East: The Triumphs and Tribulations of the Truman Administration", in Michael J. Lacy (ed.), *The Truman Presidency* (Cambridge, 1989), pp. 299–338; and Bruce Kuniholm, "Rings and Flanks: The Defense of the Middle East in the Early Cold War", in Keith Neilson and Ronald Haycock (eds.), *The Cold War and Defense*, pp. 111–35.
9. Melvyn Leffler, *A Preponderance of Power: National Security, the Truman Administration and the Cold War* (Stanford, 1992), pp. 80–81. See also "From Cold War to Cold War in the Near East", *Reviews in American History* 9, 1 (March 1981), pp. 124–30; "From the Truman Doctrine to the Carter Doctrine: Lessons and Dilemmas of the Cold War", *Diplomatic History* 7, 4 (Fall 1983), pp. 245–66; "Strategy, Diplomacy and the Cold War: The United States, Turkey and NATO, 1945–1952", *The Journal of American History* 71, 4 (March 1985), pp. 807–25; "The American Conception of National Security and the Beginnings of the Cold War, 1945–1948", *The American Historical Review* 89, 2, pp. 346–81, as well as subsequent comments by John Gaddis, pp. 382–85, and Bruce Kuniholm, pp. 385–90, and Leffler's reply, pp. 391–99. On Iran, see also Mark Lytle, *The Origins of the Iranian-American Alliance, 1941–1953* (New York, 1987), pp. xvi, xx, 150–51, who sides with Leffler in the debate (p. xx), and who appears to accept not only that the American stake in Iran was driven primarily by internal priorities but that Stalin's attitudes toward Iran may have been justified: "Azeri nationalism could easily have spread along ethnic lines into the Baku region..." and "Stalin may have had other more genuine security concerns in the Caucasus region." Louise Fawcett, *Iran and the Cold War: The Azerbaijan Crisis of 1946* (Cambridge, 1992), pp. 1–4, 107–8, 125, 150–42, 174, 178–79, 181, while emphasizing Stalin's continuing anxieties over the security of his country's vast borders, also emphasizes Stalin's policies in the region as explanations for subsequent US policies. For further insight into the Azeri question, see also David Nissam, *The Soviet Union and Iranian*

*Azerbaijan: The Use of Nationalism for Political Penetration* (Boulder, 1987).

10. Leffler, *A Preponderance of Power*, pp. 124–25, 515.

11. *Ibid.*, p. 515.

12. See "The American Conception of National Security and the Beginnings of the Cold War", cited in footnote 9, and Lawrence Kaplan's review of Leffler's recent book, "Cold Warriors: Wise: Prudent, and Foolish", *Reviews in American History* 20 (1992), pp. 411–15.

13. See footnote 2.

14. See *Sto sorok besed s Molotovym — Iz dnevnika F. Chueva* (Moscow, 1991) and the discussion of it by Woodford McClellan, "Molotov Remembers", *Cold War International History Project Bulletin* 1 (Spring 1991), pp. 17–20.

15. Vojtech Mastny, *Russia's Road to the Cold War: Diplomacy, Warfare, and the Politics of Communism, 1941–1945* (New York, 1979), pp. 35, 283, 292, 306.

16. See Wm. Roger Louis, *The British Empire in the Middle East, 1945–1951: Arab Nationalism, the United States, and Postwar Imperialism* (Oxford, 1984), p. 54, who mentions, among others: oil, a desire to make Iran a satellite, disrupting the British economy, a desire to gain access to the Indian Ocean (inherited from the tsars), an ideologically driven impulse and earth hunger.

17. See Footnote 4.

18. See Melvyn Leffler, "Was the Cold War Necessary?" *Diplomatic History* 15, 2 (Spring 1991), pp. 265–76.

# 13

# The Problematics
# of the Soviet-Israeli Relationship

## YAACOV RO'I

Soviet-Israeli relations were from the outset abnormal. However, this only became fully apparent to the world at large with the severance of diplomatic relations by the Soviet Union and the Eastern bloc countries in June 1967 and the persistent Soviet refusal to renew these relations. Indeed, it is ironic that one of the last diplomatic acts of the USSR as a major power was to renew full ties with Israel, an attempt, as it were, to correct one of the aberrations of its international conduct.[1]

It is commonly assumed by Western commentators that Soviet foreign policy was motivated mainly by considerations of great power politics. While this component was certainly not absent from Moscow's policy toward Israel, its role does not seem to have been paramount at most times. At least three other factors deserve particular attention: ideology, anti-Semitism and Soviet Jewry. The objective of this paper is to assess the significance of these factors in determining Soviet policy towards the State of Israel.

The Soviet Union is said to have supported the establishment of the State of Israel partly because it estimated that this would exacerbate the conflict between Arabs and Jews. The Arabs would never accept the existence of a Jewish state, and in this way circumstances would come into being that would enable the USSR to gain a foothold in the area.[2] Unquestionably, the USSR did consider the conflict a permanent factor on the Middle Eastern scene,[3] took every advantage of the 1948 war and, when it began contemplating potential venues for ingressions into the ex-colonial world in Asia and Africa in the early mid-fifties, was quick to realize the possibilities latent in the conflict.[4] Although the actual coincidence of interests that brought the USSR together with Egypt and Syria was the creation of the Baghdad Pact,[5] Moscow's arming of these two countries, over a period of two decades in the case of Egypt[6] and until the present with Syria,[7] was in fact tantamount to Soviet involvement in the Arab-Israeli conflict. By the early mid-sixties, the USSR was contemplating an Arab unity centred on the conflict,[8] which would hopefully bring the entire Arab world into line with the Soviet Union. This alignment would appear as a natural reaction to the American commitment to the existence, territorial integrity and security of Israel. The Soviet Union was at no stage prepared to accept the Arab slogan of destroying Israel — Moscow always recognized not only the fact of Israel's existence but also its legitimacy, even when it severed diplomatic relations.[9] Nonetheless, it could invariably go further than Washington in supporting the Arab cause.

Eventually, it was the Arab-Israeli conflict, notably President Johnson's meeting with Kosygin at Glasboro, New Jersey, in the wake of the Six Day War, that brought the Soviet Union American recognition as a Middle Eastern power.[10] Soviet leaders originally saw their support for the Arab cause as a mandate to represent the Arabs in any Great Power settlement talks in which Israel would be represented by the US.[11] The three "nos" of the Khartoum conference made direct Arab-Israeli negotiations unthinkable.[12] However, Moscow ultimately acknowledged that severing relations with Israel was a mistake from the point of view of its global and regional status.[13] Here, too, the events of the recent period, particularly Arab willingness to enter into talks with the Israelis, compelled Moscow to renew relations with Israel,[14] even if it was not able to use this step to gain points for itself and/or its Arab clients as it had initially contemplated.[15]

In addition to the regional factor, the Soviet-Israeli relationship had a manifest global aspect. Israel maintained close ties throughout with American Jewry,[16] and since the mid-sixties at least, also with the US government.[17] Since the Soviet Union as a superpower related to the various regions of the world with an eye to its standing *vis-à-vis* the West, and particularly the US, it sought alternately, and sometimes simultaneously, to vie with the West in the Middle East and to cooperate with it there. Any gain or achievement of the Soviet Union in or regarding a Middle Eastern country thus had an importance not only on the bilateral but also — and usually for the USSR more significantly — on the regional and global level. Apart from its tactical use of the American commitment to Israel to bring under its aegis the entire Arab world, or, as of the late 1970s, those states and groupings within it that adopted more radical anti-Israeli positions,[18] Moscow was able to dangle promises or insinuations of improved behaviour toward Israel in order to win for itself greater consideration from Washington. It sought, for instance, to guarantee its place at the settlement negotiating table by telling the Americans that once the

Israelis agreed to an international conference, relations would be re-established. The Americans had persistently urged the Soviets to take this step ever since *détente* had been renewed in 1985.[19]

On the level of international diplomacy, the Arab-Israeli conflict with both its regional and global ramifications, appeared to determine Soviet policy toward Israel. This factor, however, fails to explain the special nature of the Soviet-Israeli relationship. Not a few states were involved in ongoing conflicts with Soviet allies or clients. Yet the USSR not only refrained from severing ties with these states but in many cases maintained relatively good relations with them. In other words, developments connected with the conflict served as a pretext for the Soviets to take measures *vis-à-vis* Israel which were actually dictated by other components of the relationship, and which were singular to it. These elements were, as already pointed out, ideology, anti-Semitism and Soviet Jewry.

The Bolshevik party from its very inception had been extremely critical of Jewish nationalism in any of its forms,[20] for it contradicted Lenin's basic understanding that the Jews as a highly educated group would be among the first to assimilate in the dominant culture and implement the anticipated disappearance of nationalism and national differences. Zionism was not only the epitome of Jewish nationalism; it also became linked with Western imperialism following the 1917 Balfour Declaration which committed the British government to promoting a Jewish national home in Palestine. True, the support offered by the Soviet Union for the establishment of a Jewish state in part of Palestine in 1947–1948 seemed to demonstrate a change of heart. However, the short period in which Moscow both preached and practised friendship toward the Jewish state was an interlude in what was otherwise an unusually consistent policy of hostility — from 1903 through 1947, and from 1949 until very recently. This interlude, moreover, was unquestionably the result of Great Power consider-ations on both the global and regional (Middle Eastern) levels, and entailed no inkling of support for Zionism as such. The term Zionism, which had an unmitigatedly pejorative connotation, was simply removed from the lexicon of propaganda and the media for a brief while. Once the convergence of interests between the Soviet Union and Israel no longer existed, when Israel became a viable state and an official member of the international community of nations, and, indeed, even before that, the Soviets were once again condemning Zionism as a tool of imperialism.[21]

Nor was it possible or tenable to differentiate between Zionism and the State of Israel. The Jewish state not only saw itself as the realization of the Zionist dream, but was universally perceived as such, especially insofar as it claimed the right and obligation to protect Jewish minorities wherever they might be persecuted, and offered refuge to Jews the world over. The protracted, unequivocal Soviet denunciation of Zionism could only be interpreted as a campaign against Israel. Very often, too, the Soviet propaganda machine made the connection explicitly, dubbing the Israeli government and leaders as "Zionistic", with all that this epithet signified.[22] In this way, the commitment of the Soviet propaganda machine to anti-Zionism, which was an integral part of its entire philosophy, necessitated an anti-Israel position. It was only Gorbachev's de-ideologization of Soviet foreign policy, announced by him at the UN in December 1988,[23] that made a *rapprochement* with Israel at all possible.[24]

The second component that complicated the Soviet-Israeli relation-ship was anti-Semitism. Although officially outlawed — the Soviet constitution specifically denouncing discrimination against any Soviet citizen on grounds of race, nation or religion[25] — anti-Semitism was an ingredient in the Russian historical and cultural tradition, as it was in that of certain other national groups that comprised the Soviet Union.[26] A great deal has been written on both official and popular anti-Semitism in the USSR, and there can be no question that many of the Soviet leaders, including Stalin,[27] Khrushchev,[28] and Suslov,[29] to name some of the more blatant examples, manifested anti-Semitic prejudices. Israel as a Jewish state could not but be the object of antagonism and aversion for such people. Certainly, much of the anti-Israel propaganda that was generated orally and in writing in quantities that were far beyond what could have been warranted by Israel's importance for Soviet foreign policy, had anti-Semitic connotations.[30] Some of the *Stürmer*-like cartoons,[31] for example, were openly anti-Semitic. People, not only from Israel, but also from Western countries, were struck by the lack of rationale in statements made about Israel by Soviet public figures. Part of the campaign conducted against Zionism, which, as already noted, was condoned by Marxist-Leninist ideology, was also permeated with anti-Semitism, and Soviet Jews and non-Jews alike interpreted the vitriolic attacks upon Zionism as manifest anti-Semitism.[32]

Even the exceptional importance attached to Israel on the propaganda level reflected a perception of the Jewish state as the fulcrum of a world-wide conspiracy against the Soviet Union and the "forces of progress". This standpoint was part and parcel of the belief that Israel together with, and sometimes apart from, American Jewry had exceptional influence with the American administration, in the Western press and in the field of international finance.[33] This perception was not limited to periods of "stagnation", but was prevalent even as the Gorbachev administration sought ways to renew contacts with Israel.[34] It emanated from an irrational conviction that is basically inseparable from anti-Semitism. This socio-psychological aspect of the Soviet attitude to Israel permeated the ranks of the establishment, the media and various strata of society.

The third major problem that accompanied the Soviet-Israeli relationship from the very earliest days was Soviet Jewry. The presence in the USSR of a considerable Jewish minority[35] and that minority's partial identification with the Jewish state, made patent as early as 1948 when the first Israeli Minister to the USSR, Golda Meir, attended the Moscow synagogue on the Jewish High Holy Days,[36] meant that the Soviet relationship with Israel had clear implications for Soviet domestic policy. The discrimination practised by the Soviet regime against its Jews,[37] and their despair at ever attaining rectification of the wrongs done them within the framework of the Soviet body politic, made them turn to the representatives of the Jewish state as potential saviours.[38] In the same way, indications of goodwill toward Israel on the part of the Soviet authorities were seen by the Jews as promising improved behaviour towards them, while signs of animosity were interpreted as boding evil.[39]

The bond that Soviet Jews felt for Israel was demonstrated every time an Israeli sports team participated in a tournament or an Israeli artist performed in the USSR.[40] These demonstrations of sympathy were felt by the Soviet establishment to be so significant for the Jews that it continuously changed the venue and time of the performances of the Israeli delegation to the 1957 Youth Festival in Moscow in order to prevent Jews from attending.[41] Similarly, when Israeli diplomats attended synagogue in Moscow or elsewhere, the synagogue officials were forewarned that neither they nor their congregants might converse with the guests.[42] And if a Soviet Jew was so presumptuous as to receive an Israeli newspaper or a Hebrew dictionary or primer, or other such "anti-Soviet" materials from an Israeli, he would be arrested, interrogated and often given a long prison term.[43]

As early as the winter of 1948–49, rumour had it (and rumour frequently originated with the Soviet security police),[44] that the Israeli diplomatic mission was trying to win concessions from the Soviet leadership concerning Jewish emigration.[45] While this is not borne out by the evidence — except apparently for one short list of relatives of Israeli citizens[46] — by 1950, Israeli statesmen were openly calling for Soviet Jewish emigration.[47] From approximately this time, the Israeli government made periodic attempts to raise the question of Soviet Jewish emigration with the Soviet Foreign Ministry, but these approaches were consistently rebutted.[48] The Soviet powers-that-be were at no time prepared to admit that Soviet Jewry or any aspect of the Soviet Jewish question was in any way connected with Israel.[49] Their official position continued to view Soviet Jewry as a national group that stood in its own right, and to insist that its well-being was a matter that concerned only the Soviet authorities.[50]

If this applied, for instance, to cultural rights or individual discrimination, it was all the more true when it came to actual emigration, for Moscow did not sanction emigration of any sort.[51] Even when the Iron Curtain was lifted somewhat after Stalin's death,[52] emigration became possible only within the dual framework of repatriation and family reunification, that is, for individuals whose recognized motherland was not the Soviet Union and who had close relatives in that other land. Since the first condition did not apply to the Jews, whose official mother country was the Soviet Union, there was in fact no basis for discussion.

If, from the very beginning, the Soviet Jewish question was an obstacle to good relations between the two countries, once the Israeli government took upon itself the task of facilitating Jewish emigration,[53] and in the early 1960s began to do so openly at the United Nations,[54] there was little chance that relations would normalize. Indeed, when Israeli leaders asked Soviet representatives why relations were so problematic, the standard explanation was Israel's interference in the affairs of Soviet Jewry.[55] Although only circumstantial evidence is available, it is the author's firm belief that the real reason the Soviet Union severed diplomatic relations with Israel in June 1967, was to cut the ties of Soviet Jews with the Israeli Embassy in Moscow and to create conditions in which there would be no permanent or temporary Israeli presence.[56] The Six Day War served as a pretext; it provided an excellent excuse — Moscow could never openly state that it was cutting ties because of Israel's interference in its domestic affairs — and it was, moreover, a gesture toward the Arabs, at a time when Soviet prestige in the Arab world was extremely low.[57]

Under Gorbachev the gates were finally opened to Soviet Jewish emigration,[58] Jews were granted cultural rights,[59] and all religions were given the possibility to enjoy their constitutional privileges.[60] The rationale for the prolonged severance of relations was thus eliminated, and ties between the two countries improved.[61] Even then, several years passed before full diplomatic relations were renewed, partly perhaps because a number of individuals in the bureaucracy — though not Gorbachev or Shevardnadze — were anti-Semitic, and partly due to the influence of confirmed Arabists on decision-making regarding the Middle East, in particular Gorbachev's leading adviser on Middle Eastern affairs, Evgenii Primakov.[62]

If these, then, were the considerations that guided Soviet policy toward Israel, the relationship between the two countries was also compounded, to an extent, by trends and forces on the Israeli side. For although Israel ostensibly sought a normal relationship with the USSR, while the Soviets opposed this for the reasons discussed above — and their stand was undoubtedly decisive in that the relationship was anything but normal — Israel's position on certain issues precluded the fulfilment of its own declared aims.

In the first place, just as the Soviet ruling party adopted an ideological stance that in effect operated against the very existence of Israel (although this was never the official viewpoint of the Soviet government), so the attitude to the Soviet experiment in socialism was a major bone of contention among some of Israel's political parties, especially between the two leading Zionist socialist parties, Mapai and Mapam. The latter saw in the Soviet Union "the world of tomorrow", the embodiment of the socialist society it sought to establish in Israel. On the other hand, Israel's leaders, most of whom came from Mapai, entertained serious reservations regarding the possibility of too close a link with Moscow, for fear of its repercussions on Israel's domestic political arena.[63]

Secondly, no Zionist party, including Mapam, could ever forego the aspiration of "ingathering the exiles", namely, of working for the eventual immigration of Soviet Jews to Israel.[64] As long as the Soviet authorities persisted in obstructing or curtailing Jewish emigration, and indeed, refusing to acknowledge either the Jews' right to leave or the Israeli government's right to intercede on their behalf, no Israeli government or political party, except the small, non-Zionist Communist party,[65] could contemplate a normal working relationship with the USSR.

These were matters of principle and concerned the very essence of Israel's existence and political structure. They were, therefore, seen in Jerusalem as constituting even more of an obstacle to an ongoing relationship than the Soviet supply of weaponry to the Arabs, although this weaponry was designated for use against Israel and thus, in effect, the Soviets were cooperating with the Arabs toward Israel's eventual destruction. It made little difference that the Soviet Union insisted that these arms supplies were a matter of its own bilateral relationships with individual Arab states and were intended primarily to serve its own superpower status and interests.[66]

In conclusion, the Soviet-Israeli relationship was a priori destined to run aground. The temporary coincidence of interests that existed at the time of Israel's creation was posited on the desire of the two sides to terminate the British presence in Palestine and ensure the viability of the new Jewish state. Once these goals had been achieved, not only was there no longer a common objective, but the fundamental incompatibility of the two systems' *raison d'être* ruled out the possibility even of a constructive dialogue between Moscow and Jerusalem. It was not anything that Israel did or did not do, either before or after the June 1967 War, that prevented the establishment of a working relationship between the two countries. It was what Israel was — a Zionist state, predicated on a persistent striving for Jewish immigration, especially from diaspora communities suffering discrimination and persecution; a society seeking to implement its own brand of socialism, and a state surrounded by an overwhelming number of hostile countries - that sealed the fate of its relationship with the Soviet Union. The latter was a communist superpower with a significant Jewish minority to whose assimilation it was ideologically and politically committed. It had a negative predisposition toward Zionism, Judaism and Jews that it projected onto Israel, and strategic objectives in the Middle East that, in its view, could be achieved only through radical, fundamentally anti-Western nations. As long as these perceptions predominated, and Moscow, for all its usual foreign policy pragmatism, was incapable of seeing the practical advantages to be accrued from ties with Israel,[67] and as long as relations were the domain of the CPSU Central Committee secretariat and/or the KGB and MVD,[68] there was no chance of achieving a normal bilateral relationship typical of ties between a global superpower and a small regional power.

## NOTES

1. Agreement to renew diplomatic relations was reached on 18 Oct. 1991. The Soviet Ambassador elect, Aleksandr Bovin, presented his credentials in Jerusalem on 30 Dec. 1991.
2. For example, W. Bedell Smith (American Ambassador to Moscow) to Secretary of State E. Marshall, 14 Nov. 1947, *Foreign Relations of the United States, Diplomatic Papers (FRUS), 1947*, Vol. 5 (Washington, DC, 1971), pp. 1263–64, and Report by the Central Intelligence Agency, 27 July 1948, *FRUS, 1948*, Vol. 5, part 2 (Washington, DC, 1976), pp. 1246–47.
3. This was so much so that the USSR sought for many years to base its alliance with the Arabs on the common Arab anti-Israel position and to stress this factor as the optimal foundation for Arab unity (see below).
4. The first major economic agreement with the new Free Officers' regime in Egypt was signed on 29 March 1954, the same day that the Soviet Union initiated its right of veto in connection with Egypt's relations with Israel, specifically on the passage of cargoes and shipping to and from Israel through the Suez Canal. (Two months previously, the Soviet UN delegation had used its veto for the first time in connection with the Arab-Israeli conflict, to prevent the passing of a draft resolution condemning Syria for obstructing regional development projects connected with the diversion of the Jordan waters in the Syrian-Israeli demilitarized zone.)
5. The inclusion of Iraq in a Western oriented military pact changed the military balance

between the two traditional rivals for hegemony in the Arab world and made it essential for Egypt to turn for military assistance to the only power that had no connection whatever with the pact, indeed felt itself similarly threatened by its formation.

6. The last arms were supplied by Moscow to Egypt in early 1975 before the Sinai II agreement in Sept. and Sadat's unilateral abrogation of the Soviet-Egyptian Treaty of Friendship and Cooperation in March 1976.

7. Arms sales were being concluded between Moscow and Damascus even as Gorbachev was basing his ties with the US on decreasing involvement in local conflicts, including, specifically, the termination of arms supplies. In the years 1985–1989 the USSR retained its position as the world's largest arms exporter, the lion's share going to its traditional Arab clients. While there do not seem to have been new agreements since the end of 1989, and arms sales were cut to an extent by Gorbachev, it is generally thought that as of early 1992, they were still being implemented. As late as Sept. 1991, RSFSR Foreign Minister Andrei Kozyrev made clear that "the arms trade cannot be stopped technologically or economically", although he agreed that "it should acquire a more civilized character, so that the weapons trade is not carried [on] for ideological reasons": TASS, 19 Sept., 1991.

8. In this way Moscow endorsed the program laid down by the first Arab summit conference in Jan. 1964 which created the PLO and its military arm, the Palestine Liberation Army, a united Arab command and the Jordan Diversion Authority to negate the imminent inauguration of Israel's National Water Carrier. See, for example, the joint communiqué issued upon the conclusion of Algerian President Ahmed Ben Bella's visit to the USSR in May 1964: Ro'i, *From Encroachment to Involvement. A Documentary Study of Soviet Policy in the Middle East, 1945–1973* (Jerusalem, 1974), p. 374.

9. See Ro'i, "The Soviet Attitude to the Existence of Israel", in Y. Ro'i (ed.), *The Limits to Power* (London/New York, 1979), pp. 232–53.

10. For the talks between Johnson and Kosygin on 23 and 24 June 1967, see *Department of State Bulletin*, 10 July 1967.

11. This was the basic supposition underlying the Two and Four Power talks, initiated by Moscow, and held between the US and USSR and the US, Britain, France and the USSR in 1969.

12. The Khartoum conference based its affirmation of Arab unity "to eliminate the effects of the aggression" on "no peace with Israel, no recognition of Israel [and] no negotiations with it": *Middle East Record, 1967* (Jerusalem, 1971), p. 264.

13. As early as April 1987, on the occasion of a visit to Moscow by Syrian President Hafiz al-Asad, Gorbachev publicly stated that the absence of diplomatic relations with Israel was an abnormality: *Pravda*, 25 April 1987.

14. Late in Nov. 1989, Italian Prime Minister Gulio Andriotti was reported to have been told by Gorbachev that the USSR would be prepared to renew relations with Israel if it announced its readiness for an international conference or took measures toward a dialogue with the PLO: *Yediot Aharonot*, 1 Dec. 1989.

15. This seems to have been a major consideration behind Soviet policy since Moscow began dangling the bait of the renewal of relations before American and Israeli eyes beginning in the latter half of the 1970s.

16. Support for the establishment of Israel had been motivated, among others, by a desire to reach out to US Jewry. Moscow was well aware of the Jewish Yishuv's ties with American Jewry before it decided to give its support.

17. The first practical commitment of the US Administration to Israel's security came with the decision in 1963 to supply it with Hawk ground-to-air missiles.

18. After the Egyptian-Israeli *rapprochement* at Camp David and the subsequent peace treaty between the two countries, the Soviet Union lent its support to the Rejectionist Front.

19. Secretary Shultz's original demands of the Kremlin were published in *Literaturnaia gazeta*, 1 July 1985; Bush and Baker, too, persistently raised the issue with their Soviet counterparts: *New York Times*, 5 Dec. 1989; *Yediot Aharonot*, 12 Jan. 1990.

20. See, for example, J. V. Stalin, *On the National and Colonial Question* (Moscow, 1913), Ch. 5.

21. For a study of Soviet policy toward Israel at the time of the establishment of the Jewish state, see Yaacov Ro'i, *Soviet Decision Making in Practice: The USSR and Israel, 1947–1954* (New Brunswick, 1980).

22. As early as Dec. 1948, I. A. Genin in his pamphlet *Palestinskaia problema* (Moscow, 1948), pointed out that Israel's provisional government, as it then was, represented those parties that belonged to the Zionist movement and had a national-bourgeois ideology. This motif is to be found in virtually all subsequent works on Israel that appeared in the USSR.

23. At his speech to the General Assembly, 7 Dec. 1988, *Pravda*, 8 Dec. 1988.

24. True, indications of such a tendency toward Israel had been noted prior to his UN speech, but so too had his inclination to de-ideologize his foreign policy; see, for example, Mikhail Gorbachev, *Perestroika* (London, 1987).

25. See Article 123 of the 1936 ("Stalin") Constitution and Articles 34, 36 and 52 of the 1977 Constitution.

26. The Ukrainians and Lithuanians, for example, both had traditions of anti-Semitism about which a great deal has been written.

27. See, for example, Svetlana Alliluyeva, *20 Letters to a Friend* (London, 1967), p. 139 and *Only One Year* (London, 1970), pp. 148–49.

28. Thus, Khrushchev refrained from mentioning the Jewish aspect of the "Doctors' plot" when he denounced it at the 20th Party Congress in 1956. Similarly, he explained to a visiting French socialist delegation in the same year how, although the Jews had played a role beyond their proportionate weight in the population in the first years after the revolution, giving them key posts at the present would arouse justified protests from other nationalities: "Khrushchev's Views on Jews and Israel", *American Zionist* (Sept. 1957).

29. Suslov told a British Communist party delegation in 1956 that while no one would utter a word if Moscow massacred a million Armenians, a hue and cry was set up at once whenever a hair on the head of a single Jew was hurt: Hyman Levy, *Jews and the National Question* (London, 1958), and my interview with Hyman Levy.

30. For a study of this propaganda, see, for example, Baruch Hazan, *Soviet Propaganda: A Case Study of the Middle East Conflict* (Jerusalem, 1976).

31. Cf., *ibid.*, p. 153.

32. For some of the more extreme examples of patently Judaeophobic propaganda, see the many books and articles published in the Soviet Union in the 1970s and early 1980s, e.g., Lev Korneev, *Klassovaia sushchnost' sionizma* (Kiev, 1982).

33. These were all part of the standard accusations brought against Israel in Soviet publications, so much so that they have come to be widely believed among the Soviet public.

34. In addition to the undisguised American pressure on Moscow to renew relations with Jerusalem, many people in the Soviet establishment clearly believed that the road to Washington that they needed to take went through Israel. This was also without doubt one of the reasons that some, at least of the East European countries, initiated contacts with Israel in the second half of the 1980s.

35. According to the official census statistics, there were 2.268 million Jews in the USSR in 1959, just over 2 million in 1970, 1.8 million in 1979 and less than 1.5 million in 1989. The numbers themselves may not seem very significant, but it must be remembered: first, that they are probably not totally reliable — it is widely thought that some fifty percent can be safely added to the official statistics — and second, that the Jews are concentrated mostly in the country's large cities, which makes their importance disproportionately greater than their absolute numbers.

36. For a description and analysis of this demonstration of sympathy for and identification with Israel, see Ro'i, *Soviet Decision Making*, pp. 193–96.

37. This discrimination became official policy toward the end of World War II and has been described in virtually every book on Soviet Jewry in the postwar period. It was manifest both on the individual level, Jews being excluded from certain sensitive professions and some institutions of higher learning or faculties within them, or limited from entry to them by a quota system, and on the collective level, where Jewish culture was banned as of 1948–1949, see Ro'i, *Soviet Decision Making*, Ch. 7.

38. See, for example, Barukh Vaisman, *Yoman mahteret ivri* (Ramat Gan, 1973), pp. 170–72.

39. See, for instance, the reaction of Soviet Jews to the severance of diplomatic relations between the Soviet Union and Israel in Feb. 1953 and their renewal in July of that same year, *ibid.*, p. 216, and unpublished memoirs of Shmerl Goberman, "Epilog", p. 10.

40. See Vaisman, *Yoman*, pp. 247–49; Ro'i, *The Struggle for Soviet Jewish Emigration, 1947–1967* (Cambridge, 1991), pp. 63, 70–71, 269, 321–26.

41. Ro'i, *The Struggle for Soviet Jewish Emigration*, pp. 262, 264.

42. See, for example, Vaisman, *Yoman*, p. 256; Ro'i, *The Struggle for Soviet Jewish Emigration*, pp. 311–15.

43. One such person was Natan Tsirul'nikov of Leningrad who was arrested in 1960 for having received Israeli newspapers from Israeli diplomats in the Moscow Choral Synagogue.

44. For rumour and its role in the Soviet regime, see Thomas Remington, "The Mass Media and Public Communication in the USSR", *The Journal of Politics* XLIII (1981), pp. 803–17.

45. Ro'i, *The Struggle for Soviet Jewish Emigration*, pp. 34–35.

46. *Ibid.*, p. 35.

47. The first public call for Soviet Jewish emigration was made by Prime Minister David Ben Gurion in May 1950: Aryeh Ofir (ed.), *Afikim* (Kibbutz Afikim, 1951), pp. 411–12; *New York Times*, 24 May 1950.

48. For example, the approaches by Israeli Foreign Minister Moshe Sharett to his Soviet counterpart Andrei Vyshinskii in late 1950 and again in late 1951 and by Israeli Minister in Moscow Shmuel Eliashiv to both Vyshinskii and his deputy, Andrei Gromyko in July and Sept. 1951, and to Gromyko again following the resumption of diplomatic relations in Dec. 1953: Ro'i, *The Struggle for Soviet Jewish Emigration*, pp. 91, 102.

49. See, for example, Ambassador Dmitrii Chuvakhin's extrapolation from Israeli Prime Minister Levi Eshkol's reference to Soviet Jewry in his policy declaration to the Knesset in Jan. 1966, in Avigdor Dagan, *Moscow and Jerusalem* (London, 1970), pp. 168–71.

50. The 2nd edition of the *Bol'shaia sovetskaia entsiklopediia*, the relevant volume of which appeared in 1952, said that the Jews comprised several nationalities (*narodnostei*) which had, however, a common origin: the ancient Jews, a people who had lived in Palestine from the middle of the second millennium BCE until the 1st or 2nd century CE. The modern Jews were not a nation, according to this source, because they did not constitute a "stable community of people formed historically on the basis of a communality of language and territory, a common economic existence and general culture". The 1989 population census, the last to be held in the USSR, actually denied that even the Soviet Jews were a single nationality; classifying the country's population according to nationality and language, it divided the Jews into no less than four categories: Jews, Mountain Jews (i.e. the Jews of Dagestan), Georgian Jews and Central Asian Jews.

51. In the first place, the Soviet Union was by definition a closed society which, moreover, restricted freedom of movement even within the country. Secondly, emigration was perceived as indication of a shortcoming in the new socialist society that was being constructed in the USSR, and could obviously not be admitted.

52. Movement became possible in both directions, that is to and from the Soviet Union, yet the process of loosening the reins was gradual and carefully restricted. Nonetheless, delegations did visit the Soviet Union and there was even some tourism, while Soviet delegations went abroad.

53. See Ro'i, *The Struggle for Soviet Jewish Emigration*, Chs. 3, 4.

54. *Ibid.*, pp. 168–77.

55. See Dagan, *Moscow and Jerusalem*, pp. 162–64 and 182.

56. This was the clear feeling of the Israeli diplomats who were serving at the time in Moscow. Ambassador Katriel Katz had been told in so many words over half a year earlier that the Israelis should prepare for a severance of relations.

57. This was the result of the Soviet Union's failure to come to the aid of its Arab allies during the war. The dismal defeat was largely laid at Moscow's door, for Moscow was

virtually the Arabs' sole arms supplier, with all that that entailed.

58. From under 1,000 per annum in 1985 and 1986, the numbers soared to well over 200,000 in 1990, 185,000 reaching Israel. This growth was not the result of a shift in policy toward Jews specifically. Other emigrating populations, notably the Soviet Germans, also benefited from the change. The first indication of this change came with the amendment to the existing Statute on Entering and Leaving the USSR that came into force on 1 Jan. 1987 (see F. J. M. Feldbrugge, "The New Soviet Law on Emigration", and Donna E. Arzt, "The New Soviet Emigration Law Revisited: Implementation and Compliance with Other Laws", *Soviet Jewish Affairs* 17, 1 (Spring 1987), pp. 9–24, and 18, 1 (Spring 1988), pp. 17–28, respectively. The new 1991 law, which came into force on 1 July of that year, finally allowed Soviet citizens freedom of travel, in effect, without restriction.

59. As of 1989, numerous Jewish cultural associations came into being throughout the country and although many of them were not officially registered, certainly not at first, they were tolerated *de facto* and allowed to conduct courses for the study of Hebrew — formerly prohibited — and Yiddish, as well as Jewish history and culture.

60. The new law entitled "Freedom of Conscience and Religious Organizations" was passed in Oct. 1990; see *BBC/Summary of World Broadcasts*, Special Supplement, 23 Oct. 1990. In effect the law actually exceeded in a number of fields the freedom of conscience and religious worship and guarantees against the incitement of hatred or hostility on grounds of religion, which were the basic rights as expounded in the constitution.

61. Following the talks in Summer 1985 between the two countries' ambassadors in Paris, Iurii Vorontsov and Ovadia Sofer, discussions between leading officials of the two governments became regular events. Eduard Shevardnadze met several times with his Israeli counterpart and even with the Israeli Prime Minister. In 1987 it was agreed to establish consular missions, and this move was followed by commercial, scientific and cultural ties.

62. Primakov's special position and influence as Gorbachev's leading Middle East expert, as well as his unequivocal commitment to the traditional Soviet-Arab alliance, were underscored by his three missions to Baghdad as the Iraqi-Kuwaiti crisis deteriorated between late 1990 and early 1991. While Primakov does not seem to have gone officially on record as being opposed to the renewal of relations with Israel, he was reported to have been against this step.

63. For a detailed discussion of the interaction between Israeli domestic politics and Israel's relations with the Soviet Union, see Uri Bialer, *Between East and West: Israel's Foreign Policy Orientation, 1948–1956* (Cambridge, 1990).

64. Mapam was consistent in its belief in the right of Jews the world over, including the Soviet Union, to emigrate to Israel, see for example, *Divrei haknesset*, Vol. 1, pp. 860–61, 29 June 1949, and Yaacov Riftin's programmatic article in *Al-Hamishmar*, 30 April 1950.

65. The Israeli communist party, Maki until 1965 and Rakah until that party was absorbed into Hadash, at no time had more than five seats in the Knesset (out of 120).

66. Almost certainly the Soviets, who saw war as an extension of diplomacy, in the best Clausewitz tradition, never intended arms supplies to lead to war, and least of all a war in which they might become involved. From Moscow's point of view, arms enabled one to threaten war, which in turn enhanced political influence and leverage.

67. It was only in 1989–1990 that the USSR began to think in terms of commercial and technological ties and agreements with Israel, only to find that there were, indeed, not a few fields in which it could benefit from Israeli knowhow and experience.

68. The CPSU Central Committee secretariat was responsible for ideology and the MVD and KGB for internal security. With the opening of relevant archives, we hope to be able to ascertain how, indeed, policy making toward Israel in its different aspects was apportioned.

# 14

# Gorbachev and the Reunification of Germany: Personal Recollections

## ANATOLII CHERNIAEV

When Gorbachev became General Secretary of the Central Committee, and the *de facto* Head of State of the USSR, he immediately took up the German question. From the outset he sought to redefine the Soviet role in the socialist camp, the Warsaw Pact and Comecon in the context of relations with the German Democratic Republic (GDR). Gorbachev had not intended, however, to impose perestroika on the entire socialist world. He had hoped that the East European leaders would follow suit and reform their own countries.

At his first meeting with leaders of the Warsaw Pact nations during Chernenko's funeral in March 1985, Gorbachev declared that the principle of equality would henceforth govern relations between Russia and the East European states, and that outside interference in their affairs would not be tolerated. The Brezhnev Doctrine had received its death blow.

At the 27th Party Congress in February 1986, the General Secretary of the West German Communist party, Herbert Mies, reproached Gorbachev:

> Your [party] congress poses very serious problems for the socialist countries...I have spoken with Honecker. He is paying close attention to everything that is being said. But I feel that he has a certain secret fear: all the citizens of the GDR will read Gorbachev's speech; then they will hear Honecker's speech at the German Socialist Union party conference. Naturally, they will compare them. And [he] apparently feels there are certain dangers in such a comparison...After the April plenum of the Central Committee of your party I was in the GDR. At that time the CC of the SED received quite a few letters asking: "Shouldn't our approach to the problems be similar to that of the CPSU?" The leadership gave the answer in closed sessions of high level party activists: "No, it shouldn't be, although on several questions we will have to find a new approach." I noted that in the meantime, such questions had yet to arise. I spoke with the others — Zhivkov in particular. It won't be easy for them, Mikhail Sergeevich.

In the Politburo, the departments of the Central Committee and the Ministry of Foreign Affairs, there was concern over the improvement of relations between the two Germanies. Gorbachev, however, was not really affected by it. I remember how pleased I was about his positive reaction to my first intervention in the German question. In a telegram of 31 March 1986, the Russian Ambassador to East Germany, Viacheslav Kochemasov, had expressed his views on how to deal with Honecker. I commented that in my opinion the Ambassador was "fomenting suspicion" — exaggerating the dangers of relations between the two Germanies, while offering no concrete suggestions about how to formulate our policy.

Gorbachev viewed the German problem in the wider framework of his European policy. His initial concern had been with relations between the USSR and the USA, and he had devoted the utmost attention and effort to cultivating ties with Washington. Gorbachev's assumption was that a nuclear war could only be averted by bringing an end to the arms race. It was only after the Reykjavik summit that he understood that without Europe, he could not achieve his goals.

The transformation in Gorbachev's thinking regarding Europe followed a discussion he held with Margaret Thatcher in April 1987. It was reflected in a speech to the Politburo when he stated:

> We must carefully plan our work in Europe. We must regroup our scientific forces...perhaps, create a centre of European research. And we must remember that Western Europe is our major partner. We will not make a move on any matter of importance without Europe.

It should be noted that henceforth Gorbachev pursued this line on Europe actively and consistently. The majority of his meetings from 1987–1988 were with West European leaders.

Gorbachev's personal acquaintance with Europe and his understanding of its significance for the success of perestroika and the foreign policy of the "new thinking", as well as the bond of mutual trust he had established with many influential European politicians, ultimately made it easier for him to make the historic decision to support German unification.

In June 1987, he met in Moscow with Richard von Weiszäcker, the President of the Federal Republic. When von Weizsäcker raised the German question, Gorbachev affirmed:

> Contributing to the cause of global security is the duty of any state, particularly a European one. This is also true for the two German states. Their fate in 100 years *will be decided by history*. No other approach is acceptable. The consequences of taking a different path would be serious. This should be absolutely clear...Today, the existence of two German states is a reality, and one must accept this fact. The Moscow Agreement, your agreements with Poland and Czechoslovakia, the GDR

and other states, are a reality. These agreements enable the effective development of political, economic, cultural and human contacts. The Soviet Union respects the postwar realities, respects the German people in the FRG and the Germans in the GDR. On the basis of these realities, we intend to build our relations in the future. History will judge us in due course.

As it turned out, history judged much sooner. But it should be noted that Gorbachev had not excluded the possibility of German unification in his statement, and this fact did not go unnoticed. My close acquaintance with Gorbachev leads me to believe that by then, deep in his heart, he was already convinced that without a resolution of the German question and without the establishment of normal relations between these two great nations, no reconciliation would occur in Europe or the world. Nevertheless, despite von Weizsäcker's repeated attempts to draw Gorbachev out on German unity, Gorbachev carefully avoided the issue. He neither demonstrated solidarity with Honecker regarding the two German nations, nor did he compromise him.

A revealing episode occurred during von Weizsäcker's visit which sheds light on the prevailing mood in the Soviet leadership at that time. Gromyko, as Chairman of the Presidium of the Supreme Soviet of the USSR, held an official dinner in honour of the President. Von Weizsäcker's speech turned out to be twice as long as the others. Prior to its publication in the press, Gromyko ordered Iu. Kvintsinskii (then Ambassador to the Federal Republic) to shorten it to an appropriate length at the expense of passages which, in Gromyko's words, "the Soviet people would not like". These included references to the singularity of German consciousness, and (alluding to the Berlin Wall) to freedom of travel — in other words, to those passages which were probably most important to von Weizsäcker.

When the speech was eventually printed in *Izvestiia*, the Germans used every available channel to express their indignation: "You supposedly have glasnost; Thatcher and Chirac were printed without cuts," they argued. I was inundated with telephone calls from both local and foreign journalists. They wanted to know what was going on and why we were making fools of ourselves. If we were claiming that there was glasnost then glasnost had to be evident.

I called Kvintsinskii on the phone and accused him, subtly, of being "unused to glasnost, having lost touch..." He replied: "What can I do, a Minister just gave me the order..." I then telephoned Gorbachev and complained that we were acting stupidly. He responded, rather maliciously, "Leave it. This is the way to deal with Germans. They like order — *ordnung*."

Later I discovered that the question of how to publish the speech had been discussed among members of the Politburo immediately after the ceremonial dinner. Foreign Minister Eduard Shevardnadze, Party ideologist Aleksandr Yakovlev, and particularly Prime Minister Nikolai Ryzhkov, had been adamantly opposed to making any cuts. Gromyko had sulked and left the room. It turned out that he had gone to call Gorbachev, who had not been present at the dinner, and had convinced him to edit the speech.

On the following day, Shevardnadze, Kvintsinskii and I were in Gorbachev's office. He had just returned from a discussion with von Weizsäcker and was sharing his impressions with us. He clearly had taken a liking to von Weizsäcker, and the discussion had been rich in content and perspective. Our conversation turned to the publication of von Weizsäcker's speech. Shevardnadze staunchly supported me. But Gorbachev, having already agreed to let Gromyko publish the censored version, refused to change his mind. Nonetheless, I came to an agreement with Yakovlev that the full text of von Weizsäcker's address would be published in the weekly *Nedelia* and in *Moscow News*. This turnabout focused the attention of the Western press on the speech.

After that, Gorbachev met twice with Foreign Minister Hans-Dietrich Genscher, and with other West German figures — Willy Brandt, Johannes Rau, and Hans-Johann Vogel — and gave an interview to *Der Spiegel*. But in fact, there was no progress on the German question for more than half a year after von Weizsäcker's visit.

Relations with West Germany lagged behind relations with other large and influential Western states. Gorbachev sensed and acknowledged the abnormality of this situation. On more than one occasion he stressed, in closed circles and in the Politburo, that we could not have any kind of real European policy without Germany. But he was restrained by an insulting comparison between himself and Goebbels which West German Chancellor Helmut Kohl had made almost two years earlier. By accelerating the development of ties with Britain, Italy and the USA, he had, in his words, hoped to "teach the Germans a lesson".

However, time took its course. The politics of the "new thinking" demanded improved relations with Germany. Kohl, for his part, set off several trial balloons. Gorbachev responded in writing, and for the first time spoke of a new chapter in relations. Finally, they reached agreement on a visit by Kohl to Moscow in October 1988.

On the eve of the visit, Gorbachev and I were occupied with preparations for the talks. I said, "The situation, it seems, is such that the country [West Germany] is ready to go all the way with us, but the

Chancellor is not." Gorbachev responded: "And in our case it is the opposite — the leadership is ready and the country is not."

We were both mistaken. On 28 October, in the Ekaterininskii Hall, a fateful tête-à-tête took place between Gorbachev and Helmut Kohl — with Kohl's aide Horst Teltschik and myself also present. I sat, exchanging glances with Teltschik — an exceptional, witty man, who played a major role in German politics at that time, in particular in the West German-Soviet *rapprochement*.

Teltschik and I witnessed a surprising metamorphosis on that day. The two leaders had an open, straightforward conversation. While each bore the burden of past history, the talks were marred neither by ideological onslaughts nor by shades of hostility or suspicion. Once again I was able to appreciate Gorbachev's boldness and sagacity, as well as his courage in making the break with Marxism-Leninism in favour of pragmatism and common sense.

Speaking at an official dinner on 24 October, Kohl naturally brought up the question of German unification and the problem of Berlin. The next morning Gorbachev consulted Valentin Falin, the head of the International Department and former Soviet Ambassador to West Germany, and me on whether he should confront Kohl on these points at the second meeting. He even instructed Falin to prepare some notes for the meeting , "so he would not forget..." However, during the discussion he never referred to any of Falin's notes. And later he explained to us that Kohl had felt obliged to raise these issues in order to defend himself against his "allies" and the "extremists at home".

It turned out that Gorbachev had not been far off the mark. Subsequently, I found out from members of Kohl's immediate circle that he was very concerned about the reaction of the NATO allies and was wary that he "could get into trouble" when he returned. Two French papers, *Quotidien de Paris* and *Le Figaro*, which paid close attention to his speech, charged that the character of the visit cast doubt on Kohl's loyalty to the alliance. During an official press conference other Frenchmen posed pointed questions, such as:

> ...you gave so much to the Russians, and what did you receive in return? A few liberated prisoners of conscience? And what will happen now with the Franco-German alliance and other promises to the French? Isn't Kohl now veering towards the East?

Kohl also noted veiled accusations of a similar nature in the American press. Unexpectedly, it was the British who reacted calmly.

In any event, the talks between Gorbachev and Kohl produced a mutual trust, which quickly developed into a genuine friendship. This relationship played a singular role in accomplishing the unification of

Germany without "blood and iron". It is symbolic that the meeting which brought them closer took place around the time of Gorbachev's December 1988 address to the UN. There, with the whole world watching, he proclaimed that the Soviet Union's transition to a fundamentally new international policy was irreversible.

It was agreed between the two leaders that Gorbachev would pay an official visit to West Germany in the summer of 1989, and that with regard to the process of *rapprochement* between the two states, both visits would be viewed together as a single step towards the emergence of a new level of relations.

One of Gorbachev's main objectives during the visit was to get advice from Kohl on how to conduct himself in the international arena, and in particular with the newly elected American President, George Bush, and his Secretary of State, James Baker. The Administration had got off to a slow start after taking office at the beginning of 1989, and Gorbachev had become suspicious that the new President might shelve everything that had been achieved under Reagan.

In response to suspicions voiced by Gorbachev regarding the Americans, Kohl asserted:

> Yes, Bush is entirely different from Reagan. But one should not forget that he inherited a formidable legacy, particularly in the economic sphere...However, in a short time both Bush and Baker have demonstrated their political distinction. They are forceful — both the President and his Secretary of State. This should not be underestimated. It should be exploited...I can assure you: Bush personally can and wants to do business with you. And his close circle is also inclined towards doing business. One example is the Arab-Israeli conflict, and the change in the style of the White House in relation to the states involved in the conflict. You can, in terms of your orientation, begin to adjust yourselves to partnership with the United States.

For the Germans, Gorbachev's visit had direct and significant results. The ecstatic and sincere welcome which the Germans gave Gorbachev, the unusual nature and obvious message of the Joint Agreement signed in Bonn, which recognized the right of the Germans to self-determination, marked the beginning of the process of German unification.

Gorbachev told Kohl that the Americans, the French, the Belgians and the Italians, but most significantly the East Germans, already understood the importance of Soviet-West German relations, and that it was West Germany which would be the USSR's main partner in the building of a new Europe. The obvious conclusion for the East Germans was that the Soviet Union would no longer constitute an obstacle to reunification.

In autumn 1989, events unfolded in the communist countries of Europe which swiftly brought about a fundamental change on the entire European scene, but which, at the same time, threatened to undermine all that had been achieved toward ending the Cold War. It was precisely then, following the collapse of the communist regimes in Hungary and Poland, that the Berlin Wall was toppled, and Honecker and Zhivkov fell from power. Developments in East Germany showed clearly that the process which had been unleashed would bring to an end not only an entire stage in the history of socialism, as we tended to think at the time, but also to "Yalta" and the Stalinist legacy in Europe, and would lead to a reassessment of the consequences of Nazi Germany's defeat.

The situation was coming to a head. Intensive exchanges took place between Gorbachev and the leaders of many of the Western states. Intuitively, Gorbachev felt that the unification of Germany was inevitable. He had abandoned ideological concerns about the disappearance of the socialist spearhead in Central Europe. Judging by his discussions with the SED General Secretary Egon Krenz, and by diplomatic statements, he was still counting on the emergence of a transitional period in East Germany which would facilitate the introduction of perestroika after Honecker's dismissal. Even Kohl had seemed to share these views. Gorbachev's main fear was that the tide of reunification would sweep away the achievements of the pan-European process, and would lead to bloodshed. Therefore, he insisted that Kohl not give in to emotions, use reunification as an election issue or take any steps which might lead to a breakdown of the process.

This is well reflected in the conversation that took place between Gorbachev and Kohl on 11 November 1989:

> Gorbachev: All shifts entail instability. Therefore, when I speak of preserving stability, I mean that we, from all perspectives, must carefully calculate our steps in regard to one another...It seems, Mr. Chancellor, that at the present time an historic transition towards other relations and another world is occurring. And we must not, through our own clumsiness, allow this shift to be endangered — let alone prod developments towards an unanticipated path, towards chaos, by rushing them. This would be undesirable from all points of view...And I hope you will use your authority and political weight and influence to ensure that all the others act within bounds appropriate to the time and its demands.

> Kohl: Mr. General Secretary, a session of the FRG government has just ended. If you had been present, you might have been surprised at how our assessments coincide. This historic hour demands appropriate responses, historic decisions. In German, there is a very important concept of "judging by one's eye". It means having a sense of proportion, the ability, in planning actions, to allow for their possible consequences,

and possessing a sense of personal responsibility. I would like to assure you that I am acutely aware of our responsibility...I consider it a great success that relations between the USSR and the FRG have reached the high level where they stand at present. And I particularly value the good personal contacts which have developed between us. In my view, our relations have transcended a strictly official level...I expect that they will continue to develop in the future. I am prepared for this to happen. I understand that personal relationships do not alter the essence of problems, but they can ease their resolution.

Gorbachev: I think that the solidity, which is characteristic of the Germans in both countries, will aid in decisively resolving all questions which arise and in dealing with the long-term processes and changes.

West Germany's allies in NATO objected to the rapid reunification of Germany. This was apparent from Gorbachev's various meetings with Western leaders. Their position was presented by George Bush, as recorded in the following excerpts from his talks with Gorbachev on 2 December 1989 in Malta.

Bush: Kohl knows that several Western allies who publicly support reunification — providing that is what the German people want — are worried about the prospect.

Gorbachev: Yes, I know. And this point of view was explained to the Chancellor. But contrary to your allies and to you, I say openly: there are two German states, that is what history has willed. So let history deal with how the process develops and what it brings in the context of a new Europe and new world. Kohl has repeatedly asserted that he recognizes his responsibility, and that he will observe the agreements that we reached in Bonn. In sum, this is the issue to which we must pay utmost attention in order to avoid a setback in the changes which are now underway.

Bush: Agreed. We will not undertake any premature actions, or attempts to hasten a solution of the reunification question...However strange it may seem, on this question you, Mr. Gorbachev, are in the same boat as our NATO allies. The most conservative of them welcome your approach. And at the same time, they are forced to think about a stage, when the concept of the FRG and GDR will become history. I will act cautiously on this question. And our Democrats can go ahead and accuse me of being timid. I have no intention of jumping over the Wall, because too much is at stake on this issue.

Gorbachev: Yes, jumping over walls is not a good occupation for a President (laughter).

Bush: If Bush and Gorbachev can be satisfied with the changes in progress, it will be a good thing. But I will not be tempted into taking actions which look appealing but which might have dangerous consequences.

It should be pointed out that the identification of Gorbachev's position with that of West Germany's European allies in NATO was inappropriate. The allies apparently wanted to use Gorbachev to delay the process of unification. Their assumption was that the USSR had a great interest — both practical and ideological — in such a delay. However, they underestimated Gorbachev's pragmatism. He realized that resistance to the inevitable, particularly violent resistance, was bound to cause that very chaos which he wished to prevent.

In January 1990, Gorbachev held a closed discussion on the German question in his office at the Central Committee. He summoned his aide Georgii Shakhnazarov, Yakovlev and myself. Upon arriving, we found Ryzhkov, Shevardnadze, KGB chief Vladimir Kryuchkov, Chief of Staff Sergei Akhromeev, and Falin and his deputy Rafael Fedorov. The discussion, at times acrimonious, lasted four hours.

I spoke first and urged that we firmly orient ourselves towards the Federal Republic, since we no longer had political leverage in East Germany. To put it more bluntly, we had to seek a "mutual understanding" with Kohl and not with the SED. I opposed the invitation of Prime Minister Hans Modrow to Moscow, and even more firmly rejected the idea of Gorbachev meeting with SED Party Chairman Gregor Gysi. On the latter point, no one supported me.

Falin and Fedorov remained fervently committed to the SED. They were supported by Yakovlev and Shakhnazarov. To everyone's surprise, Fedorov, an expert on Germany, argued that "in West Germany no one was interested in reunification". Shevardnadze supported me, as did Ryzhkov, although with the proviso that "not everything should be given away to Kohl". Kryuchkov was ready to join whichever side prevailed, noting by the way that the SED "as such" no longer existed and that the state structure of the GDR was falling apart.

But there was unanimous support for my proposal to take the initiative in forming a group of "the Six": the four victors in World War II (the USSR, USA, England, France) and the two Germanies (the FRG and GDR) for discussing problems connected with the process of reunification.

It was finally agreed, as summed up by Gorbachev, that we would promote the formation of a Group of Six. Our orientation would be towards West Germany, but the SED would not be ignored altogether. Modrow and Gysi would be invited for an official visit. There would be closer coordination with London and Paris, perhaps facilitated by Gorbachev making a short trip to both capitals. Lastly, Akhromeev would prepare a troop withdrawal from the GDR, despite the fact that this would create a domestic problem of housing some 100,000 officers with their families.

On 11 February, a dramatic telephone conversation occurred between Kohl and Gorbachev in which they acknowledged the fact that Gorbachev had taken yet another giant step on the road towards the peaceful unification of Germany.

> Gorbachev: On the point of departure there is an agreement that the Germans should make their own choice. And they should be made aware that this is our position.
>
> Kohl: You mean to say that the question of unity is for the Germans themselves to decide?
>
> Gorbachev: Yes...Given the present situation.

But the concept, on which they apparently agreed, and which presumed the inevitability of German reunification, was not so easy to implement. At the beginning of May, when Shevardnadze was expected to attend the first "four-plus-two" meeting (as the Group of Six came to be called), a heated discussion took place in the Politburo. Gorbachev made a statement strongly opposing the entry of a united Germany into NATO. He would let the talks in Vienna and START treaty negotiations break down rather than allow it. A more moderate memorandum was presented by Shevardnadze, Yakovlev, Kryuchkov and Defence Minister Dmitrii Yazov. But at the meeting, aside from Shevardnadze, the others kept quiet. And they did not consult me.

On the morning of the next day, I wrote Gorbachev a memorandum in which I protested that members of the Politburo were discussing whatever issues they pleased and making decisions on them, despite the fact that they were not specialists and did not possess all the facts. As a result, a new position on the German question was taking shape, influenced by ultra-conservative Politburo member Egor Ligachev and his warnings that "NATO [was] approaching the borders of the [Soviet] Union!" This argument was reminiscent of those used in 1945. It was obvious that Germany would join NATO in any case and once again we would "miss the boat". Instead of concretely and firmly establishing the terms for our compliance, we clearly chose the path of failure. The results were indeed in keeping with this decision.

From the encoded telegrams of Shevardnadze and from the reports he made upon returning from the "four-plus-two" meeting, it became clear that we had lost out because the Politburo had refused to ratify the agreement. Kohl and Baker declared the meeting to be "historic", and announced that obstacles to unification no longer existed. The press wrongly depicted Shevardnadze's position as sabotaging the European process and the reunification of Germany.

Gorbachev tried to recoup his losses during his visit to Washington at the end of May 1990. The German question was discussed repeatedly and not without considerable stridence. Gorbachev insisted that Germany enter simultaneously into NATO and the Warsaw Pact. Bush did not bother to hide the fact that a fundamental difference of opinion existed between the two sides. A compromise formula was finally devised in the following fashion:

> Gorbachev: So, let's formulate it this way: The United States and the Soviet Union are in favour of a unified Germany, of achieving a final settlement which takes into account the outcome of the Second World War and of [Germany] deciding for itself which alliance it will join.

> Bush: I would propose a slightly different version: The USA unequivocally favours the membership of a united Germany in NATO, however, if she chooses otherwise, we will respect and not dispute it.

> Gorbachev: Agreed. I accept your formulation.

Helmut Kohl arrived in Moscow in July 1990, in order to finalize the agenda for the reunification of Germany. He was articulate and energetic, playing a fair but tough match. He was prepared to make major concessions, but in the end achieved his main objective — a unified Germany with membership in NATO. Gorbachev did not even object this time — nor did he propose diluted variants regarding NATO. These were the very "realities" which he almost always took into consideration in foreign affairs.

Here is how he characterized his resolve regarding the German question a month after Helsinki, in a highly confidential discussion with Bush:

> You will probably agree that events in Eastern Europe, and mainly German affairs, were much more difficult for us than for the USA. I will tell you openly that colossal efforts, enormous pressure, and political will were called upon, in order to overcome, in spite of ourselves, outdated approaches which appeared unshakeable, and to keep up with the demands of changing realities. To this day, I am forced to clarify this position in our country, to prove the need for new thinking, for new approaches to what is happening in the world, and to justify these steps. This is not always easy, all the more since there are people in the West, who make analyses based on the old thinking, and this complicates my position.

Kohl handed over to Gorbachev a draft (subsequently accepted in full), which, in his words, was intended to seal the past and open a period of *rapprochement* and friendship between the two peoples. Kohl asked Gorbachev to wait before involving the Foreign Ministry, and to let Teltschik and myself continue working on the text. We were less concerned with secrecy, however, and I broke my silence, confiding in Shevardnadze and Ambassador Kvintsinskii, but only in them.

In order to reinforce what had been achieved, Mikhail Sergeevich brought his friend Helmut (henceforth they were on a first name basis) to his native region — Stavropol. They secluded themselves in Arkhyz — a small pastoral resort for VIPs. There they spent almost the entire night at dinner and further negotiations. The discussion covered the nature of the future friendship agreement, partnership and cooperation, the temporary presence of Soviet troops, transitional measures, and the final settlement. The agreements, which were finally signed on 9–10 November 1990 during Gorbachev's visit to an already united Germany, laid the legal, political and moral foundations for normal relations between the German and the Soviet peoples.

# 15

# On The Road To German Reunification: The View From Moscow

## VYACHESLAV DASHICHEV

From the end of World War II, the German question became a cornerstone in the expansionist policy of the Stalinist regime. This policy led to the creation of a postwar status quo based on Soviet domination of Central and Eastern Europe and the division of Germany and the Continent. The blockade of Berlin, the Berlin Wall, the treaties of the Warsaw Pact countries with the Federal Republic between 1970 and 1973 and even the signing of the 1975 Helsinki Act by Brezhnev were congruent with this Stalinist and later neo-Stalinist line pursued by Krushchev, Brezhnev, Andropov and Chernenko. This policy was motivated throughout by socialist messianism mingled with superpower arrogance, and imposed by repressive, totalitarian regimes which prevented any substantive debate.

When Gorbachev rose to power, he adhered to this dogmatic stance. In his book *Perestroika*, published in 1987, Gorbachev restated that in the wake of World War II:

> ...the European states, in accordance with the concrete conditions and opportunities, made their choice: Some of them remained capitalist while others moved toward socialism. A truly European policy and a truly European process can only be promoted on the basis of recognition of and respect for that reality.[1]

The policy towards Germany remained intact.

> There are two German states with different social and political systems. Each of them has values of its own. Both of them have drawn lessons from history and each of them can contribute to the affairs of Europe and the world. And what will be in a hundred years is for history to decide. For the time being, one should proceed from the existing realities and not engage in incendiary speculations.[2]

This was also the prevailing view in the Central Committee *apparat* and in the Foreign and Defence Ministries. For most of the party functionaries and diplomats, who were blinded by ideological prejudices and isolated from reality, the status quo appeared to be the best guarantee for Soviet security interests and for stability in Europe. They believed that the United States, France and England had basically come to terms with the situation on the Continent and would not be willing to accept a change in the German question.

The expansion of the Soviet sphere of influence to East and Central Europe engendered a powerful anti-Soviet coalition of all Western powers and their allies, and hurled the Soviet Union with its limited resources into a dangerous confrontation with the entire West. This clash led to excessive militarization of the country and to the debilitation of its economy. It strengthened the totalitarian regime and prevented any fundamental reform of the political and economic system. In short, it sentenced the Soviet Union to isolation from the Western community and to political, economic and intellectual backwardness.

When Eduard Shevardnadze became Foreign Minister, he demanded and promoted close cooperation between academics and diplomats in order to stimulate "new thinking" in the foreign policy apparatus, where it had been stifled under Gromyko. It was extremely difficult to convince the dedicated guardians of the postwar order that the expansionist foreign policy of Stalin and his successors was ruinous for the nation's interests and welfare and that it held great dangers for peace. "But it was useless to point out," as Shevardnadze later wrote in his memoirs, "that even though we had lived 45 years without a war, a war was actually going on — precisely because of the order established in Europe after 1945."[3]

Change hinged on removal of the political and ideological causes of the East-West confrontation. The increasing indications of crisis in the economic and political spheres in Eastern Europe from 1986 until 1988 convinced me that these countries were on the verge of great political upheavals which could fundamentally alter the entire postwar structure of Europe. The situation was particularly dangerous in the German Democratic Republic, because of its strategic position adjacent to the NATO countries.

Therefore, when the Foreign Ministry's Academic Consultative Council, which I headed, was due to meet in June 1987, I placed a discussion of the German question on the agenda. I was unaware at the time that by 1986 Shevardnadze had already understood that it would become the crucial issue for Russia's relations with the West. However, he found it impossible to even broach the subject. When I raised the German question in the International Department of the Central Committee, I was told bluntly that it had been settled and that there was nothing to discuss. Nevertheless, I decided to start spreading my ideas. I wrote a 26-page analysis entitled "Some Aspects of the German Problem" and presented it to the members of the Academic Consultative Council as well as leading officials in the Foreign Ministry and the International Department of the Central Committee. As a result, the June Council meeting was postponed several times and took place only on 27 November 1987.

In the course of the Council's deliberations, I challenged the prevailing assumption that the postwar order in Europe, based on military parity and nuclear deterrence, would remain stable and reliable in the long run. I warned that the trend toward national self-determination and toward national unification had been increasing markedly not only in West Germany but also in the German Democratic Republic (GDR). As a consequence of the systemic crisis in the countries of East and Central Europe as well as in the Soviet Union,

> ...the model of socialism as established and developed in the GDR, has been unable to prove its advantages to the common people in the two German states. For most of them, the interests of socialism are taking a backseat to national interests. This erosion of socialist values will continue...

I argued that the continued existence of two German states was very negative for the Soviet Union. It was bound to further consolidate Western Europe as a nucleus of power in which the Federal Republic would be able to play a leading political and economic role, and would lead to a West European military alliance based on the *Bundeswehr* and Anglo-French nuclear forces. From the economic and technological point of view, it would widen the gap between the Federal Republic and the GDR. Finally, it was likely to inflame national feeling in the Federal Republic and the GDR and strengthen the efforts by citizens of both countries to find a solution to the German question.

Consequently, the Soviet Union would have to face numerous complicated problems. It would have to counteract the attraction presented by the Federal Republic to the population of the GDR, diminish the destabilizing impact of the German question in Europe, and determine the limits to *rapprochement* and cooperation between the two German states. Just as complicated were the repercussions of the reduction of US troops in Europe on the emergence of Germany as the leading West European power. Thus, the German question would continue to threaten peace and stability in Europe.

The time had come, therefore, to consider and discuss the option of reunification. If this option should prove to be inevitable, Moscow should at least take the initiative while it was still able, without waiting until the course of events forced it to act.

Under the circumstances prevailing at that time, the only

conceivable and acceptable basis for German reunification seemed to be the neutrality of Germany. But it turned out that even Stalin's 1952 concept of a neutral Germany was entirely rejected. Distinguished diplomats and other senior officials at the Council meeting, with the single exception of Iurii Davydov from the USA and Canada Institute, criticized me sharply and rejected my ideas and recommendations. I was even accused of political transgressions. Such was the atmosphere in the Foreign Ministry at that time, decisively influenced by figures like Politburo member Egor Ligachev and International Department head Valentin Falin. Gorbachev, too, remained mired in traditional stereotypes of foreign policy thinking on the German question. In fact, there was little change in Soviet policy on the issue of German reunification until 1990. The Soviet leadership was taken by complete surprise when the Berlin Wall was toppled on 9 November 1989. Two weeks later, Gorbachev still did not consider German reunification an urgent issue. His inaction was not, as some claimed, an effort to pacify the conservatives, but stemmed from his illusion that the GDR leadership under Egon Krenz, the new head of the Communist party, would be able to carry out the political and economic reforms needed to save the socialist GDR.

The subsequent radical change in policy towards Germany was forced upon the Soviet leadership primarily by the course of events and by the broad mass movement for national self-determination in the countries of East and Central Europe. A second contributing factor was the fresh approach which Shevardnadze introduced into Soviet foreign policy on key questions, such as the relationship of the Soviet Union with the countries of East and Central Europe and with the West. The chief problem in this regard was the arduous and long process of abandoning the heritage of Stalinist foreign policy, as reflected in the Brezhnev Doctrine, and recognizing the right of national self-determination. It was important at that point to convince the political leadership of the damage being inflicted on our national interests. On 18 May 1988, an edited version of my article entitled "East-West: In Search of New Relationships", was published in *Literaturnaia gazeta*. This was the first sharp public criticism of our previous foreign policy. While explaining the erroneous principles upon which our German policy had been based, I blamed Stalin and his successors for the global confrontation, the division of Europe and the Cold War.

One week later, the American Ambassador, Jack Matlock, invited me to his residence and told me that he had sent my article to President Ronald Reagan and to Secretary of State George Schultz prior to their visit to Moscow. The Ambassador said that the American President had welcomed the ideas presented in my article, since they would help him reach a better understanding of the problems which needed to be solved at his summit meeting with Gorbachev. I was very pleased.

An article published in *Pravda* on 29 August 1988 soon dampened my enthusiasm. There, Falin, and the journalist Lev Bezymensky, presented an apologetic view of Stalinist policy in Europe from the end of World War II and a defence of the European postwar order. They contended that the United States and the other Western powers alone were responsible for the confrontation between East and West.[4]

On 8 June 1988, another collision occurred between those advocating the traditional approach and myself, this time over the issue of the Berlin Wall. In reply to a journalist's question at a press conference at our Embassy in Bonn, I declared that the Berlin Wall was a relic of the Cold War and would disappear in time under changed political and economic circumstances. On 10 June, *Neues Deutschland*, the East German Communist party daily, carried a piece about my statement which ended with the following words: "The dogs may bark but the caravan moves on." Later, I learned that this piece was written by Honecker himself.

On 19 April 1989, I presented our leadership with a memorandum advocating reunification, and also sent a copy to the International Department of the Central Committee. From the latter I received a written reply saying that such a proposal was neither in the interests of the Soviet Union nor of the West, and that my analysis of the situation was dubious.

My efforts to enlighten our Ambassador in East Berlin, Viacheslav Kochemasov, in the autumn of 1988 and in the spring of 1989, also proved futile. The staff of our Embassy there, however, was more attentive.

Nevertheless, despite the attempts by Falin, Ligachev and others to hinder them, Shevardnadze and Gorbachev were gradually succeeding in forging a realistic foreign policy, free of the dogmas and burdens of the Stalinist era. At the 19th Conference of the Communist party in June–July 1988, Gorbachev renounced the principle of paternalistic relations between the Soviet Union and the countries of East and Central Europe. Shortly afterwards, the Warsaw Pact countries accepted international law as the basis for their mutual relations. On 3 March 1989, Gorbachev consented to the introduction of a multi-party system in Hungary. Three months later, the Soviet leadership recognized the non-communist Polish government of Tadeusz Mazowiecki. Then, in a joint statement in Bonn on 13 June 1989, Gorbachev and Kohl proclaimed their commitment to the "self-determination of all peoples and states". Gorbachev followed this up with a speech to the

European Council in Strasbourg in July, proclaiming himself to be in favour of a "voluntary, democratic community of European peoples". In August, the Soviet Defence Council instructed Soviet troops in East and Central Europe not to intervene in domestic conflicts. One month later, the Soviet leadership did not react when the Austrian-Hungarian border was opened to East Germans seeking to escape to the West. On 9 October 1989, during mass demonstrations in the streets of Leipzig, Soviet troops were ordered to remain in their barracks.

On 26–27 October 1989, when the revolutionary processes in East and Central Europe were in full swing, the Council of Foreign Ministers of the Warsaw Pact confirmed the right "of all peoples to self-determination and free choice of its social, political and economic development without interference from outside". This was the death blow to the Brezhnev Doctrine.

On 9 November 1989, the Soviet leadership reluctantly accepted the destruction of the Berlin Wall, despite conservative demands "to deploy special strike and defence divisions on the frontiers in order to save the GDR and to prevent reunification".

Did this chain of decisions by Gorbachev and Shevardnadze reflect a premeditated withdrawal from the position of Soviet dominance in East and Central Europe? Had the new architects of Soviet foreign policy finally understood that the Soviet Union had become the policeman and oppressor of East and Central Europe and that this role was a senseless, unnecessary burden on their country? Or, had they realized that the position of dominance could not be maintained and that they had to yield to new exigencies and realities? The West Berlin commentator Peter Bender expressed one view when he stated, "Gorbachev did not give up anything that had not already been lost, ideologically, politically and economically..."[5] But neither did Brezhnev possess anything in East and Central Europe; nonetheless, he ordered tanks into Czechoslovakia in 1968 in an effort to nip reform there in the bud. Gorbachev could have reacted similarly, but he chose not to. Shevardnadze was of the opinion that the use of military force in the GDR could result in a third world war. This was a responsible, reasoned judgment. Moreover, the use of force in the GDR could have meant the end of perestroika, a return of neo-Stalinism, and the fall of Gorbachev. It is to Gorbachev and Shevardnadze's credit that they were well aware of the worst consequences of using force on German soil and chose to avoid it.

When, in October 1989, Gorbachev made his well-known comment in East Berlin that "life punishes latecomers", he was alluding not to the reunification of Germany but rather to Honecker's refusal to introduce reforms in the GDR. Moscow's faith that Krenz, and later his successor Hans Modrow, were capable of carrying out such reforms was misplaced. The GDR regime collapsed under the onslaught of the national movement of the German people.

Not until 10 January 1990 did Gorbachev openly state in a meeting with Modrow in Moscow that "in principle" the Soviet Union was not opposed to the unification of Germany. During his discussions with Chancellor Helmut Kohl on 10 February, Gorbachev took the decisive step toward recognizing the German people's right to self-determination, stating that it was up to the Germans to determine "in what kind of a state, within which time frame, at what speed, and under what conditions this unity can be realized".[6]

Gorbachev went on to state that reunification was predicated on ensuring the "security and interests of Germany's neighbours and of the other states in Europe and the world", as well as the inviolability of their borders. In this way, the domestic and international aspects of reunification became closely linked for the first time. Gorbachev and Shevardnadze had compelling reasons for stressing this connection. The Foreign Minister later wrote in his memoirs:

> The conviction that the existence of two German states was a reliable guarantee for the security of our country and the whole continent had become too deeply rooted in the minds of our people. They were convinced that an enormous price had been paid for it and that it would be inadmissible simply to forget it. The memories of the War and the victory were stronger than the new concepts of the limitation on security, and we could not help but take this conviction into account.[7]

Shevardnadze was not referring to the ordinary citizen, who had no objections to German unification, but to the political and military *nomenklatura* whose existence, power and privileges depended on the preservation of the old order. Gorbachev and Shevardnadze also had to face the Party apparatus, which intimidated the public by invoking images of an alleged enemy. In introducing their "new thinking" about Germany, Gorbachev and Shevardnadze had to take all these factors into account. This explains the often contradictory and inconsistent actions of Soviet diplomats. For example, the Soviet leadership unanimously rejected Chancellor Kohl's Ten-Point Plan of 29 November 1989, which foresaw the creation of confederate structures in Germany. At one point, the leadership demanded the neutralization of Germany, at another dual membership in both NATO and the Warsaw Pact for a united Germany. Subsequently, it proposed membership for the Federal Republic in NATO and associate status in NATO for the Eastern part, then German membership in the Alliance but not in its integrated military command — a status similar to that of France.

All of this not only demonstrated the absence of a clear Soviet policy toward Germany after 9 November 1989, but also the desire of the conservatives in the Party apparatus to delay, if not halt the process of German unification. There were even demands in the press that the "sovereign rights" and "social structures" of the GDR be maintained.[8]

The decisions made by NATO at a July meeting in London were conducive to the reduction of conservative influence on our policy toward Germany and to achieving a compromise solution on security questions related to that country. They indicated a change in the doctrine and strategy of the Alliance through the reduction of NATO forces and constituted a declaration that the Alliance no longer regarded the Soviet Union and the Warsaw Pact countries as enemies.

The stormy progress towards reunification threatened to derail all plans of the Soviet Union and the Western powers, and put their leaders under intense pressure. The "four-plus-two" negotiations were a direct outcome of this pressure. At the first meeting of the Six in Bonn on 5 May, Shevardnadze suggested separating the internal and external aspects of German reunification. However, the idea of preserving Four Power rights even after Germany was unified was both unrealistic and counterproductive. In June, Gorbachev met with Bush in Washington and the Soviet leader retracted this proposal.

Just as puzzling was the Soviet proposal made at the "four-plus-two" meeting in Berlin on 22 June, prescribing a five-year transition period for German reunification. The Russians suggested that the international obligations of both German states (such as membership in NATO and the Warsaw Pact, and Four Power rights) should remain in force after unification. The Western side rejected this proposition.

Again it seems that Shevardnadze was forced to adopt these tactics because of the pressure exerted by the conservatives, who protested strongly against the Western demand to integrate a unified Germany into NATO. High-ranking members of the Soviet military and political establishment could not accept this idea. They were capable of looking at the German reunification issue only from the perspective of the outdated theory and practice of European power politics. As a result, the problem of Germany's membership in NATO threatened to become the main obstacle on the road to German reunification.

In February 1990, I discarded the concept of German neutrality which I had presented in my talk at the Academic Consultative Council in November 1987. At the Foreign Policy Forum of the German Free Democratic party in early March 1990 in Hannover, I presented new terms which would take into account Soviet security interests and make Germany's membership in NATO acceptable to the Soviet government. The proposed conditions for a unified Germany to join

NATO were the following:

- The territory of the former GDR would remain outside the NATO area.
- The *Bundeswehr* would be drastically reduced.
- Nuclear weapons would be withdrawn from German territory and Germany would renounce the production and stockpiling of nuclear, biological and chemical (ABC) weapons.
- NATO strategy would be reassessed.

On 20 March, in a telephone interview from Moscow to the German daily *Die Welt*, I again insisted that "one cannot look at the security interests of the Soviet Union from the viewpoint of the 1950s and 1960s". I suggested that on our side, old stereotypes still existed, for example as far as the military and political status of a united Germany was concerned. Such ideas stemmed from the assumption that it was necessary to maintain the principle of the balance of power in Europe. While the principle of parity was essential during the period of confrontation and the Cold War, this balance of power no longer existed. The demand for a united Germany to remain outside NATO was, in essence a call to dissolve the Alliance. It was clear that NATO could not exist without the Federal Republic and that the Western powers were not prepared to break up NATO. Therefore, this demand was unrealistic.

A few days later the Foreign Ministry spokesman stated at a press conference that my views were unofficial and that the decision not to allow a united Germany into NATO was final.

US diplomacy in general, and Secretary of State Baker, in particular, contributed a great deal toward overcoming the stalemate over German membership in NATO. The Western powers presented the Soviet leadership with an extensive program of security guarantees. Noteworthy was Baker's 9-point plan, which fixed the borders of a united Germany, restricted Germany's production and stockpiling of chemical weapons, proposed that NATO reassess its force size and prohibited NATO expansion into the territory of the GDR. The plan further called for German economic assistance to Moscow.

After the introduction of monetary union on 1 July, German reunification could no longer be delayed. Poland, Hungary and Czechoslovakia also came out in favour of German membership in NATO. The Soviet leadership was threatened with isolation and a *fait accompli*. Rather than continue its opposition, it was more in its interests to have a say in laying down the security status of a united Germany in treaties.

Gorbachev's political victory at the 28th Party Congress created uniquely favourable circumstances for accepting German entry into

NATO. The compromise reached by Kohl and Gorbachev at their meeting in Moscow and then in the Caucasus from 15–16 July, recognized the full sovereignty of a unified Germany in NATO. The *Bundeswehr* would be reduced by 42–45 per cent, and Soviet troops would withdraw from the former GDR within three to four years. Finally, it was agreed that no NATO facilities, foreign troops or nuclear weapons would be allowed on the territory of the former GDR.

The road to German reunification lay open. The results of the negotiations between Kohl and Gorbachev were approved by the other "four-plus-two" members on 17 July in Paris. On 12 September, at the last "four-plus-two" meeting in Moscow, the final settlement was signed by the six Foreign Ministers. The next day Shevardnadze and Genscher signed the Soviet-German Treaty on Good Neighbourliness, Partnership and Cooperation.

### NOTES

1. Mikhail Gorbachev, *Perestroika*, English edition (London, 1987), p. 193.
2. *Ibid.*
3. Eduard Shevardnadze, *The Future Belongs to Freedom* (New York, 1991) p. 234.
4. Valentin Falin and Lev Bezymenskii, "Kto razviazal kholodnuiu voinu?" *Pravda*, 28 Aug. 1988.
5. Peter Bender, "Im Osten ein Neues Zwischeneuropa", *Tagesspiegel*, 5 May 1991, p. 6.
6. *Pravda*, 2 Feb. 1990.
7. Shevardnadze, *op. cit.*, p. 234.
8. See, for example, *Komsomol'skaia pravda*, 10 May 1990: "Since we have proclaimed the principle of free choice, then we must be consistent to the end and grant the Germans the right to decide themselves about their domestic affairs. Why should we put ourselves in the position of being the guardians of the old order and thereby uselessly evoke unfriendly feelings by the Germans in both Germanies toward Soviet policy? In any case, Stalinism and its embodiment in the GDR regime has already lowered the reputation of the Soviet Union with the Germans. Would it not be better to start laying the foundations for relations with the future Germany on the principles of honest good-neighbourliness, by ceasing to depict it as an enemy, and by taking into account the enormous change in the Germans' psychology and their way of life since they learned the lessons from their national catastrophe of 1945, and turned toward democracy and peace?"

# Part Four

## CHANGING PERCEPTIONS
## OF RUSSIAN FOREIGN POLICY

# 16

# Politics and Morality in Soviet Foreign Policy

## ALEXANDER TCHOUBARIAN

The emergence of a new era in the development of the Russian state has created opportunities to carry out an extensive study of the genesis and consequences of Soviet foreign policy. In the past few years considerable resources have been invested in the re-examination of Soviet history. From the outset Soviet historians posed as unreserved apologists for their country's foreign policy, which they regarded as the only correct model. The trend has now shifted towards utter negation of even the positive elements of Soviet foreign policy. If we examine the entire Soviet experience as historians, not as political scientists, we should succeed in producing an unbiased analysis of Soviet foreign policy which might be beneficial.

The situation in Russia during this transition period is far from simple. Obviously, the immediate aim of historians at the Russian Academy of Sciences is to make a contribution to the country's development, in particular in the sphere of diplomacy. However, our efforts as historians must be geared more broadly to the entire academic and political community.

The present generation, which has not yet joined actively and wholeheartedly in reviewing the past, will gain relatively little from the research being carried out at present. It is the future generations that will profit the most. Russian historians must strive to create a conducive environment and to formulate a new theoretical framework. Examining the complex subject of politics and morality in international affairs is an essential component of this process.

Many historians in Russia and abroad are sceptical about the possibility of applying moral values to foreign policy, whose main goal is the promotion of national and state interests. On the other hand, a number of world forums and congresses have addressed the problems of international affairs and foreign policy from a moral and ethical point of view. This is primarily a result of the situation that has emerged in the late twentieth century, when we are faced, probably for the first time ever, with the problem of establishing a new world order. It is with great difficulty that Russians are transcending the ideology of hostility and confrontation. Yet, within the last year we have begun to speak about partnership, even alliance, with the United States and West European countries. But, what is the aim of such relations? In World War II, alliances were forged for the sake of the struggle against fascism. Today, however, alliances should reflect a higher purpose — namely, human values, which inevitably embrace ethical and moral principles.

How are moral principles manifested in the formulation of foreign policy? First, they are found in joint action taken to foster human rights, and the freedom and independence of individuals and nations; second, through the promotion of issues such as world peace and security and environmental protection. One might say that all this can hardly be relevant while the former USSR is being rent by sharp conflicts, and while similar conflicts are now raging in various parts of Europe, the Middle East, America and Asia. Historians, however, must be farsighted and attempt to discern not only present-day realities but also the main trends of the future.

Soviet historians were working in a stagnant environment, basing their research on postulates, dogmas and principles that were accepted in the USSR. Any analysis of Soviet foreign policy should take into account aspects of its past, such as over-ideologization, over-politicization, irreproachability and alleged superiority — all of which eroded the moral principles of that policy.

The whole process started back in 1917, when Soviet policy was being formulated. From its incipience, Lenin's concept of foreign policy did not include a moral perspective, for this policy was to be based on objective principles of class struggle and class interests. However, it should be stressed that just before 1921, especially in connection with the Genoa Conference, certain changes could be discerned in Soviet foreign policy, in particular, the attitude toward pacifism. In 1921–1922, the Soviet authorities publicly recognized pacifist circles in the West. As a result, a desire for cooperation in the economic and political sphere immediately became evident. However, in the 1920s and 1930s this trend was abandoned by Stalin in favour of totalitarianism, which denied pacifism and humanism.

The notorious Molotov-Ribbentrop Pact was probably a classic example of this violation of moral and ethical principles. The Pact was not only an illegal document, but an amoral one as well, since it ignored the interests and rights of other countries and peoples and provided for a division of the world into spheres of influence. It should be noted that on the eve of the Second World War, the prevailing mood among the Soviet Union's Western partners, primarily Britain and France, was similarly ruthless. Human values in general, and a perception of fascism as a threat to the whole of humanity were conspicuously absent from the thinking of all future members of the coalition. This was the reason behind their failure to unite prior to World War II.

An analysis of the postwar realities and of Soviet policy in particular, shows that even after the defeat of fascism (following a brief period of cooperation and accord), the USSR reverted to a confrontational model in its foreign policy. This policy was likewise adopted by the US and its Western partners. Ethics and morality were totally absent in the making of foreign policy and conflict took the most acute forms. Had anyone in the Soviet Union dared to assert then that moral and ethical behaviour could be dictated by politicians, he would have been not only mocked and denounced by the public, but severely punished.

In the 1980s, new patterns of thought emerged in the Soviet Union. The World Congress of Historians, held in Budapest in 1980, precipitated the first study groups on the idea of peace in the history of the USSR, and these began examining the subjects of pacifism and humanism. A volume entitled *An Anthology of Peace*, prepared in cooperation with an American team, focused on the moral and ethical pacifist tradition in history — including the Russian pacifist heritage which, until then, had been studied little by Western historians.

Such studies in the context of the history of the twentieth century are of immense importance for present and future generations. Hopefully, they will arouse the interest of young people in the concepts of pacifism and humanism, as well as in those individuals who sacrificed their lives for their beliefs, and in those who were bold enough to take to the streets in order to uphold common human interests.

Russia is now undergoing a transformation in which the national idea is filling the vacuum formed due to the collapse of communism. National awareness and national development represent, in principle, progressive forces — especially in the period of transition from totalitarianism to democracy. However, the national idea should also cherish individualism, democracy and universalism.

There were two major attempts in the twentieth century at setting up institutions based on universal principles: the League of Nations, which eventually proved a failure, and the United Nations. In the future, the United Nations is likely to pursue a pragmatic policy of promoting human rights on a worldwide scale. One of the major achievements and assets of Russia in the past few years is that it has become a part of that global process; it is learning to think in terms of those traditions in history which further human and civil rights, independence and freedom. These are the principles that should prevail in foreign policy.

In this context, it is of immense importance today to reveal the essence of national and state interests. Assuming that foreign policy is geared towards advancing state interests and ensuring the country's security, we must introduce significant changes in our approach to these issues. One country's national interests should not be realized at the expense of others. Ideally, national interests should correspond to the interests of humanity. Then foreign policy would be moral, humane and ethically just. Historians must trace humanism back to its origins in world history and examine its evolution, as well as its manifestations, in the twentieth century.

Morality in foreign policy is only part of the greater issue of morality in history. In the past, this subject was totally ignored in Soviet historiography, having been regarded as a deviation from the Marxist-Leninist concept of history. It is not very popular in Western historiography, either. Studies of ethical and moral aspects of history make it possible to extend the scope of historical research and to bridge the gap between science and politics. While touching on those subjects, the historian examines, as it were, his own moral position and feels more keenly his responsibility to society and humanity.

# 17

# International Affairs at the End of the Cold War

## Igor Lebedev

The radically new situation in world affairs resulting from the break-up of the USSR and the emergence of the Commonwealth of Independent States, calls for a thorough examination of the responsibilities inherited by the "new Russia". The course of history is irreversible. But the question remains: Will Russia assume the role of successor?

In the legal sphere, the Russian Federation has expressed its willingness to fulfill commitments undertaken by the USSR in the most important of 16,000 treaties it concluded. It has reconfirmed its readiness to ratify and implement all agreements on arms control, especially those relating to strategic weapons cuts and the reduction of troops and weapons in Europe, as well as other agreements, including those passed in the UN, on global and pan-European issues. A few of the less important agreements will probably be declared invalid, should they prove inapplicable under current circumstances.

With regard to Russia's historical legacy, the issues are far more complex. Despite the plurality of views on current developments, the dynamics and inner logic of events remain unchanged. Even today we find ourselves hostages of the past. Rarely do we experience sudden breaks in historical continuity or can we claim that a particular epoch belongs to the past. Yet, it seems that we are now witnessing just such an historic opening, when the end of the Cold War between the two Great Powers offers an opportunity to inaugurate a new era of partnership.

It has been said that history is the most doctrinaire and politicized scholarly field in Russia. This has broad implications for diplomacy, since current policy is being formulated largely on the basis of past experience. It also affects the question of Russia's historical accountability. The appearance of a Russian state which, on the one hand, has emerged quite recently and, on the other, has age-long experience in foreign policy activity to rely upon, presents other states with two alternatives: to accept Russia unconditionally into the community of nations as an ally, or to put obstacles in the way of its attempts to join this community by holding Russia responsible for mistakes made by the Soviet regime.

Fortunately, the former approach seems to predominate. For instance, when George Bush received Boris Yeltsin during his first visit to the United States as Head of State, the American President emphasized that the two leaders were meeting as friends, not foes. According to Bush, that historic encounter was further proof that the Cold War had ended and a new era had begun. President Yeltsin's reply was in the same vein: "From this moment on we shall no longer regard each other as potential enemies, as it was previously in our military doctrine."[1] Russians are impressed by the fact that American scholars have compared Yeltsin's visit to the United States and his meetings with world leaders to the Yalta and Potsdam conferences. Such assessments constitute a major departure from the Cold War mentality.

The onset of the Cold War, shortly after the end of World War II, redefined relations between the former members of the Grand Alliance. The Cold War was a complicated global phenomenon which permeated virtually all aspects of international affairs, including the military and political spheres, bilateral relations, and international trade and economic policy. It was also manifest in manoeuvres and conflicts on regional issues — not only in Europe and the Far East but also in the Middle East, Africa, the Caribbean and South Asia.

It is difficult to say what the key factor in that confrontation was: adherence to ideological principles, or the pursuit by both sides of great power politics and the use of pressure tactics to gain influence. What is clear is that together, these two factors generated a policy of brinkmanship.

An objective, in-depth study by diplomats and scholars of the origins and conduct of the Cold War, would be of immense importance in filling in some of the "blank pages" of history, and drawing conclusions for the future. Knowledge and comprehension of history are a substantial guarantee for avoiding miscalculations and mistakes in our current efforts to improve the international climate.

Following is a brief look at Russia's current stand on problems emanating from its confrontation with the United States from the second half of the 1940s to 1980. The two main features of the Cold War era, the subordination of international relations to ideology and imposition of policies from a position of strength, have been rejected. Russia's leaders have attempted to alleviate mutual distrust by renouncing the use of psychological warfare, as well as Russian involvement in the arms race and ideologically-based conflicts. International relations, grounded in sober economic policies and common sense, are naturally more stable than a balance of fear and suspicion. The more farsighted experts have long been aware of this. American political analyst Theodore Sorensen declared back in 1990 that "the touchstone of our nation's security concept — the containment of Soviet military and ideological power — is gone".[2]

The direct threat of a global nuclear conflict has passed. New realities are now being created in international politics and the current disposition of Russian-American relations is the moving force behind these changes. The continued improvement of relations will, no doubt, contribute positively to resolving major international issues.

It is extremely significant that the United States and the entire world community now recognize the special responsibility vested in Russia by virtue of its status as a nuclear power. There is a real opportunity to radically cut strategic offensive and tactical nuclear weapons and resolutely pursue a policy of halting nuclear tests and eventually stopping them altogether. The short-term goal of Russian diplomacy is to achieve radical cuts in nuclear weapons, put an end to the arms race and find a way to achieve minimal nuclear sufficiency; the ultimate aim is liquidation of nuclear arsenals and the creation of a modern security system.

In the post-Cold War era guiding principles for Russian-American relations have been established. They include:
- refusal to regard one another as potential enemies, transition to a system of relations based on friendship and partnership, mutual trust, respect and commitment to the principles of democracy and economic freedom;
- an end to the arms race and reduction of strategic arsenals;
- active joint efforts to prevent the proliferation of weapons of mass destruction and related military technology;
- limitations on the proliferation of state-of-the-art conventional weapons systems;
- establishment of a new system of international relations, based on rejection of aggression and political diktat, peaceful settlement of regional conflicts, an enhanced role for the UN and peaceful changes in the world;
- prevention of relapses into confrontation and force on the international scene;
- a readiness to strive for the promotion of common values and ideals of democracy, the supremacy of law, morals, respect for human rights, including the rights of national minorities;
- expansion of Russian-American bilateral relations, cultural contacts,

exchanges with state and public organizations, promotion of tourism;
– promotion of free trade and investment, and economic, scientific and technical cooperation between the two countries;
– pursuit of a joint struggle against terrorism and drug trafficking, and in support of trade and environmental protection measures.

Both sides welcome the end of the Cold War and share responsibility for formulating a new approach to the framework of cooperation, and even alliance, that will accord with the spirit of the times. It is widely believed in Russia that in the near future the traditional concept of "alliance" will have to be reassessed. Until recently, alliances were established by countries exclusively to contain other countries. They divided regions rather than united them. This phenomenon reached its peak during the Cold War era. A new approach to forming alliances is required, which will be based on the alignment of countries in response to radically different but very real threats. Russia and the United States must cooperate for the sake of their common goals of reducing stockpiles of nuclear arms, banning and eventually eliminating chemical weapons, and providing living conditions and an environment fit for human beings.

Both sides should liberate themselves from the mutual distrust which has affected their relations. A calculated, responsible and considerate approach will decisively and resolutely advance the cause of peace, while disregard for the "balance of interests" could lead to destabilization.

Currently, plans for material support to the Commonwealth of Independent States (CIS) are being drawn up by the world community. In order to avoid past mistakes, Russia needs to call upon historical precedent. Thus it is showing great interest in the experience of the Marshall Plan, introduced in 1947.

It should be pointed out, for example, that on the issue of historical responsibility, Russia has openly condemned past mistakes. Russia has reassessed the 1956 events in Hungary and the 1968 events in Czechoslovakia, which, it should be remembered, occurred in an atmosphere of confrontation between the two hostile blocs, when international relations were distorted by ideological considerations. It is now felt that the former members of the socialist bloc should not become its enemies. On the contrary, it is only natural that there be cooperation between them and the Russian Federation.

This process of reassessment has led to the declassification of documents. Crucial information about the 1968 events in Czechoslovakia, for example, may be found in *Vestnik* No. 24, 1991 (a publication of the Ministry of Foreign Affairs of the Russian Federation), which includes cable correspondence between Prague and Moscow during that period. Moreover, the Ministry of Foreign Affairs of the Russian Federation reached an agreement with the US Department of State, on releasing confidential correspondence between Nikita Khrushchev and John F. Kennedy between 22 October and 14 December 1962 during the Cuban Missile Crisis. The collection constitutes exceptionally valuable historical material for diplomats and researchers.[3]

A dispassionate approach to the legacy of Soviet foreign policy, which will assist in establishing Russia's identity and responsibilities, is essential for the stability of the entire world. To quote from a somewhat unexpected source — the article "To the Stalin Mausoleum", which was heavily criticized in Russia and published in the United States by an author using the pseudonym "Z": "Even though after seventy years the road to the putative 'radiant future' of mankind no longer leads through Moscow, the road to world peace still does."[4]

## NOTES

1. *Diplomaticheskii vestnik* 4–5 (1992), p. 13.
2. Theodore C. Sorensen, "Rethinking National Security", *Foreign Affairs* (Summer 1990), p. 1.
3. These documents were published jointly by the Foreign Ministry of the Russian Federation and the US Department of State in special May 1992 issues of *Mezhdunarodnaia zhizn'* and *Problems of Communism*.
4. Z., "To the Stalin Mausoleum", *Daedalus* (Dec. 1989), p. 296. The American historian Martin Malia later admitted authorship of the article.

# 18

# From Cold War To New World Order

## VIKTOR KUVALDIN

The end of the Cold War, like its genesis, cannot be pinpointed precisely in time. Rather, the transition was gradual, reflecting circumstantial changes in the international arena. Since it is generally agreed that the Cold War is now a thing of the past, the time has come to reflect on the nature of the conflict.

In the first place it is essential to establish the primacy of either politics or ideology as the motivating factor in the Cold War, for this determines our whole perception of it, including its periodization, its causes and results, and the forces driving its leading figures. Moreover, it enables us to understand the characteristics of the postwar world order. If the basis for the Cold War was entirely ideological, one might assume that it began in October 1917 and ended in August 1991, with the downfall of the communist regime. In fact, the ideological conflict created only the preconditions required for global confrontation between the two superpowers. The specific circumstances that brought about the confrontation itself arose in the early years following World War II and prevailed for the next four decades. Throughout this era, political considerations took precedence over ideological ones — although the two were often intertwined. The actions of both powers were motivated by real or imagined national interests, not by ideological differences, however deep these may have been.

The Cold War was a complex phenomenon which should be divided into several distinct phases. It can be classified as a war in the narrowest sense only when referring to the period from 1947 to 1962. At that time, there was a real possibility of deliberate escalation leading to a military clash. The Cuban Missile Crisis revealed the danger of pursuing this type of policy and led to a degree of caution which essentially removed the threat of global conflict from the agenda.

The well-known characterization of the years 1962–1985 as a

period of "neither war nor peace" is extremely fitting. A desire seems to have existed, not so much to expand, as to fortify existing spheres of influence. Both the United States and the Soviet Union sought to avoid direct confrontation. The antagonism between them was guided more by the course of events than by will. For example, the superpowers did not initiate, but rather were drawn into the two most dangerous military conflicts of that period — the wars in Vietnam and Afghanistan.

In the second half of the 1980s, the Cold War was gradually superseded in world politics by a new model of relations between the superpowers: the transition from enmity and confrontation to mutual understanding and cooperation.

It is highly significant that the Cold War ended a year and a half prior to the collapse of the Bolshevik system. Events during that period demonstrate that the USSR could have taken an active part in the establishment of the new world order, even without renouncing the primacy of socialism. The successful development of relations between China and the West during the 1970s and 1980s confirms that there is nothing preposterous about such a proposition.

The initiative for bringing about an end to the Cold War was taken by the Soviet Union. A sober assessment of both the domestic and international situation led the new Soviet leadership to seek normalization of relations with the West. Towards the middle of the 1980s the arms race had become an unbearable burden for the faltering Soviet economy. Gorbachev's radical reforms could only be carried out if drastic cuts were made in the military-industrial complex to which all economic activity was subordinate. No less important was the demilitarization of all public life: eliminating the "besieged fortress" mentality, renouncing force as the sole means of resolving conflicts, transforming both the army and KGB into normal state institutions, and channeling the nation's enormous creative potential into productive activity.

Domestic exigencies had become more acute because of the demands of foreign policy. Towards the middle of the 1980s it became clear that the Soviet Union could no longer claim superpower status. Its allies were primarily underdeveloped countries in the Third World whose interests were purely mercenary. The deadlocked war in Afghanistan had revealed the incompetence of the huge Soviet military machine. Moreover, the West had reached a level of technological superiority that the USSR could not feasibly attain. Thus, the idea of achieving strategic parity was totally unrealistic. This pointless and dangerous game had to be terminated with minimal losses to the USSR.

The shift in foreign policy was made possible by a revolution in the consciousness of certain elements of the Soviet élite. This fact has been underestimated by both Western and Soviet researchers, although studies carried out by Moscow's "think tanks" had detected a sense of discontent among the intelligentsia, high government officials, leading economists and even members of the party apparatus. Of course, none of these people went beyond the bounds of the system in seeking remedies for the chronic illnesses of socialist society, but they clearly understood that things could not continue as they were. The sphere of foreign policy presented a range of opportunities for bold reform, in particular because there the conservative opposition was weaker. The appointment in summer of 1985 of Eduard Shevardnadze to the post of Foreign Minister in place of the veteran diplomat Andrei Gromyko, reflected the desire to take a fresh look at the outside world.

Gorbachev's "new political thinking" was neither a tactical ploy, nor a means of camouflaging devious schemes. He might sooner be accused of a certain degree of naïvité, of not fully comprehending the harsh realities of international politics, or of underestimating the significance of national and state interests in global politics.

Impressing a new map of the world on the minds of a large segment of the Soviet political élite was just part of the fundamental process of reassessing communist dogma, which took place in the USSR towards the end of the 1980s. Even those who remained true to socialist ideals to the end tried to reinterpret them along Western lines.

The priority given to democratic principles in the official interpretation of socialism paved the way for the reintegration of the Soviet Union into Europe and brought about the irreversible collapse of the Manichaean world view. In contrast to the eras of *détente* under both Khrushchev and Brezhnev, the issue was now one of total revision of the fundamentals of foreign policy. Of course the process was far from simple or straightforward. Gorbachev's foreign policy met with very strong opposition from the party apparatus, the military-industrial complex, the army and conservatives. This opposition increased considerably in the late 1980s, when it became clear that the end of the Cold War would leave the Soviet Union markedly weaker and stripped of its superpower status.

The loss of Soviet supremacy in Eastern Europe substantially undermined Gorbachev's domestic policy. Among the population, especially the older generation, there was noticeably increased concern over a foreign threat. In addition, the memory of World War II with its enormous losses and sacrifices was an unfavourable background for the politics of the "new thinking".

Anti-communist revolutions in the so-called socialist countries of

Eastern and Central Europe served as a threatening *memento mori* for the Soviet *nomenklatura*. A considerable segment of the privileged élite lined up in open opposition to Gorbachev and began attacking his foreign policy. The Soviet President had to manoeuvre more skillfully than ever to fight off these conservatives and reactionaries.

The process of formulating a position on the Persian Gulf, between Iraq's annexation of Kuwait and the actual outbreak of war, provides substance for assessing the direction in which Soviet foreign policy evolved during the final period of the country's existence. Liberated from the Cold War legacy, the former superpower sought possibilities to create a more humane and just world order.

The annexation of Kuwait by Iraq came as a total surprise to Gorbachev, who immediately adopted a firm stance against the Iraqi invasion. This was not an easy decision. The Soviet Union was tied to Iraq by a Treaty of Friendship and Cooperation. Thousands of Soviet specialists, whose lives could have been in danger, were employed in Iraq. Substantial Soviet economic and political interests were at stake. In addition, the broader context of relations in the Middle East, and in the Arab world, where the Soviet Union had significant influence, had to be taken into consideration.

The task was not made any easier by domestic political concerns. It was during this period that the conservatives launched a counter-attack, in an effort to regain their lost status. A broad-based process of democratization opened the government to criticism from all sides. Six Muslim republics with a population totalling 60 million demanded that special attention be paid to the fate of Iraqi civilians.

Under these complex circumstances, the Soviet leadership pursued a policy aimed at restraining Iraq and re-establishing the independence and territorial integrity of Kuwait. Throughout, Gorbachev sought to resolve the conflict by diplomatic means, in an effort to avoid unnecessary victims and future complications. With these goals in mind, Moscow tried to influence the Iraqi regime using whatever connections were still intact. An agreement in principle on this course of action was achieved at a meeting between Gorbachev and Bush in Helsinki on 9 September 1990.

It appears that the United States, not fully trusting its former rival, did not keep the Soviet Union informed of its military plans. Confronted by unilateral action on the part of its new ally, the Gorbachev regime was forced to consider independent diplomatic steps which would allow it to defend the legitimate interests of the USSR in the Persian Gulf. However, these steps did not infringe on the USSR's agreements with the United States or violate the united front in the struggle against Saddam Hussein.

This conflict struck a harsh blow at Gorbachev's vision of the new, post-Cold War world order. The tireless efforts of the Soviet leader to achieve a peaceful solution did not succeed in preventing a massive use of force or heavy human losses. All the parties involved in the conflict were given an object-lesson in world politics: force remains the most decisive and intelligible argument. Mikhail Gorbachev, the "prophet" of the "new political thinking", was weakened as a direct result of the war.

The process of parting from the Cold War was no less difficult for the Americans than for the Russians — although it was less dramatic. A willingness in principle to renounce the ideology of global confrontation was evident at the Geneva and Reykjavik summits in 1985 and 1986. However, United States' foreign policy activity was complicated by the anti-communist beliefs of the President and his advisers and, moreover, was implemented with excessive caution during 1987–88, the final years of the progressively paralysed Reagan Administration.

Nor can it be said that the Administration of George Bush got off to a quick start in foreign policy, particularly in US-Soviet relations. The President's highly professional staff was in no hurry to redefine the American position in the face of new realities. The process of policy reformulation dragged on until the summer of 1989, and even longer in regard to the Soviet-American dialogue — until the Shevardnadze-Baker talks at the end of September.

In Malta, the two Presidents reached a mutual understanding on the major issues, which opened the way to peaceful transformation of the postwar order in Europe, liquidation of the East European communist regimes, unification of Germany and an intensification of the Helsinki process.

The dismantling of Cold War political structures has offered new opportunities, but has posed serious new problems, as well. The disintegration of the Soviet Union has created a political vacuum in many regions. The rapidly changing "rules of the game", have contributed to the atmosphere of uncertainty and instability. Numerous zones of strife have emerged in the centre of Eurasia and major international conflicts have already erupted (for example, in the Persian Gulf and Yugoslavia).

A political vacuum cannot exist for long. The end of the Cold War has generated an urgent need for the major powers to reassess their positions. This is all the more pressing in light of the destructive potential of modern weaponry. The Gulf War, which was the first international crisis in the post-Cold War era, forced the United States and Europe, the Muslim states, the Soviet Union, the countries of Asia and the UN, to take a stand in a changing world. The anti-Iraq coalition which was formed, and behind which lay a wide range of national interests, may to a great extent be viewed as an embryonic prototype for the new world order.

At present, the contours of this new order are still vague. We cannot even say for certain whether the system of relations will have single or multiple centres. Without question, the United States has emerged as an unrivalled superpower — unlikely to face any military challenge in the foreseeable future. On the other hand, doubts persist over America's ability to maintain its status as world leader. The country's economy is unstable, in particular as a result of huge military expenditures. America has also been drained by the exhausting super-power confrontation, and is in need of a respite to put its somewhat neglected house in order.

Of course, not everything is in the hands of the United States. It is difficult to determine the extent to which other leading powers such as Japan, Germany, Russia, China and India will tolerate American supremacy. It is doubtful that they will be satisfied with a subordinate role. In the long term they will probably aspire to having a voice in establishing the future of the vital Eurasian region. Perhaps these powers will join forces in order to strengthen their position *vis-à-vis* the USA.

In contrast to the United States, Russia must rebuild its foreign policy from the bottom up. While Russia is the recognized legal heir to the Soviet Union in the international arena, it is, in fact, a different state and is unable to follow the course set by Gorbachev. Russia faces a long and difficult period of domestic transformation, of defining the contours of national and state interests, and of searching for its place in the global constellation of power. At present, the only thing which can be stated with a reasonable degree of certainty is that in the foreseeable future its role will be significantly more modest than that of the USSR in its day, and that its sphere of interests will be limited to Eurasia. The fundamental priorities of Russian foreign policy will be determined by a harsh domestic struggle, whose outcome will depend largely on the new social forces which emerge.

# 19

# Moscow and the Gulf War: The Policies of a Collapsing Superpower

## CAROL R. SAIVETZ

The "new political thinking" of former President Mikhail Gorbachev revolutionized Soviet domestic politics and led to a reassessment of Moscow's role in the international political system. The obvious economic decline of the Soviet Union was probably the major factor in its decisions to sign arms control agreements, cut the cords with Eastern Europe, and end its costly involvement in regional conflicts. For both domestic and foreign observers, the "new thinking" and its policies signified the diminishing superpower status of the Soviet Union. Gorbachev's critics on the right argued that Moscow should remain committed to the old ways and retain an independent foreign policy; "new thinkers" on the left questioned whether being a superpower was worth the cost.

On 2 August 1990, Iraq invaded and occupied neighbouring Kuwait. Over the years, the USSR had enjoyed a long-standing political and military relationship with this Middle Eastern state. Moscow had helped to develop the Iraqi oil industry, had signed a Treaty of Friendship and Cooperation (1972) and sold an estimated $14 billion worth of arms to Baghdad. Nonetheless, in the context of the tremendous international changes then taking place, including the US-Soviet *rapprochement* and efforts to end regional conflicts, the attack on Kuwait became a test of both the "new political thinking" and the Kremlin's superpower status.

This chapter will explore Moscow's policies in the Gulf in light of the decline in the former USSR's power and status in world affairs. The first section will examine the policies pursued by Moscow as the crisis unfolded,[1] and the second will look at the debates surrounding the decline of the Soviet Union and moves to salvage its prestige and position after the war. The final section will analyze the impact of the war on Soviet and post-Soviet Middle East policies.

When a crisis which had been brewing for several months erupted on 2 August 1990 with the Iraqi invasion of Kuwait, US Secretary of State James Baker and Soviet Foreign Minister Eduard Shevardnadze were meeting in Irkutsk. The next day, Baker and Shevardnadze returned to Moscow, where they issued a joint statement condemning the invasion and demanding the withdrawal of Iraqi forces. Earlier, an official Soviet spokesman had called for the "urgent and unconditional withdrawal of Iraqi troops from Kuwaiti territory".[2] The Soviet Union also announced that it had suspended arms shipments to Baghdad.

Despite Moscow's condemnation of the invasion and support for US initiatives at the United Nations, Kremlin leaders were under pressure to act differently for two reasons. First, there was apparently heated debate within decision-making circles about whether voting for an international economic embargo against Iraq, and for the use of force to uphold this embargo, would jeopardize the lives of those Soviet civilian and military personnel still in Iraq. Second, voices were heard among the conservatives urging the USSR not to abandon its commitment to Iraq. Indeed, from the outset, Gorbachev indicated that Moscow would maintain ties with Saddam Hussein.

A month later, on 9 September, Gorbachev and President George Bush met in Helsinki to discuss events in Europe and the Gulf crisis. Despite growing cooperation between the two superpowers, differences in their approaches to the Gulf had surfaced by the time of the summit. Moscow had only reluctantly gone along with the UN Security Council Resolution authorizing the use of force to police the embargo on Iraq, and Gorbachev himself also seemed somewhat sympathetic to Baghdad's attempts to link the Kuwait crisis with Palestinian issues.[3] Nonetheless, in their joint statement, the two leaders reaffirmed their support for the resolutions of the Security Council and intimated that if those were not sufficient, then further action would be necessary. Yet, when pressed at a news conference about the use of force and Soviet participation in military action, Gorbachev reiterated his preference for a peaceful resolution to the conflict.[4]

The question of Soviet participation in the military coalition formed by President Bush, haunted Soviet politicians throughout the crisis. In a major address at the UN in late September 1990, Shevardnadze soundly condemned Iraq for violating international law and pointed out that the UN could "suppress acts of aggression". He called for the revitalization of the Security Council's Military Staff Committee to deal with the unfolding crisis and, most significantly, offered to contribute Soviet troops.[5] It should be noted that this was not the first call for the empowerment of the Military Staff Committee. In the later stages of the Iran-Iraq War, the USSR had also urged the Committee into action so as to replace the then growing US naval presence with international troops under a United Nations flag.[6]

Shevardnadze's comments elicited strong condemnation from several quarters within the Soviet Union. When the issue was debated in the Supreme Soviet, some delegates criticized the mere suggestion that the USSR should send troops abroad. Given the high Soviet casualty rate in Afghanistan, the reluctance to become involved in yet another Third World conflict was understandable.[7] Others argued against Soviet participation on wholly conservative grounds. They did not want to see Soviet troops arrayed against long-time ally Iraq.

As events in the Gulf developed, Soviet policy toward the crisis exhibited these conflicting pressures. Rhetorically, the Gorbachev regime continued to support the United Nations and the US effort to compel the eviction of Iraqi troops from Kuwait. This policy was conducted under the direction of the Foreign Ministry and those "new thinkers" who saw Iraq's attack on Kuwait as immoral. Simultaneously, Gorbachev seemed to respond to a group composed of the so-called Arabists and those who could be labelled neo-conservatives.

This second group was represented by Evgenii Primakov, an old Middle East hand and former director of both the Institute of Oriental Studies and the Institute of World Economics and International Relations. Primakov, paradoxically, was also a "new thinker" who had penned one of the early seminal pieces on new political thinking and foreign policy.[8] Moreover, he had vast experience in the Middle East and a long-standing personal relationship with Saddam Hussein. Primakov argued forcefully that the USSR should pursue an independent foreign policy. In a television interview he asserted, for example, that "the Soviet flag has been shown, and it is being perceived very positively. We are a superpower and we have our own line, our own policies, we are demonstrating this point."[9]

Unable to choose between these two approaches and policies, Gorbachev pursued both simultaneously. As noted above, while supporting the Security Council resolutions, the USSR kept communications with Baghdad open, thus providing Moscow with manoeuverability as the crisis dragged on. The Soviet Ambassador to the UN, Iulii Vorontsov, continued to work with the US and the Security Council, while at three different times, Primakov was dispatched to Baghdad to see if face-saving measures for Saddam Hussein could be devised and war could be averted.

Primakov traveled to Baghdad on 4–5 October, and again on 28–30 October. His ostensible assignment was to work out details for the evacuation of Soviet citizens stranded in Iraq because of the crisis; his main task was to try to convince Saddam to withdraw. In a series of articles in *Pravda*, Primakov described his negotiations.[10] During that first trip, Saddam tried to convince the Soviet envoy that Kuwait was an integral part of Iraq; but he also allegedly acknowledged that under certain circumstances withdrawal from Kuwait could be effected. According to Primakov, Saddam Hussein did agree to the repatriation of Soviet citizens, but at a relatively slow pace. During the second Baghdad trip, Saddam supposedly sought assurances that if he withdrew from Kuwait, US troops would be removed from the region. However, for all practical purposes, Primakov left Baghdad empty-handed.

By late November, Gorbachev was apparently convinced that Saddam could not be induced to leave Kuwait voluntarily, and the USSR — albeit reluctantly — voted for Security Council Resolution 678, authorizing the use of all necessary means to liberate the country. Soviet verbal support for the UN resolutions earned Moscow a $1 billion credit line from Kuwait, a $4 billion loan from Saudi Arabia, and a $175 million investment in a joint Soviet-Saudi bank located in Alma Ata. Nonetheless, Gorbachev, supported by the French, succeeded in persuading the Security Council to build a delay until 15 January into the resolution.

As war became inevitable, the diplomatic line pursued by Shevardnadze came under increasing criticism and he ultimately resigned in December 1990.[11] The critics included supporters of Saddam and radical proponents of the Arabist line, as well as those who were concerned about the significant US presence so close to Soviet borders. Finally, they were joined by observers who felt that Moscow was losing its ability to determine its policy independently. This conservative coalition was strengthened by domestic events. Gorbachev's shift to the right became apparent from October 1990 when he rejected Shatalin's "500 Day Plan" for the transition to a market economy, and was confirmed by the crackdowns in Lithuania and Latvia in January 1991. The resulting ascent of the military and the KGB virtually guaranteed that vociferous criticism of US policy and of Soviet support for that policy would be heard. Once the Gulf War began on 16/17 January, these denunciations reached a climax. The United States was accused of wanting to destroy Iraq and Saddam Hussein and of pushing the USSR to the sidelines. Moreover, the Soviet military wanted to protect the Iraqi military establishment that it had worked so hard to create. The Supreme Soviet, at the instigation of these conservative groups, passed resolutions urging Gorbachev to seek an end to the war as quickly as possible.

This set the stage for Primakov's third mediatory trip to Baghdad. Following a month of intensive coalition bombing designed to destroy Iraqi command and control facilities, the Soviet envoy was sent to Baghdad to devise a final plan to avoid the total destruction of Iraq. Soviet efforts resulted in a vaguely worded agreement according to which Iraq would withdraw from Kuwait in 21 days in return for the annulment of the other Security Council resolutions.[12] Even with several modifications, the plan was rejected by President Bush, and the ground offensive began on 24 February.

It is important to note why this last-ditch mediation effort was launched. In the first place, it represented a continuation of the Arabist line, that is, an attempt to save Iraq and Saddam Hussein. As a corollary, we can presume that there was tremendous pressure from the Soviet military to save the Iraqi military establishment and to avoid the humiliating defeat of a force armed with Soviet weaponry. Over the course of the war several articles appeared in both military and civilian publications questioning Western claims of superiority. Some even alleged that Soviet weapons would have performed better in Soviet — rather than Iraqi — hands. It was further argued that if Moscow's efforts had led to a negotiated cease-fire and Iraqi withdrawal, then Gorbachev might have been able to placate the Arabists and neo-conservatives and to pursue the "new political thinking" simultaneously.

As noted at the outset, the Gulf War came at a time of unprecedented international change. Additionally, glasnost at home facilitated the open and far reaching debate about Gulf policies and, of course, other foreign policies as well. In some respects, the debates may be summarized as public discussion about whether or not the USSR was to remain a superpower and, if so, the costs that this would entail.

Reluctantly, Soviet international affairs specialists concluded that superpower status depended upon economic and political power as well as on military might. Thus, the acknowledged economic failures of the Soviet Union and the image of the Soviet leadership lurching from one political crisis to another, all cast doubt on Moscow's international standing. In the words of Georgii Mirskii, an outspoken critic of Soviet policy in the Middle East:

> A nation's international standing depends to a tremendous extent on the state of its internal affairs, the authority and stability of the system that exists within it and the capacity of its leadership for achieving recognition of its domestic policy in the outside world. It is in this respect that our affairs are currently far from dazzling.[13]

"New thinkers", therefore, grappled with several interrelated questions. Given the Soviet Union's new domestic circumstances could Moscow afford to be a superpower? Was there a cheaper way to remain a superpower? Could the Kremlin retain its superpower status through new policies? At issue was not only the fact that Soviet citizens were immersed in their domestic problems, but also that the oscillations in Soviet domestic politics held definite repercussions for Middle East politics and foreign policy in general. In addition, there was the question of what the USSR could offer its clients. As a *New Times* correspondent wrote: "The role and weight of a state are determined by its economic and diplomatic achievements. The Soviet Union can be on a par with the United States only in arms transfers."[14] And, as several observers noted, military equipment which was routinely transferred to Middle East clients in the past, could in fact create a threat to the USSR itself.[15]

This line of thinking led Soviet commentators to conclude that the changed circumstances necessitated a new approach to Moscow's global role and the adoption of new tools with which to pursue the Kremlin's foreign policy objectives. No consensus, however, existed among the leadership on precisely those foreign policy objectives. Some analysts argued that the Soviet Union was torn between redefining its role in the world and following older doctrinaire policies.[16] A *New Times* columnist maintained that the Arabist/neo-conservative line represented a "misinterpreted vision of state interests".[17] And Aleksandr Bovin, the outspoken *Izvestiia* political observer, noted that future Middle East policies must be determined by Soviet interests — in particular, establishing relations with Israel and not giving in to the Arabs. This, however, did not exclude support for Palestinian statehood.[18]

Primakov's trip in February 1991 and Soviet proposals for postwar security arrangements in the Gulf, reflected both the signs of weakness and disarray noted above and the desire to seek an easier — and less costly — way to remain a force in the Gulf and the Middle East. The visit demonstrated a slightly differentiated foreign policy line and constituted, in many respects, a declaration of independence. In the words of Bovin: "The operation to rescue Iraq was meant to have one more political effect — to stress the autonomy and independence of the USSR's Near East policy..."[19] And in a longer analytical piece in *Moscow News*, Andrei Kortunov argued that Washington and Moscow have similar, but not identical interests in the Gulf region.[20]

In addition, Primakov's mission and the Soviet mediation effort were clearly designed to enhance Soviet prestige and perhaps guarantee the Soviet Union a future role in the region. If it had been successful, the USSR would have won accolades and worldwide gratitude. The Kremlin would have shown that it was a responsible and trustworthy member of the international community. Moreover, if those negotiations had led to regional security arrangements in which the Soviet Union played a role, then Moscow's stake in the Arab world would have been secured.

With the cessation of hostilities at the end of February, calls for new security arrangements became more pressing. Within hours of the cease-fire, Aleksandr Bessmertnykh, Shevardnadze's successor, held a news conference in which he outlined steps to ensure that hostilities were not renewed. These measures included: an urgent meeting of the Security Council; international discussions of a security system; the participation of Iraq in that security system; and a study of arms supplies to the region.[21] In a detailed statement following Baker's trip to Moscow on 16 March, Foreign Ministry Spokesman Vitalii Churkin outlined a six-point Soviet plan for peace in the region:

1. The states of the region should have the key role in defining the new structures; however, "the arrangements must promote the interaction of all countries connected to the region, as well as the interaction of states that do not directly belong to it but make an important contribution to sustaining peace and stability there".
2. There should be a limitation on the sale of arms to the region. Moreover, the area should be cleared of nuclear, biological and chemical weapons.
3. The presence of foreign troops should not exceed the levels reached on 1 August 1990.
4. Economic cooperation should be implemented so as to facilitate the reconstruction of the region.
5. The United Nations should guarantee compliance with any formal accords elaborated. To this end, the Security Council's Military Staff Committee should be reactivated.
6. Finally, the causes of regional instability, including the Arab-Israeli dispute, should be removed.[22]

A careful analysis of this scheme reveals several important points. First, the plan responded to the very genuine Soviet security concern about long-range missiles possibly targeted on the USSR, or about some future use of nuclear, chemical or biological weapons which could, at the least, contaminate regions of the Soviet Union. Second, the proposals were clearly responsive to Arab concerns. They implicitly recognized "linkage" between a settlement of the Gulf crisis and the Arab-Israeli dispute. Moreover, they prevented Iraq from becoming a pariah nation. Third, the plan sought to eliminate the massive US military build-up in the Gulf. Not only were all troop levels to be reduced, but activation of the Military Staff Committee might prevent future unilateral action by Washington. Last, as in

Bessmertnykh's earlier proposals, the plan was designed to guarantee the Soviet Union a major say in regional affairs.

Taken together, these proposals indicated that from the period prior to the attempted coup in August until the ultimate collapse of the Soviet Union in December 1991, Moscow was determined not to abandon its role in this geopolitically important region. In fact, if anything, the new rhetoric and policies were designed to maintain the Soviet Union's Middle East stature. The Kremlin's status would be enhanced by being the co-convenor of a Middle East peace conference and the revitalization of the Military Staff Committee would assure Moscow a regional role. Finally, the reduction of foreign troop levels would also eliminate one of the Arabists' and neo-conservatives' consistent criticisms of Moscow's past policies. Beyond the specifics of a settlement for the Gulf crisis or even some sort of long-term security arrangement, the USSR — until December — was apparently searching for a transformed regional role. As a Soviet television commentator noted:

> It is not just growth in our customary links with our traditional partners in the zone of the Middle East that is required. What is needed is a qualitatively new level of relations with the Gulf countries, that is, Saudi Arabia, Kuwait, Oman, Bahrain, and the UAE. Ties with Egypt, Syria, and other Arab states need to be substantially expanded...I want to give a special mention to the fact that in the light of this future work, the absence of diplomatic relations between our country and Israel is a legacy of the evil past...[23]

That Moscow saw its superpower status ensured by just such a policy may be seen in Aleksandr Bessmertnykh's trip to the Middle East in May 1991. The Foreign Minister traveled to Syria, Jordan, Israel and Egypt. The visit to Damascus was part of the continuing relationship with Syria while those to Amman and Cairo represented enhanced ties to moderate Arab states. The six hours in Israel highlighted the transformation in Soviet policy: Bessmertnykh was the highest ranking Soviet official ever to visit Israel.

The crisis precipitated by the failed hardline coup in Moscow in August 1991 is beyond the scope of this chapter; nonetheless, several preliminary points that relate to Soviet policy in the Gulf, and to the Middle East more generally, need to be made. It would seem fair to assume that military dissatisfaction with the conduct of Soviet foreign policy, which was manifested during the fall of 1990, increased, and may have been one of the factors contributing to the coup attempt. It has been reported that three of the conspirators in the coup feared that the USSR was becoming too dependent on the United States.[24]

In the autumn, movement toward a Middle East peace conference accelerated. The Madrid meetings were an outgrowth of the defeat of Iraq and the changed Middle East balances that resulted from the war, as well as of the continuing weakness of the Soviet Union in the aftermath of the attempted coup. Uncertainty over who was in charge in Moscow enhanced the US role as broker and probably also convinced the Syrians and the Palestinians to participate in the meetings. Moreover, the USSR re-established diplomatic relations with Israel as a quid pro quo for participation in the scheduled peace conference.[25]

The collapse of the Soviet Union and the creation of the Commonwealth of Independent States (CIS) raise a series of new questions about the participation of the CIS and/or individual successor states in the Middle East. What will be the policies of Russia and the Ukraine toward the Arab-Israeli conflict? Will the foreign policies of the Central Asian republics be Islamic in content? Will the Muslim successor states become significant actors in the Middle East?

Some of the most interesting questions revolve around the future role of the Muslim successor states. Geography alone would dictate that they become part of an enlarged Middle East state system. At issue is whether or not these new nations will follow the secular and pro-Western, Turkish model or the Iranian fundamentalist example. Saudi Arabia and Egypt, both US allies and fearful of Iranian influence in Central Asia, have provided money and religious teachers to explain mainstream, non-radical Sunni Islam to the Central Asians. Israel, also anxious to prevent the radicalization of the Central Asian states, has provided much needed expertise in irrigation techniques and has established diplomatic relations with several of the Muslim successor states. Ultimately, the foreign policies of all fifteen of the former Soviet republics will be determined in large measure by two factors: the resolution of internal power struggles and economic exigencies. In the Central Asian states and in Azerbaijan, power struggles are taking place between factions that favour Islamization and those inclined toward a more secular orientation. That is why the intense bidding war between Turkey and Iran for influence there is so significant.

As for the second factor, all of the former republics have sought links with those outside powers which can provide economic and technical aid. They have reached out to Western institutions, and the Central Asian states and Azerbaijan have turned as well to the Middle East. Iranian officials have made several high profile trips to Central Asia and Azerbaijan and have tried to mediate in the dispute over Nagorno-Karabakh. Nonetheless, Tehran has little to offer economically. Turkey has been more forthcoming, but its economy too, is troubled. Saudi Arabia could provide substantial economic help, while

Israel, as noted above, has provided agricultural expertise.

Currently, it is clear that post-Soviet policies toward the Gulf and the Middle East are in a state of flux, if not suspension. For the non-Muslim successor states, "classic" foreign policy concerns are definitely secondary. This detachment was most evident when Boris Yeltsin failed to attend the opening round of regional Middle East peace negotiations convened in Moscow in February 1992. Although foreign policy is of lesser importance for Azerbaijan and the Central Asian states too, their involvement with the Middle East seems to be assumed.

Ultimately, the collapse of the Soviet Union leaves a power vacuum in the Middle East. Old clients, such as Iraq, have lost their patron, and none of the successor states is in a position to fill the void left by the USSR's disintegration.

## NOTES

1. An earlier version of the first section of this chapter was presented at a meeting of the Canadian Professors for Peace in the Middle East, in Toronto, in June 1991. The author wishes to thank Paul Marantz for his comments.
2. TASS, 2 Aug. 1990, in *FBIS-Sov*, 3 Aug. 1990, p. 3.
3. It seems that Shevardnadze hoped to delay the use of military force to police the embargo, but urged united Arab action to settle the crisis. See for example, *Izvestiia*, 10 Aug. 1990. Moreover, several Soviet statements — from Gorbachev, Shevardnadze and others — all seemed to accept Saddam's demand that the Kuwaiti crisis be settled in the context of a larger Middle East settlement. See, for example, Gorbachev's press conference in Helsinki, Moscow TV, *FBIS SOV*, 10 Sept. 1990, p. 11.
4. Gorbachev press conference, *op. cit.*
5. Shevardnadze's speech at the UN, TASS, 25 Sept. 1990, *FBIS-Sov*, 26 Sept. 1990, p. 4.
6. See the discussion in Carol R. Saivetz, *The Soviet Union and the Gulf in the 1980s* (Boulder, 1989), p. 105.
7. For example, Vitalii Churkin, the Foreign Ministry spokesman said on 15 Jan.: "The Soviet Union is not and cannot remain neutral in the conflict. However, it will not send troops to the united forces mainly because of internal political reasons, the tragic memory of the Afghan war." Budapest Television, in *FBIS-Sov*, 16 Jan. 1991, p. 8.
8. Evgenii Primakov, "A New Philosophy of Foreign Policy", *Pravda*, 10 July 1987.
9. See Primakov's television interview, 31 Oct. 1990, in *FBIS-Sov*, 1 Nov. 1990, p. 9.
10. A good example is "The War Which Might Not Have Been", *Pravda*, 27 Feb. 1991, pp. 1, 7.
11. See Shevardnadze's resignation speech, Moscow Domestic Service, 20 Dec. 1990, in *FBIS-Sov*, 20 Dec. 1990, pp. 11–12.
12. See TASS, 22 Feb. 1991, *FBIS-Sov*, 25 Feb. 1991, p. 10.
13. Georgii Mirskii, "After Desert Storm", *Literaturnaia gazeta* 6 (March 1991), p. 1.
14. Leonid Mlechin, "Is Moscow on the Wrong Side", *New Times* 7 (Feb. 1991), p. 16.
15. See for example: Major-General Vadim Makarevsky, "The Threat from the South", *New Times* 34 (Aug. 1990), p. 12.
16. See for example, "The World Pays Saddam's Bills", *New Times* 9 (March 1991), p. 17: "The Soviet Union is torn between its superpower status and the syndromes of Afghanistan, Tbilisi, Vilnius, etc. We would like to start a new life, but the old sins drag us back into the past."
17. Leonid Mlechin, "Will Iraq Outlive Saddam Hussein", *New Times* 9 (March 1991), p. 20.
18. Aleksandr Bovin, "Do No Harm", *Izvestiia*, 19 March 1991, p. 6.

19. *Izvestiia*, 7 March 1991.
20. Andrei Kortunov, "USSR-USA: Tested by Crisis", *Moscow News* 11 (March 1991), p. 3. The author was on the staff of the Institute of the Study of the USA and Canada.
21. TASS, 28 Feb. 1991, *FBIS-Sov*, 28 Feb. 1991, pp. 7–8.
22. TASS, 16 March 1991, *FBIS-Sov*, 18 March 1991, pp. 14–16.
23. TASS, 23 March 1991, *FBIS-Sov* 25 March 1991, p. 2.
24. Stephen Kinzer, "Three in Coup Feared US Dependency", *New York Times*, 7 Oct. 1991.
25. Historically, the USSR had claimed that it would re-establish diplomatic relations with Israel only after it would be included in a peace conference. Israel, for its part, stated repeatedly that it would agree to Soviet participation in an international conference only *after* diplomatic relations were restored. Thus, each side received what it had wanted from the other.

# 20

# Domestic Aspects
# of Soviet Foreign Policy

## ALEXANDER DALLIN

As we study the characteristic traits of Soviet foreign policy — some constant, some variable — we are drawn to an examination of its sources. And we find that it is ultimately impossible to identify and explain these traits without looking at the domestic roots of foreign conduct.

By its very nature, this dimension of foreign policy has always been more difficult to study, especially at a distance, from the outside. For political reasons it has, until recently, constituted something of a taboo for Soviet scholarship. While the linkage of internal and external policy choices in the USSR was explicit and emphatic both at the beginning and at the end of the Soviet era, during most of the intervening period discussion of the politics of foreign policy was as impermissible as that of domestic policy; and a diversity of foreign policy outlooks was deemed even less legitimate than alternative perspectives on policy choices at home. Orthodox Soviet analysts were of course trained to see the foreign policy of any state as an extension and extrapolation of its domestic base — the class structure and correlation of forces — but they could scarcely suggest the existence of any alternative to the "general line" pursued by the Soviet leadership.

Fortunately such constraints have now been lifted. And as we begin a new phase in the study of what has become a truly historical subject, we can point to this dimension as a major gap in our understanding that remains to be filled, and try to specify, at least in summary fashion, some of the variety of domestic inputs that need to be identified.

For Lenin, the Treaty of Brest-Litovsk was a prerequisite for stabilization and recovery at home. It legitimized dealing with the adversary; it affirmed faith in time as an ally; and it established the priority of internal over external objectives: the survival of the Soviet state came before the promotion of revolution abroad. Lenin was candid and articulate on these points.[1]

Similarly, Gorbachev was explicit in linking the foreign policy identified with the "new thinking" to the needs of Soviet perestroika. This was not the only reason for the policy of normalizing international relations, nor was it sufficient to assure the success of domestic reforms. But reducing the strain in foreign affairs, as well as cutting Soviet defence expenditures, was part of a strategy of keeping the international equation constant at times of stressful transformations at home. The domestic scene again took precedence over the foreign.[2]

Finally, there was the spurious linkage, notoriously evident in Stalin's claims to have uncovered evidence of an amalgam of domestic and foreign enemies, tying would-be plotters at home to some variant of Gestapo-CIA-Titoist-Zionist-Trotskyite agents. This practice requires no comment.

On most occasions such linkages between domestic and foreign policies were not so advertised. The same logic as in the earlier examples prompted a policy of general appeasement (for example, towards Japan and Germany) during the most difficult period of forcible collectivization of agriculture and the first Five-Year Plan. Especially since in the so-called Third Period it was accompanied by the "ultra-left" Comintern effort to make trouble behind the potential enemies' lines, such a policy was in no sense adventitious. It would be important to establish in what terms it was discussed in advance.

Another instance of a tacit linkage relates to the years of the Nixon-Brezhnev *détente*. The "liberalization" of Soviet emigration policy in the 1970s was presumably part of Moscow's side payment to the United States — whether or not it was specifically labeled as such — for a short-lived improvement of relations. No doubt, it was discussed in high state and Party circles (and probably attacked for permitting American interference in matters of domestic Soviet jurisdiction). If there were memoranda submitted and Politburo discussions on this trade-off, or others like it, it would be important to have knowledge of them.

If we compare the pursuit of foreign economic ties in the Brezhnev and in the Gorbachev years, a significant difference comes to mind: while in the years after the 27th CPSU Congress the effort to make the Soviet Union an active member of the international economic community was an organic part of the program of reform, in the years of so-called stagnation, the attempt to increase participation abroad for the sake of economic and technological benefit was, it seems, intended as a substitute for structural reform. Was it indeed conceived in this way by its sponsors, and how was the policy defended on the inside?

While capabilities and intentions need not coincide, "objective" indicators of internal strength or weakness typically influence corresponding foreign policy postures (though of course other variables also influence risk-taking, such as the perception of opportunities abroad or the dread of nuclear war). In the early days of the NEP, Lenin sent the Soviet delegates to Genoa as "businessmen, not Bolsheviks".[3] When in the early months of the German invasion in 1941 the situation was close to desperate, Stalin was prepared to welcome British troops on Soviet soil; when later in the war the Soviet outlook improved remarkably, Stalin wanted no foreign forces to threaten his monopoly of power. Khrushchev almost stumbled into nuclear confrontation in Cuba, perhaps exaggerating Soviet capabilities.

Of course, much still depended on the "subjective" perception of "objective" data. Gorbachev's predecessors and their advisers were apparently prepared to ignore the implications of a serious slowdown in economic growth and a budgetary deficit for the conduct of foreign policy. For a while it was possible to deceive both oneself and one's adversary. But by the mid-1980s it had become more costly and more difficult for the Soviet Union to "keep up" with the United States, especially in research and development of the most advanced weapons technology — and the new leadership drew appropriate lessons from this fact.

Other structural sources of foreign policy preferences include the particular bureaucracy in which a given actor functions and his or her role within it. In a famous *Pravda* cartoon of the 1920s, Foreign Commissar Chicherin was shown tearing his hair out in despair as Comintern head Zinov'ev made incendiary speeches.[4] It is plausible that a high official concerned with foreign trade — Anastas Mikoian, for instance, or Leonid Krasin, who was dispatched to England in 1921 and 1926 to recover markets destroyed by the Comintern's subversive activities — should have been inclined toward a more moderate foreign policy that would not be likely to jeopardize international commerce. But position within the system at home is not a certain indicator of foreign policy preferences: individual inclinations, background and commitments can override the validity of the general rule that "where you stand depends on where you sit".

Analysts of Soviet foreign policy are divided between those who perceive Soviet decision making as an essentially vertical, authoritarian system, and those who view it in terms of a "conflict model", in which various figures — in this case, members of the Soviet élite — differed over foreign and domestic policy orientations and priorities. The latter approach is an important corrective to the traditional image. We know of anecdotes about individuals — Maxim Litvinov, Marshal Budionnyi, Academician Evgenii Varga — but here much remains to be learned. Clearly, these were often not so much power struggles as contests of rival orientations and policy preferences.[5]

A number of studies deal with the significance of esoteric disputes in Soviet academic journals — for instance, the prospects in the Third World (from national-liberation movements to economic development, to alignment with the USSR);[6] the place of competing images of the United States;[7] the importance of arms control and the future of nuclear weapons.[8] Do such scholarly divergences reflect prior policy differences at the top? Do they mirror the contents of Politburo debates? Or, do they seek to influence potential policy makers? Case studies would be of value here.

The whole process of foreign policy decision making deserves close study. No doubt, there were substantial variations over time and over different issues. Stalin might or might not have listened to some comrades but the decisions were unmistakably his. This was not the case with his successors. One of the best examples of a confrontation over foreign (as well as domestic) policy is the Khrushchev-Molotov duel at the Party Central Committee plenum in July 1955. As will be discussed below, here were two widely differing sets of underlying assumptions — essentially Stalinist and anti-Stalinist.[9]

Were there similar disputes over the Cuban Missile Crisis, the invasion of Afghanistan, arms control agreements, the Sino-Soviet conflict? We are not sure. Is it accurate to say that, in general, over time, a widening circle of officials and consultants was involved in the preparation for major foreign policy decisions? And what was that process of preparation?

There is room for investigation of institutional rivalry over matters of foreign policy — most obviously, between the International Department of the Party Central Committee and the Ministry of Foreign Affairs. The role and outlook of the security services require study, as does the input of the military establishment and of the academic institutes.

Key personalities need to be examined — not only those who had direct responsibility for foreign conduct — but also others, like Andrei Zhdanov and Mikhail Suslov whose status seems to have given them an inordinate influence on Soviet policy. Individual variations in world view, in political styles and temperament and in policy advocacy are among priority topics for research.

This is not the place to argue the role of ideology in Soviet perceptions and policy making. But clearly there have been — to use conventional language — left and right communists and left and right policies competing which, at times, have reflected fundamental differences in outlook, style and objectives. How much congruence was there between domestic and foreign outlook here? Did the Muscovite hawks and doves divide much like the "friends and foes of reform"?[10] Is it accurate to suggest that there was much fluidity in the Khrushchev years, little congruence in the Brezhnev years, but more than accidental coincidence in the Gorbachev era, between "friends and foes of reform" and "friends and foes of *détente*"?[11] The difference in outlook between Litvinov, and Molotov or Zhdanov, was dramatic. But even between Khrushchev and Molotov the unstated underlying assumptions in 1955 pointed to significantly different world views.[12] In recent years, the remarkable "new thinking" of Eduard Shevardnadze in foreign policy quite naturally has invited bitter attacks, overtly and covertly, from a whole battery of "hardliners", be they Nina Andreeva, Egor Ligachev or Colonel Victor Alksnis. Here too we must look for constants and variables. While these foreign policy orientations may seem to correlate with broader categories reminiscent of "Westernizing" or "Slavophile" movements, they would not seem to be congruent with views concerning the survival of the Soviet state, federalism and the new Commonwealth.

There has been a good deal of ignorance and confusion in Western accounts about the relation of the Communist party to Foreign Ministry policy. For instance, it would be important to answer questions concerning intentions in 1948–50 when, under the banner of the new Cominform, communist parties from Europe to India and Japan were advised to adopt a more militant stance. The same would apply to more recent years and encompasses the whole question of how Moscow looked upon the comrades abroad.

Finally, it is the "big issues" that of course await study: what were the leading figures' expectations of conflict and war, their assumptions of the incompatibility of the capitalist and socialist world, their perceptions of a hostile encirclement, their hopes and fears? Did they believe what they were saying in public? Perhaps most critical, can any new light be shed on the ostensibly "aggressive" intentions of the Soviet leadership — not in terms of the morality or inevitability of an expanding socialist universe (though that too deserves study and documentary substantiation) but in terms of concrete plans and policies?

An additional aspect that deserves mention concerns the extent to which political figures in the Soviet Union unconsciously carried over assumptions of how to deal with partners and adversaries, styles of in-fighting and habits of asserting and exercising authority, from the domestic scene to the international.[13]

In the post-Stalin years, there was an uneven trend in the direction of broadening the circle of those concerned with foreign affairs. However, the recent change in the relationship of Russian state and society has ushered in a qualitatively novel situation in which public opinion polls and a multiplicity of social movements and political parties have begun to deal with questions of foreign policy.[14] Their impact, if any, remains to be studied; moreover, the problems of multi-ethnicity add a new complexity to conduct abroad and invite future studies. So of course do the breakdown of the Communist party and the disappearance of the International Department.

Clearly not every foreign policy issue is "linked" to a domestic policy focus; nor does a clear set of domestic orientations and policy preferences of a given individual always permit identification of a congruent foreign policy choice. Large segments of the *nomenklatura* have not been involved or interested in foreign policy, which has been outside their universe of experience or competence.

Nonetheless, perhaps this sketch suffices to underscore the need for research in each of the areas mentioned above and for access to all possible — including previously inaccessible — sources. Only after we have a better grasp of them can we attempt to assess the relative importance of the international environment, the decision makers' calculus and domestic politics in the formation of Soviet foreign policy.

In studying the history of Soviet foreign policy, it is useful to bring together Soviet researchers and foreign scholars. Thus, one might try to identify the causes of wrong or dangerous judgments — in the Soviet establishment as well as abroad — by going back to the participants and to the written record. The same is likely to be true in regard to the big interpretive questions for which there are no documents to provide definitive answers.

NOTES

1. See A. O. Chubarian, *Brestskii mir* (Moscow, 1964); and John W. Wheeler-Bennett, *Brest-Litovsk: The Forgotten Peace* (London, 1956).
2. M. S. Gorbachev, *Time*, 9 Sept. 1985; also his *Perestroika* (New York, 1987).
3. Cf. Carole Fink, *The Genoa Conference* (Chapel Hill, 1984); George F. Kennan, *Russia and the West under Lenin and Stalin* (Boston, 1960), Ch. 14. See also E. H. Carr, *The Bolshevik Revolution*, Vol. III (New York, 1953).
4. Deni, in *Pravda*, 19 July 1924.
5. See, for example, Robert Darst, "Unitary and Conflictual Images in the Study of Soviet Foreign Policy", in George Breslauer (ed.), *Analyzing the Gorbachev Era* (Berkeley, 1989).
6. See, for example, Jerry F. Hough, *The Struggle for the Third World* (Washington, DC,

1986); Elizabeth K. Valkenier, *The Soviet Union and the Third World* (New York, 1983); William Zimmerman, *Soviet Perspectives on International Relations, 1956–1967* (Princeton, 1969); Gilbert Rozman, *A Mirror for Socialism: Soviet Criticism of China* (Princeton, 1985).

7. See Alexander Dallin, "The United States in the Soviet Perspective", in Christoph Bertram (ed.), *Prospects of Soviet Power* (New York, 1980); Morton Schwartz, *Soviet Perceptions of the United States* (Berkeley, 1980); Franklyn Griffiths, "The Sources of American Conduct: Soviet Perspectives and Their Policy Implications", *International Security* 9 (Fall 1984), pp. 3–50.

8. See Samuel B. Payne, Jr., *The Soviet Union and SALT* (Boston, 1980); Coit Blacker, *Under the Gun, The Portable Stanford* (Stanford, 1986); and David Holloway, *The Soviet Union and the Arms Race* (New Haven, 1984).

9. See Alexander Dallin, "The Domestic Sources of Soviet Foreign Policy", in Seweryn Bialer (ed.), *The Domestic Context of Soviet Foreign Policy* (Boulder, 1981), pp. 366–67 and fn. 86.

10. Stephen F. Cohen, "Friends and Foes of Change", in Cohen et al., *The Soviet Union Since Stalin* (Indiana, 1980), pp. 11–31.

11. See, for example, George G. Weickhardt, "Foreign Policy Disputes in the Gorbachev Succession", *Soviet Union* 16, 1 (1989), pp. 29–54.

12. Compare the three volumes of *Khrushchev Remembers* with Feliks Chuev's *Sto sorok besed s Molotovym* (Moscow, 1991).

13. James M. Goldgeier, "Soviet Leaders and International Crises: The Influence of Domestic Political Experiences on Foreign Policy Strategies", Ph.D. diss. (Berkeley, 1990). An additional subject that has recently attracted interest among Western scholars is the extent and nature of "learning" by political figures — from experience, from errors or failures, or from historical precedents. For both case studies and generalizations applied to Soviet foreign policy, see in particular the volume, George W. Breslauer and Philip E. Tetlock, (eds.), *Learning in US and Soviet Foreign Policy* (Boulder, 1991), especially the chapters by George W. Breslauer, Franklyn Griffiths, Jonathan Haslam and Robert Legvold. A variant approach argues that Soviet élite competition did in fact take precedence over "learning" and served to inhibit learning from failure and experience. See Richard D. Anderson, Jr., "Competitive Politics, Learning, and Soviet Foreign Policy", in Breslauer and Tetlock, *op. cit.* For other recent formulations of domestic/foreign linkages, see Jack Snyder, "The Gorbachev Revolution: A Waning of Soviet Expansionism?" *International Security* 12 (1987/88); James Richter, "Action and Reaction in Soviet Foreign Policy: How Leadership Politics Affect Soviet Responses to the International Environment", Ph.D. diss. (Berkeley, 1988).

14. An early example of such an initiative is Anatoly Gromyko and Martin Hellman, (eds.), *Breakthrough/Proryv: Emerging New Thinking* (New York, 1988).

# Notes on Contributors

LEV BEZYMENSKY is the former editor of the journal *Novoe vremia*. He has published numerous works on German-Soviet relations, among them *The Barbarossa File* [in Russian] (Moscow, 1972).

ANATOLII CHERNIAEV was the personal aide to Mikhail Gorbachev and chief adviser on foreign policy from 1986 until Gorbachev's resignation. He is now a consultant at the Gorbachev Foundation.

FRANCIS CONTE is Professor of Russian and Soviet History at the Sorbonne and at the Institute of Political Studies in Paris. His recent publications include *A Political Biography of Christian Rakovskii* (New York, 1990) and *Gli Slavi* (Turin, 1991).

ALEXANDER DALLIN is Professor of History and Political Science at Stanford University. Among his many publications are *German Rule in Russia, 1941–1945* (rev. ed. Boulder, 1981) and *Black Box: KAL 007 and the Superpowers* (Berkeley, 1985).

VYACHESLAV DASHICHEV is a renowned expert on Germany at the Institute of International Economic and Political Studies of the Russian Academy of Sciences. He was personally involved in the process of German unification.

RICHARD K. DEBO is Professor of History at Simon Fraser University in Vancouver. His major publications are *Revolution and Survival: The Foreign Policy of Soviet Russia, 1917–1918* (Toronto, 1979) and *Survival and Consolidation: The Foreign Policy of Soviet Russia, 1918–1921* (Montreal, 1992).

ALEKSEI FILITOV is a senior researcher at the Institute of General History of the Russian Academy of Sciences. He has published several works on the history of World War II and postwar international relations, including the monograph *The Cold War: Historiographic Debates in the West* [in Russian] (Moscow, 1991).

CAROLE FINK is Professor of European International History at the Ohio State University. She is the author of *Marc Bloch: A Life in History* (Cambridge, 1989) and co-editor of *Genoa, Rapallo, and the Reconstruction of Europe in 1922* (Washington, DC, 1991).

GABRIEL GORODETSKY is Director of the Cummings Center for Russian and East European Studies and Academic Adviser to the Staff College of the Israeli Defence Forces. He has published extensively on Soviet foreign policy and the history of the Second World War. His major publications include *The Precarious Truce: Anglo-Soviet Relations, 1924–1927* (Cambridge, 1977) and *Stafford Cripps' Mission to Moscow, 1940–1942* (Cambridge, 1984).

JONATHAN HASLAM is a Fellow and Director of Studies in History at Corpus Christi College, Cambridge, and Assistant Director of Studies in International Relations at Cambridge University's Centre of International Studies. His most recent publication is *The Soviet Union and the Threat from the East, 1933–41* (London, 1992).

MARTIN KITCHEN is Professor of History at Simon Fraser University in British Columbia, Canada. His recent publications include *British Policy Towards the Soviet Union, 1939–1945* (London, 1986), *Europe Between the Wars* (London, 1988) and *A World in Flames: A Concise History of the Second World War in Europe and Asia* (London, 1990).

BRUCE R. KUNIHOLM is Director of the Sanford Institute of Public Policy and Chairman of the Department of Public Policy at Duke University. His numerous publications include the book *Origins of the Cold War in the Near East: Conflict and Diplomacy in Iran, Turkey and Greece* (Princeton, 1980).

VIKTOR KUVALDIN is a leading researcher at the Gorbachev Foundation. Between 1989 and 1991 he was a foreign policy consultant to President Gorbachev.

IGOR LEBEDEV is a former diplomat who served at the Soviet Embassy in Washington during the periods 1974–1980 and 1983–1986. He is currently Director of the History and Records Department of the Ministry of Foreign Affairs of the Russian Federation.

MIKHAIL NARINSKY is Deputy Director of the Institute of General History at the Russian Academy of Sciences. His publications include *Great Britain and France in Post-War Europe, 1945–1949* [in Russian] (Moscow, 1972), *Classes and Political Parties in France, 1944–1958* [In Russian] (Moscow, 1983), and the collective work *Europe in the Twentieth Century: Problems of Peace and Security* [in Russian] (Moscow, 1985).

ANITA J. PRAZMOWSKA is a Lecturer in Central European History at the London School of Economics. Her recent publications include *Britain, Poland and the Eastern Front, 1939* (Cambridge, 1987) and *The Warring Allies: Britain, Poland and the Soviet Question, 1939–1943*. Forthcoming.

YAACOV RO'I is a Senior Fellow of the Cummings Center and a Professor of History at Tel Aviv University. He is the author of numerous studies, including *From Encroachment to Involvement* (New York, 1974) and *The Struggle for Soviet Jewish Emigration 1948–1967* (Cambridge, 1991), editor of *USSR and the Muslim World* (London, 1984) and co-editor of *Soviet Jewish Culture and Identity* (New York, 1991).

CAROL R. SAIVETZ is a Fellow at the Russian Research Center and a Lecturer in Social Studies at Harvard University. She is the author of *The Soviet Union and the Gulf in the 1980s* (Boulder, 1989) and co-author of *Soviet-Third World Relations* (Boulder, 1985). She also edits the journal *The Soviet Union in the Third World* and is co-editor of the book *In Search of Pluralism: Soviet and Post-Soviet Politics*. Forthcoming.

ALEXANDER TCHOUBARIAN is Director of the Institute of General History of the Russian Academy of Sciences. He has published extensively on European history and the history of international relations, including his work *The Brest Peace* [in Russian] (Moscow, 1964). He recently completed a book entitled *The European Idea in History in the Nineteenth and Twentieth Centuries: A View from Moscow* (London). Forthcoming.

TEDDY J. ULDRICKS is Professor of History at the University of North Carolina, Asheville. He has written a number of works on the Russian Revolution and on Soviet foreign relations, including the book *Diplomacy and Ideology: The Origins of Soviet Foreign Relations 1917–1930* (London, 1979).

# Index